Redes I wnside
from
[signature]

Xmas
1953

THE HUNGRY SHEEP

By the same author

THIRTY-NINE MONTHS
THE RULING FEW
BEYOND THE IRON CURTAIN

THE HUNGRY SHEEP

by

SIR
DAVID KELLY
G.C.M.G., M.C.

The hungry sheep look up, and are not fed,
But swoln with wind, and the rank mist they draw,
Rot inwardly, and foul contagion spread . . .

Milton, Lycidas

LONDON
HOLLIS & CARTER

MADE AND PRINTED IN GREAT BRITAIN
AT THE CHAPEL RIVER PRESS, ANDOVER, HANTS
FOR HOLLIS AND CARTER, LTD., 25 ASHLEY PLACE
LONDON, S.W.1

First published 1955

To SOPHIE

FOREWORD

THE following pages cover vast fields in which there is abundant room for more distinctions and further discussion. I would gladly have anticipated this criticism but for one reason—it would make the book intolerably long. The brevity due to this fact does not mean that I am not fully conscious of all that can be said in qualification of my conclusions, or that I have been arrogantly indifferent to other considerations. It only means that I have found it difficult enough to express my own views in the space available.

While I take the sole responsibility for all the opinions contained in these pages, my warm thanks are due to Lord Coleraine for most helpful criticisms on Part I; to Mr. Douglas Woodruff for advice on the whole book; and for that of my wife and my son Bernard particularly on questions of form, and for that of my son Lawrence particularly on some matters of substance.

D. K.

THE THEME ANALYSED

PART I

THE SURFACE

and confusion between foreign policy and diplomatic method, discredited professional diplomacy and for it substituted negotiation by politicians at international conferences. Character and technique of nineteenth-century diplomacy, its essentially pacific outlook. Stabilizing influence of nineteenth-century Monarchies. In decade 1904 to 1914 eclipse of diplomacy was contributory cause of war; disastrous consequences of accidental temporary influence of Chiefs of Staffs. German General Staff's evil influence continued during 1914–1918 War, but practically all peace initiatives were of completely undemocratic origin and they received no popular support. Demagogy and nationalism prolonged the 1914 War, made an unworkable vindictive peace treaty, and made smooth the way for Nazism by accelerating the disruptive effects of the War on Europe. International relations from 1918 to 1948 dominated by lack of realism and loose, woolly and uncritical formulas. In trying to correct weakness of League of Nations by establishing Security Council and right of Veto, the United Nations Charter ignored fundamental objectives of Soviet policy. Other weaknesses of world assemblies. Failure of the conference system. Conditions for the success of an international conference; basic preliminary agreement, mutual will to compromise, confidential discussion, patience, settlement to be defined in precise terms. Contrast of Congress of Vienna and the Versailles Treaty. General comparison of effects on international relations of middle-class opinion and uninformed mass-opinion. The wishful thinker's paradise in 1918. Misunderstanding of the origin and militant left-wing character of Nazism; and of the differences between Nazism and Fascism.

Sir E. Crowe's memorandum of 1907; British foreign policy based on Free Trade. The Free Trade régime had taken over a commercial and industrial supremacy built on protection of both industry and agriculture; temporary factors masked a decline relative to other nations which pursued the historic English policy of mercantilism. By the 1890's Free Trade had become a religious dogma which assumed that it had created the industrial lead and that the new mass electorate would continue to accept the *laissez-faire* principles of the classical economists which were part of Free Trade system. The Free Trade régime conferred great benefits on other countries, especially the undeveloped areas; but it created a lack of balance in the home economy, which proved unequal to the strain when in the 1914 War another break with tradition was made by taking part in a European war with a full-scale land Army, and refusing to end the war in time by a negotiated peace. The four assumptions of the Banker's paradise.

The English liberal tradition as applied both to independent and subject peoples is an unconscious expression of insular self-confidence: assumption that all foreigners are imperfect Englishmen and only need opportunity to imitate them. Nationalism in Asia a Western importation. Macaulay's Minute on Indian education: assumption that Hindu culture would be replaced by English Victorian way of life. Most serious consequence of insular pride is attempt to impose British Parliamentary Government in Africa on chaos left by dissolution of tribal institutions and just when Parliamentary institutions are admittedly threatened in Britain itself. Practical result is transfer of power to oligarchy of uprooted intelligentsia; an evasion of the responsibilities incurred to the majority by the disruption of their previous social organization. Refusal even to consider alternative policy of Belgian Congo, consisting of restriction of White settlers, good government, good wages, no colour bar—and no politics: consequent absorption of native intelligentsia into business administration.

Balance of power principle now global. Britain no longer capable of war singlehanded. No World association can work owing to strength and revolutionary objectives of Communist Powers. Answer lies in North Atlantic Union. Free Trade is no longer possible; answer is return to balanced economy and encouragement of productive effort. Need to reassess strategic position which has been changed by loss of Indian Empire and restriction in wartime of Mediterranean highway. New weapons and Soviet Power by increasing English interdependence with Western Europe impose more realistic attitude in relations with other members of the Commonwealth. How far do the new weapons of mass destruction affect our foreign policy. Recapitulation of short-term objectives: Policy must conform to the degree of armed strength available. Need to develop North Atlantic and European connections in every way. Policy must be adjusted more quickly to changed circumstances. Foreign policy ultimately depends on balanced economy and productive energy at home. Colonial policy should concentrate on social and economic development rather than the imposition of unsuitable British Parliamentary institutions.

PART II
THE DEEPER CURRENTS

Daily lives of " practical " people profoundly influenced by ideas without their knowing it. Soviet system not inevitable but result of imposition by tiny minority of the Marxist philosophy without which it is unintelligible. Practical results of Hegelian idea on Soviet postwar policy, of German racial idea on the course of the War, of the Nationalist idea in Asia. Indirect influence of ideas in creating a climate of bewilderment and loss of confidence, e.g., influence of Shaw and Wells on English middle classes. History of ideas is complicated by action of chance, by dominating personalities or their absence, by free will or physical pressures. Ideas subject to selective force of characters and circumstances. They can lie dormant for long periods. They have latent explosive force and can issue in series of delayed-action explosions. They develop in forms which their originators seldom foresee and often do not desire. While some ideas are creative, others rationalize and strengthen existing tendencies and conditions, e.g., English Utilitarians. Interaction of ideas and institutions; no single formula assigning general priority to either.

his conception of cultures as living organisms each with its " prime symbol." Professor Toynbee's theory of challenge and response, withdrawal and return. Impressionist classifications of Schubart and Berdyaev. Professor Sorokin's " great cultural supersystems " the phases of which are distinguished by the sense of values in each phase, which may be " ideational," " idealistic," or " sensate." Advantages of his classification which is the most flexible and comprehensive of the various systems, though basically the same. His criticisms of the others; and the significant points of agreement with them.

Pessimism of cycle sociologists about our civilization finds counterpart in disillusionment of Shaw and Wells, in change from conventional Utopias to future as seen by Aldous Huxley and George Orwell, and in conclusions of Alexis Carrel and Durkheim. Durkheim's study of suicide led him to condemn both nineteenth-century individualism and the Modern State. General argument is that our civilization has become unbalanced owing to undue predominance of purely materialist interests and consequent substitution of standards of quantity for standards of quality. Characteristics of mass civilization: its effects on intellect and artistic creation. " Progressive education " typified official recognition of mediocrity as standard of value in education. The mass civilization caters for wealth and poverty at the expense of the middle classes who have been, broadly speaking, the real guardians and transmitters of quality values. Growing divorce between art and intelligence, and between art and society; consequent tendency of the arts to become eccentric and inhuman. Nemesis of anarchy in art and thought is growth of the State as only authority left. From Hippolyte Taine to Crichel Down. Effects of 1914 War which killed not imperialism but liberal democracy and undermined Socialist democracy. Liberalism the result rather than the creator of nineteenth-century conditions and perished with them. By its errors in philosophy and psychology Liberalism dug its own grave. Socialist democracy had to fight on two fronts—Fascism and Communism. New power groups turning to " science " and expert planning. Handicaps of the pure scientist in practical affairs. Fallibility of economists and statisticians: conflicting opinions and false predictions. Historically, loss of quality values has been eventually followed by material decline as well. North America though in first phase of prosperity is more typical mass-civilization than Western Europe, where there are more surviving quality values. Conclusion that our civilization has typical elements of disintegration, but this is not inevitable if reintegration is willed strongly enough.

English opinion still identifies modern psychology with pioneer system of Freud. His achievement in directing attention to influence of irrational sources inside the personality, the active rôle of the unconscious, through his technique of " free association "; but being adept of most extreme form of late nineteenth-century materialism he used his clinical work as basis for a complete superstructure of *a priori* theory. Freud's doctrine was closed mechanical system which reduced all values to manifestations of repressed " libido," with no objective existence, derived all mental processes from biological functions, and treated human personality as having no continuous mental life. His psychology was built up on his determinist philosophy, not on his clinical research which was used to justify his theories. His obsession in practice with sex caused breakaway of Adler and Jung. Adler's school of comparative individual psychology treated personality as total unit and primarily as a member of society. Shifted the emphasis from biological functions to specifically human non-animal factors. Adler's doctrine of the will to power, the will to live in society, and the inferiority complex due to frustration of the will to power. Conflict causing neurosis treated as spiritual conflict between man's infinite pride and finite limitations; aim of psychiatry to promote harmony between personality and laws of Nature and society. Later schools of psychology following Adler's lead have tended to solve patients' difficulties by new social relationships and emotional transference and away from search for infantile conflicts and infantile eroticism. Stress increasingly laid on social-cultural relationships and spiritual aspects of personality. Meanwhile Freud's other chief disciple Jung had developed study of the collective unconscious. His doctrine of the " archetypes," "compensations," " loosening of the opposites," strikingly justified by his accurate predictions and acute analysis of developments in Germany before, and under, Nazism: contrast with lack of guidance from School of Freud. Jung's conception of aim of psychotherapy as education towards independence and moral freedom of the individual.

7. The Libel on the Cavemen 174

The pioneers of anthropology and the comparative study of religions started with fixed presuppositions that whole life of man was governed exclusively by mechanical forces of evolution working through natural selection from lower to higher forms. All evidence either distorted to fit the theory or rejected because incompatible with it. Hence four main assumptions: (a) that earliest man had no religion, then developed animism, magic, fetichism, and " evolved " from these through polytheism to monotheism; (b) that slavery, human sacrifice, cannibalism and sexual promiscuity were characteristic of very primitive society; (c) that all arts evolved by slow stages through lower to higher forms; (d) that material and spiritual development advanced on parallel lines. Closed unscientific approach of older anthropologists illustrated by their reaction to discovery of Cave Art which contradicted all the orthodox assumptions about palaeolithic man. Classic example of Sir J. G. Frazer. Modern anthropology based on concept of culture-circles. Distinction between primitive and primary cultures and their mixture in secondary and tertiary cultures. Monotheism an essential feature of primitive culture; growth in technical knowledge has no relation to moral and spiritual qualities or rational faculty. On the contrary, growth of higher material civilization in river valleys is accompanied by blood sacrifices, animism, magic, ritual cannibalism, and divorce of religion from morality. Matriarchal agrarian culture associated with moon-worship, patriarchal hunting culture with sun-worship. Patriarchal pastoral culture tends to preserve monotheism. Fusion of all three later cultures the basis of the " historic " cultures, i.e., those with documentary records and monuments and complex organization. Comparative study of historic religions distorted and scrambled by evolutionary presuppositions which were incompatible with fact of unique character of Jewish National religion and of the early Christian

Church. Contrast with the religion of Babylon and Assyria; of
Egypt; of the Aztecs. Spiritual degeneracy in religious systems of
India and China. Contrast of the Christian Church with Gnostics
and Manichaeans. Slavery associated with material progress; it
represents a constant human tendency.

A symposium in *The Listener*: views of Sir E. Barker, Professors
Toynbee, Barraclough, Cole, Messrs. Taylor, Bertrand Russell, Canon
Demant and Mr. Dawson. The Greek and Roman contributions
restated. Wide rejection of Greek insistence on form, balance, and
general principles, and ignorance of extent to which European civilization is rooted in Greek and Roman framework. Misunderstanding of
the nature of the Barbarian " invasion." Essence of Western tradition as transmitted from Greece through Rome to mediaeval Europe
was the will to integrate the fragmentary into defined intelligible
" wholes," contrasted with constant tendency elsewhere to fragmentation, formlessness or deformity. Tendency of religion to
degenerate into cult of evil and cruelty always allied to tendency of art
to degenerate into cult of disharmony, chaos and contradiction.
Illustrations from India and America before the Spanish Conquest.
Significant indications of revival of this tendency in our civilization
accompanying gradual abandonment by Western peoples of their
traditional values. The significance of Cubism. Cult of evil in
recent literature. Western tradition has represented integration of
best elements in Greek-Roman culture, Christian doctrine and the
vitality of the Northern Barbarians. Its abandonment is at the
heart of our crisis which is essentially spiritual, and not *primarily*
political, economic, or biological. Though vitality and will to power
have been factors in European expansion, the Western tradition in its
full sense is not identical with Europe; it is in harmony with the true
nature of man and is shared by all members of the human race who
accept—and in the measure that they really assimilate—the full
Christian tradition in which the best Greek-Roman elements are
incorporated. Defence of the tradition against Professor Toynbee
and Bertrand Russell, who would identify it with technology or power
politics. Illustration from Spanish colonial policy.

Propaganda myth of spiritual and moral superiority of the East over
the West. High Brahmin and Buddhist theosophy is rooted in profound pessimism; existence and personality are essentially evil, world
of appearance is unreal and irreformable. Western logic and Western
conception of Law are unknown. Rewards or penalties are dis-
tributed through process of reincarnation, therefore caste system
represents working of inexorable law. Overstressing of purely
spiritual leads to disorder and acceptance of arbitrary tyranny just as
does overstressing of the purely material. Hence in all religions
which over-emphasize pessimistic negation of matter, tendency is
towards passive acceptance of social and political abuses and loss of
personal freedom. This has been general characteristic of Asiatic and
Russian history. Affinity of German philosophy with spirit of Asia.
Real meaning of theory that Asia has been the home of toleration.
Strength and weakness of Islam.

Permanent factor of division inside Europe represented by the
struggle inside Germany between the Christian order and the old
Germanic mythology. Geographical factors and limiting of Roman
frontiers intensified by rise of non-German Prussians. Character of
primitive German soul: Pantheist, revolutionary, and dynamic,
instinctive rejection of stability or finality. Cult of will, the " eternal
becoming," rejection of pure reason, reappear in philosophy of Kant
and Hegel, nationalism or Stateworship of Fichte or Hegel, pessimism
of Nietzsche and Schopenhauer, and finally Nazism. Mediaeval
attempts at German unification on Christian-European basis.
Turning-point was in the consequences of German Reformation and
its French offshoot, Calvinism. Need to distinguish Luther's
personal beliefs, the driving-force behind their success, the actual
consequences, and his personality. His fundamental doctrine:
salvation through faith alone without works, and hatred of reason.
Social and economic consequences of "faith without works." Success
due to his alliance with the German princes against the peasants'
revolt. Luther a pure romantic and incarnation of primitive German
soul; egoism, imagination, energy, entirely governed by will and
feeling. Calvin provided firm base for German religious revolt.
Effects on education, position of women, belief in demonology and
witchcraft. Puritan movement in general a stab in the back for
Western tradition.

Underlying crisis of our civilization is primarily spiritual and due to
a succession of false ideas about human nature. Purpose of Part One
is to suggest some results in practice of false or confused thinking and
loss of standards of judgment, e.g., confusion between diplomacy and
foreign policy, about the relation of armed strength and policy; in
the prevalence of unreal formulas in international affairs and in
defeatism and lack of realism in British colonial policy. Basic idea of
Part Two is that the human personality is unique, being (a) capable of
ranging between opposite extremes and (b) only subject to mechanical
evolution in matters of technology. In the nineteenth century,
psychology, anthropology, the comparative history of religions,
history and sociology were re-created on basis of false assumption of
evolutionary moral progress derived from false biological analogy.
Recent research indicates that this materialist pre-supposition is
contrary to facts. Effect of subversive criticism, even without
establishing new ideas, in undermining confidence and creating
"loss of nerve." Inner contradictions of nineteenth-century
Liberalism and its final breakdown. Real meaning of " Western "
tradition and " Western " values becomes clear when contrasted
with the other major traditions which are rooted in pessimism and
lack of form and balance: their inherent tendency to loss of personal
freedom, the cult of evil, absence of the rule of Law. Partial breakdown of Western standards and bankruptcy of false philosophies
leave no brake on tendency of crowd civilization and uprooted urban
masses to spiritual disintegration and unlimited authority of the
State. As the fundamental cause of social disequilibrium is the loss
of the Western spiritual values, the ultimate disintegration of our
Western civilization can only be arrested by a return to those values.

Part I
THE SURFACE

PROLOGUE

WHEN the late Mr. Ford made his famous remark that " history is bunk " he presumably meant that the study of past and present events (for last week is already history) provided no clear guidance for the future. That so practical a man could reach this conclusion does suggest that historians in the main had failed to solve this great problem of how to distinguish the surface of the stream of events—wars, revolutions, governments, industrial changes— from the underlying currents of ideas, impulses, personality, and pure chance. For practical purposes, as a method of approach, there is much to be said for Spengler's division of the human story into static realized events which he called the World as Nature, to be learned by scientific methods, and the underlying, dynamic life which he called the World of History, to be grasped by intuition, as a picture, in terms of analogy and symbols.

What I am suggesting is that the most hopeful method in speculating about the future of our society is to start with the surface facts which can be measured and weighed, and having built up some coherent pictures of the surface, attempt to explore the more hidden, less tangible sources. For the surface picture will change rapidly, but the underlying factors are " variable constants " which have been at work since the beginning of our race.

Applying this method, the first step is to have a look at the surface world as it is in 1955, the world of politics and economics and the nucleus of Uranium 235 which our scientists have unfortunately learned to smash with neutrons—as a preliminary to their combination of nuclei of hydrogen and heavy hydrogen, a still more unfortunate discovery for our race, as I understand no one yet claims that this reaction can be of any use except for destruction on a colossal scale. Naturally the main trends of any period are more obvious to the later historian than they can be to the contemporary actor, whose only advantage over

3

the historian is that he can know the outlook and motives of his own people, whereas the sense of the past is the rarest of all gifts.

What will seem to any historian of 1984 the most out-standing factors of our surface world of 1955? I would suggest: the unique character of the Soviet Empire; the birth of the Atlantic Union; the revolt of the greater part of Asia against the control by the West; the abandonment since 1918 of the Old Diplomacy in favour of World Assemblies and public negotiation by Conferences; the place of Britain in World Affairs, and the prospects of the European Depen-dencies especially in Africa; and the development of the new weapons of mass-destruction.

Chapter One

THE UNIQUE CHARACTER OF THE SOVIET EMPIRE

(a) The Elephant and the Whale

THE Soviet Empire is unique in two ways. For the first time in history, the whole flat land-mass from the Elbe to the Pacific—what the late Sir Halford Mackinder called the Heartland of the World—is controlled by one Government. Mackinder regarded the two Americas, Britain, Japan, Malaya and Australia as satellite planets around the "World-Island," meaning Africa and Asia and its European peninsula. In the World-Island lay the Heartland—the area bounded by the Baltic, the Danube and the Black Sea, the Arctic Ocean and the Himalayas; the great drainage area everywhere traversable by land, but to which access by a maritime power can be denied. He included Asia Minor and Persia; with these exceptions, the whole area, including Mongolia, is now in the Soviet Empire. He expounded the formula that the ruler of East Europe would command the Heartland; the ruler of the Heartland would command the World-Island; the ruler of the World-Island would rule the World. All rulers of the Heartland hitherto (from the Huns and Mongols to Tsarist Russia) had failed from lack of man-power and communications (as had the Arabs and the Norse pirates); what he feared was the control of this vast area by Germany, and he hastened the production of his book in 1919 in the pathetic hope that it would be studied by the Versailles peacemakers.

Writing of Germany in 1919, he observed that "the end of the present disorder may only be a new ruthless organization, and ruthless organizers do not stop when they have attained the objects which they at first set before them," and asked with equal foresight, "Is it not productive power which now counts rather than dead wealth?" In fact it was the Germans who

studied and adopted his thesis, so that Hitler's main preoccupation was not war with England, which he hoped to avoid,
but the conquest of Russia.   Still hoping against experience,
the publishers brought out a new edition of Mackinder's book
in 1944 believing it might still be useful for the peacemakers.
Among the many subjects for thought suggested by the geo-
grapher is the possibility of a securely based Land-Power
taking to the sea—the elephant beating the whale in his own
element.   The Cretan civilization was destroyed by the Doric
Greeks of the Mainland, Carthage, greatest Sea Power of
Antiquity, was literally destroyed by the Roman farmers.   The
French Navy from Colbert until the Revolution was better
built and equipped than the English, and the fate of Canada
and India was decided by the persistent priority given in the
French Court to the game of European Dynastic Politics, so
that at critical moments they could not defend their colonies
adequately.   The Imperial German Navy was a completely
artificial creation, competing as a late Victorian joke with the
Horse Marines, but in 1914 it proved a formidable rival in all
arms, as our losses in capital ships at Jutland proved; so
though these examples may be exceptional, they afford some
basis for Mackinder's caution that we must " still reckon with
the possibility that a large part of the great Continent might
some day be united under a single sway " (as it now is) " and
that an invincible Sea-Power might be based on it."

This " single sway," unlike Attila the Hun's or the Mongol
Khans' who depended on their wild, light cavalry living on
the country and their mares' milk, controls in the Russian
Empire itself a population nearing 210 millions whose industrial production in 40 years increased 14 times over while
that of the world increased $2\frac{1}{2}$ times and that of the United
States increased $3\frac{1}{2}$ times.   Their share of the World's Industrial Production increased between 1913 and 1950 sixfold—
from 2·3 per cent to 14·2, while that of the United States
increased by one third—from 27·4 to 36·3.   Soviet coal
production rose from 28 million tons to 261, and the target is
500 million.   At the peak period of the war, when the old
industrial areas in European Russia were largely in German
occupation, the remainder of Soviet industry claimed a

production of 40,000 aircraft, 120,000 guns, 30,000 tanks and armoured cars; in 1950 the civilian delivery was announced as 137,000 tractors, 54,000 combine harvesters, 400,000 lorries. In the same year more than 800,000 new students entered the universities and technical high schools, more than 500,000 technicians entered industry from the higher and secondary technical colleges. A decree of October, 1940, envisaged the annual call-up of a million boys and girls between fourteen and nineteen years old for specialist training in trade, railway and factory schools, for periods varying from six months to two years. Gigantic schemes were under way—the 700 miles Amu-Daria-Caspian irrigation canal, great canal schemes in the lower Volga region linked with mammoth hydro-electric plants planned for Kuibyshev, Stalingrad, Tsimlyansk and Kakhora. The old industrial areas—Moscow, Donbas, the Caucasus—continue to expand, but supplemented by the great new development areas in the East—the middle Volga, Urals, Kuzbas, Karaganda and Central Asia. The production of machine tools had risen in 1950 to 50 per cent above the pre-war records, engineering industry as a whole had risen in 10 years by 83 per cent.

Now the significant feature of this really stupendous development is the priority steadily given to the industries which are essential for war—the metallurgy, oil, electrical, transport. The turnover tax, which is levied on everything produced and delivered, and accounts for more than half the revenue, has been nearly all re-invested in heavy industry; the ratio of investment in the production of capital goods to that of investment in consumer goods has been about 7 to 3; in 1951 10 per cent of the national income was re-invested in consumer goods, 24 per cent in capital construction. Since all production and distribution is controlled from the centre, there is no real distinction between civil and military engineering; and the " Defence Budget " cannot be compared with that of free countries, since equipment can be transferred from one Ministry to another, and contracts are replaced by book-keeping transactions. It is then no matter for surprise that a peace-time army of at least 175 divisions can be maintained together with a very formidable Air Force and a Navy which is particularly strong in the Submarine arm. On July 28th, 1954, it was stated officially in the House of Lords that the Naval manpower in the Soviet Union had risen from 600,000 in 1951 to 750,000. An Admiralty statement on August 26th estimated that in two or three years the Red Fleet would comprise about 30 Cruisers, 150 Destroyers, 500 Submarines, 500 Motor Torpedo Boats, 1,000 Minesweepers. It referred to the high quality of the Cruisers and large ocean-going Submarines, probably annually produced at the rate of 6 and 60 respectively, to the presence of 85,000 men in the Naval Air Arm, and to the probable use of long-range torpedoes, mines with complex anti-sweeping devices, tactical atomic weapons and guided missiles. But all this refers only to the Soviet Empire proper. This Empire has not only absorbed since 1939 the Baltic States, Bessarabia and parts of Finland, Poland, and Czechoslovakia; it has acquired effective physical control through Communist governments and armies of occupation of the European satellites—Poland, Hungary, Czechoslovakia, Eastern Germany, Bulgaria, Roumania, and part of Austria, and these mean a population of over 88 millions, a large auxiliary industry, and 70 additional divisions. Last but not least, it is estimated that nearly half the population of the U.S.S.R. are under 21 years of age, as compared with one third in the U.S.A. and less than one third in the U.K. The great land mass not only has a vast population; it is a virile, young population, increasing by well over two millions a year.[1]

The greatest weakness of this formidable system arises from the long-drawn-out conflict between the Socialist Revolution and the Peasant, who saved the Revolution of 1917 but has been resisting it, sometimes actively, always passively, ever since. In 1929 Stalin ended Lenin's policy of compromise

---

[1] The form in which U.K. population statistics have been published has obscured the fact that even if present trends were changed, a heavy fall in the total population is inevitable. For over a generation the net reproduction rate (i.e. the number of surviving girls per 100 women) and the gross rate as well, was below the minimum required to maintain a stationary population. When the total population begins to fall, the national industrial product will fall still faster, and decreasing demand for capital equipment will cause increased unemployment. (See R. F. Harrod, *Britain's Future Population*, Oxford, 1943.)

and began the process of converting the peasants into members of amalgamated collective farms. He succeeded by 1938 at the cost of 10 million peasants dead or deported, the loss of half the livestock of the country, and a concession of far-reaching significance—that each peasant retained a personal allotment of about 1¾ acres. Wherever Party vigilance has been relaxed, the farm-members have reduced their labour-days and have also frequently encroached on the collective lands. Concealed until 1953 by a statistical blackout, there has been a decrease since 1928 of 8·9 million cows (2·1 million in 1952) and since 1940 of 10 million acres under grain. A great effort in 1950 to remedy the decline by further amalgamations, more machinery, more Party organization, having failed, the facts were published in 1953 and 1954 and Khrushchev launched a great drive, consisting on one hand of all-round financial inducements to the existing farms and encouragement of private breeding, and on the other hand a furious compaign to reclaim 75 million acres of virgin and waste land. So it goes on, a constant see-saw between theory followed by decline in production, relaxation followed by improvement; and it is a permanent dilemma, for, as Lenin saw, " small peasant owner-ship breeds capitalism every hour." The permanent co-existence of a nation of peasant proprietors and one of wholly controlled factory workers is impossible—but the alternative is an increasing population with decreasing food production.

(b) An Empire controlled by Dogma: an all-embracing logical system

How has this tremendous expansion been achieved? This question brings us to the second main feature in which the Soviet Empire is unique and without precedent. Mackinder—to quote him for the last time—wrote in 1919 that there were two types of government—those run by men who thought on strategical, " realist " lines, and those of which the rulers thought in terms of moral idealism, economics, sentiment or prejudice. His example of the former was Prussian academic thought, dominated since Jena by strategical thinking. The Soviet Empire is a new category, and its second unique feature is one that is still very imperfectly realized. It is despotically controlled by a central government which has combined the military strategical habit of mind with the systematic application of a logical comprehensive philosophy, of which the principles are interlocked and serve as guides in the regulation of every branch of activity.

This control of all action by theory is utterly alien to the modern Western mind, and it is expressed in a technical jargon which is boring as well as alien. In consequence the free peoples have instinctively refused to take it in, and this refusal to study its implications is a great asset for the Soviet ruling class—for it is like backing a horse or buying shares on the basis of wishful thinking in ignorance of the form and record of the horse or the Company.

Lenin and Stalin took over the whole Marxist doctrine, but they took over Russia as well, and they therefore soon worked out a qualifying clause which by its practical implications and without departing from the essentials of Marxism, produced results totally unexpected by the early revolutionaries. This qualification was based on their discovery that the proletarian revolution had occurred, not as Marx had foreseen, in the most highly industrialized countries but in a very backward agricultural country which six years of war and revolution and civil war had left bankrupt and disorganized. The new qualifying principle was that, instead of a simultaneous world revolution, the third historical epoch (the first and second being first the feudal and then the capitalist epoch) had started with "socialism in one country." The dictatorship of the proletariat in Moscow (i.e., the leaders of the Communist Party) must therefore play two parts; on the one hand to work for the world revolution, and on the other to protect the Socialist headquarters from premature strangulation by the inevitably decaying but still powerful world of capitalistic imperialism. Hence the basic system of the ownership by the community of all the means of production and distribution, the complete elimination of the employment of one man by another man for his personal enrichment, must be combined with the transformation of a backward mainly agricultural country into a great workshop which would eventually rival and surpass Western Europe and the United States, and be protected by an overwhelming military force.

This combination of the old social democracy with the old strategic imperialist thinking of Peter the Great and Catherine and the Prussian General Staff, was facilitated by the fact that Marxism itself was essentially a fighting creed, based upon a purely materialist conception of the world. Marxism was based on two cardinal assumptions; first, that the material world is the primary fact, and all ideas and institutions and customs are secondary and change with the material basis; and secondly that all the changes in the basic material world arise from a struggle between inner contradictions. When the fight between the contradictions reaches a point at which the change becomes inevitable, this must be accomplished by a revolution. It was therefore natural and logical that from the beginning Lenin and Stalin interpreted their ideology in military strategical terms—the two opposing " camps " of imperialist capital and socialism, the liberation " front " in the Colonies and the " front " of the Colonial oppressors, and most notably in the theory of "strategy" and "tactics" which without any doubt is the key to Soviet policy over the last thirty years.

This means briefly that the permanent strategy is the promotion by every means of the World Revolution, taking all possible action to aggravate the contradictions between labour and capital, between the colonials and the colonial powers, and between the rival capitalist states themselves; the tactics are the line over a given short period, during which the defence of socialist Russia imposes conciliatory or disruptive tactics to check a coalition of the essentially hostile capitalist powers. When Stalin in 1927 told an American labour delegation that the existence of the two opposed systems did not exclude the possibility of agreements, he frankly added that the limits to these agreements were set by the rivalry and conflict between the two systems and that agreement was only possible within the limits permitted by the two systems. He completely endorsed Lenin's statement that the existence of the Soviet Republic side by side with imperialist states for a long time was unthinkable; one or the other must triumph in the end, and before that end, a series of frightful collisions would be inevitable.

A very important corollary of the military conception was
that Socialism could in the last resort only replace Capitalism
by force; all attempts at evolutionary peaceful reform were a
dangerous illusion, and for this reason " Attention must be
concentrated on fighting the so-called left wing of social
democracy, that left wing which by playing with left phrases
and thus adroitly fooling the worker, is retarding their defection
from social democracy. It is obvious that unless the left Social
Democrats are smashed it would be impossible to overcome
Social Democracy as a whole." These basic Stalinist concepts
of strategy and tactics, and the necessity of revolution by force,
have guided Soviet policy for many years. They explain the
support of Hitler in the early thirties by the German Communists, the support of the League of Nations and Popular
Fronts when it became obvious that Hitler had been the wrong
horse to back, the reversion to tough revolutionary strategy in
1946, and the gradual return to tactics, already apparent to
close observers before the death of Stalin when the Marshall
Plan and the beginning of the Atlantic Community revealed
that the tough line had been an error of judgement. It was
the tragic error of Benes and Masaryk in Czechoslovakia that
they failed to appreciate this irreconcilable opposition to all
reformers, and to this day the Labour and Socialist groups in
Western Europe find the greatest difficulty in accepting its
implications. It is fascinating to observe how the same logic
has conditioned the whole course of the internal development
of the U.S.S.R. The problem which faced Lenin and Stalin
inside Russia and still faces Khrushchev and his colleagues, was
and is, how to combine a completely Socialist structure, with
its lack of the personal profit motive, with a gigantic increase
in industrial production, and this with a people who though
possessing many natural gifts and capable of great energy over
short periods, have been noted throughout history for their
tendency to the exact contrary of all those qualities of pleasure
in hard work and discipline and thoroughness which char-
acterize the Germans.

The Stalinist solution can be summed up in two words,
inequality and penalties. He discovered that Socialism, far
from being identical with social equality, could not be made

to work with it; and by scrapping social equality and political democracy, he made Marxism a practical proposition. Political democracy, equality, and Socialism (i.e., State ownership of the means of production and distribution) are three separate things each of which is separately practicable; but they cannot be combined. Before 1914, the Western Socialist Parties had tacitly dropped Marxist economics, as was shown by the small circulation and infrequent editions of Marx's works and their patriotic line-up in 1914; Lenin and Stalin saved it by eliminating equality and representative Parliamentary government. For the Capitalist motive of making profit out of the labour of others, Stalin substituted a system of rewards through the differential allocation by the State of salaries and privileges; and when the State is the universal provider, it is obvious that everything material which appears to make for enjoyment and happiness becomes a privilege. So the nature of the individual's services to the State became the deciding factor not only in the amount of his monied salary, but of his housing, travel and holidays, the education of his children; once more, Russia presents the familiar spectacle of the vast majority, " hewers of wood and drawers of water," and the new *élite* hierarchy of experts in every field whose children start life with ever-increasing advantages. This new aristocracy, in Moscow, in the Provinces, and in the various Soviet Republics, extends from the men at the top to " honoured workers " of science and engineering and art, including the theatre, and their privileges vary with the group to which they belong. They not only can possess both town flats and country houses, and enjoy special privileges and priorities in all amusements as well as travel and holidays; they have special privileges in regard to death duties and income tax (which is very much lower than in the capitalist countries). They can and do acquire the best furs and jewellery, their own motor cars, even their houses, and they can leave these to their successors.

But it was soon found that although these dazzling incentives were sufficient for the naturally ambitious and intelligent, they were not adequate means of getting the maximum of work out of those whom nature had not so endowed. For those whom the carrot would not tempt, the stick was necessary, and the

Labour Code and the whole method of applying social benefits were gradually elaborated for their benefit. The factory recruit brings his school and residence certificate and from that moment his record is kept in his labour book which is returned to him if the Director instructs him to leave the factory. He has become a private soldier in the army of industry. The first time he is late for periods amounting to twenty minutes in a month, he or she must work with a black mark for at least three months with the loss of a week's wages in each month and the loss of accrued social benefits to date. For repeated offences or real absenteeism, the penalties are prison or the labour camp (forced labour incidentally is laid down in the corrective Labour Code and was defended by Molotov in the large Soviet Encyclopaedia). The loss of accrued social benefits is a serious matter, for the whole welfare system has been organized, with the object which Schvernik as head of the trade unions explained as far back as 1933: " To secure a privileged position for the shock workers and long service workers we must use the social insurance weapon so as to promote the attachment of the worker to the undertaking." For example, a man at 60 has the right to an old age pension if he has performed 25 years' work without a break, and women at 55 after 20 years' continuous work; but the penalty of loss of accrued benefits means that those so penalized must start afresh to accumulate their continuous period. The national health system is similarly—and explicitly —organized to encourage the hardworking and efficient and penalize the less successful.

The severity of the penalties varies with the importance attached to the industry; thus the 1952 edition of the Criminal Code lays down that in the case of transport workers, violation of traffic regulations which could lead to damage, accidents, delay in departure of trains and ships, standstill of wagons and boats and any action which might cause a non-fulfilment of transport plans, is punishable by loss of freedom of up to 10 years—unless the offence is obviously malicious in which case " the highest measure of social defence is applied." There are no unemployment benefits, and the functions of the Trade Unions is to assist the Government by raising production

" norms," promoting stakhanovite methods, spreading the knowledge of new techniques and boosting state loans and lotteries. Why not? If the individual's rights are merged in those of the community as a whole, work is a social duty; bad work is therefore sabotage, and no one should change his work unless authority agrees that the change will be for the benefit of the community. If work is to be rewarded according to its social value, then inequality in rewards is surely reasonable. Similarly, holidays, games, etc., should be considered as methods of making the citizen more fit for discharging his social obligations and the responsible brain-worker is entitled to better living conditions and recreation than the plain labourer.

The same inexorable logic permeates the whole Soviet social structure. The artist has no right to show off his virtuosity by playing with bourgeois decadent techniques; whether he be, writer, painter or musician, dramatist or film producer, his business is to work with " socialist realism " in union with the " progressive class," and this can only be ensured if he adheres closely to the propaganda line laid down by a central committee, interpreted by its " agitprop " department, and worked out by committees representing his own profession. The results may be, and mostly are, devastatingly dull, but how else can you avoid dangerous thoughts and images? The scientist also must dedicate himself to the direct service of the community, as interpreted by the proletarian dictatorship; he has no right to amuse himself with sterile research and still less to busy himself with researches which, as in the case of the Western geneticists, actually conflicted with the known principles of Marxist science and soviet social engineering. Even if Lysenko and Michurin genetics are repudiated, the system would not be changed, any more than by Stalin's repudiation of Marr's philology. There is a right to free speech, but rights must not be abused, and the citizen must not abuse this right by anti-social statements; and who can judge whether a statement is anti-social or not except the Party? Then sex; the bourgeois emotional attitude must be replaced by a rational, civic approach. So adultery is banned from the theatre, the films, the press and fiction, and divorce has become difficult, costly and highly discouraged. I have never seen anything to compare with the Puritan atmosphere of Soviet Russia; though not yet Orwell's " 1984," it is on the way!

Now this is all very well for the pure socialist logician, but one can well imagine that it is not to the taste of everyone and the plain fact is that the Labour Code and the total mobilization of the individual for the building up of the great socialist Russia is only enforceable by the machinery of the total Police State. The last Tsars, theoretically autocrats, totally failed; there were strikes, peasant revolts, and the intelligentsia were in a chronic state of revolt. But the Tsarist Secret Police, the Okhrana, numbered only a few thousand, and Tsarist bureaucracy was notoriously corrupt and inefficient. To ensure the total subordination of the individual to Stalinism, the MVD, running into millions, has been built up, with its agents in every factory, in every block of dwellings, its deputy commanders and their assistants in every unit of the Army, Navy and Air Force, in every Government department. So the system requires and could not dispense with the support of the Police State. Not only does it require the support of the Police State; when innocent questioners at popular lectures ask about the Marxist prediction that " the State must wither away " under Socialism—whereas obviously no State has ever been so omnipotent and ubiquitous before—the stock official answer is that which Stalin gave to the 18th Party Congress in 1939, when he said the State would wither away when the danger of military attack from abroad was removed. But the basic feature of the doctrine is that danger from abroad can only cease with the triumph of the World Revolution, and that the dying capitalist Powers must of their nature be irreconcilably hostile; it is obvious that if the doctrine of world revolution were abandoned, the justification for the Police State would disappear with it.

(c) A camouflaged Imperialism

The doctrine not only provides the reason for the Police State, the compulsion of labour, and the total mobilization of all forms of activity in the service of the Soviet State. It is also the cement which holds together the many nationalities now submerged in the monolithic State. In 1921 *Pravda* estimated the " Great Russians " at 75 millions and the minority races at 65 millions, and gave a list of 33 of these latter. There are in fact far more, but it is difficult to give a precise number as there are so many sub-divisions. Some 30 millions spread over several Republics are Moslems of Turkish stock. The total population has increased to well over 200 millions, but the proportion of minorities is probably higher still, on account of the absorption of more national minorities as a result of the last war.

The absolute control of this immense polyglot Empire from the central headquarters in Moscow, forming in fact one monolithic Empire—a strange phenomenon which has been so little considered—is entirely dependent on the maintenance of the doctrine. The Federal Constitution of January, 1924, superficially resembles other Federal Constitutions except that it goes further by allowing in theory the right to secede. Look at it more closely, and you will find that, first, it is assumed that all the Republics, members of the Federation, are Communist governments; and secondly that the Federal Government, while nominally leaving strictly internal matters such as justice, education, agriculture or public health to the individual republics, reserves to itself the right to lay down the general principles even in all these local matters. Not a single action of the local republics is outside the Federal Government's right to lay down and in practice to enforce the directing policies. There is no clear-cut division between Federal and local powers, but there are three types of ministry; the Central Ministry, its counterpart local Ministry, and a type of two-headed Ministry called " Union Republic " Ministry. The Union Republic type of ministry, which in reality means Moscow, includes those of Foreign Affairs, Finance, Labour, nationalized industry, collection of farm produce, inspection services, justice, State security, internal affairs. This classic example of " double-think " functions smoothly because all the " autonomous " Republic Governments are composed exclusively of Communists hand-picked by Moscow. They have a superficial resemblance to the " sister republics " set up by the French Revolution, but the French had not the advantage of the Communist doctrine and the system of the dual Ministry. Under this ingenious façade, the Central Government in Moscow has for 30 years pursued a policy of imperialism which has had no counterpart in any of the so-called Western imperialist systems.

The typical example is offered by the Tadjiks, a primitive Moslem people living between Afghanistan and Tashkent. In about 15 years, the Tadjiks had become a cotton-growing, instead of a rice-growing, people; agriculture had become collectivized with enforced deliveries of meat and wheat, the traditional craftsmen and handworkers had been eliminated and State enterprises substituted, with the deliberate creation of a genuine proletariat which the unprogressive Tadjiks had lacked. The Arabic alphabet had been replaced first by Latin, and then by Russian; Sunday had been substituted for the Moslem Friday and so on. By the middle thirties, the Russian language had become compulsory in all schools, and the years immediately preceding the war were marked by many thousands of arrests and the final elimination of the elements of opposition which in the early twenties had actively resisted the occupation by the Red Army. This elimination synchronized with the final triumph of Soviet industrialization, and we hear now of the exploitation of coal, petroleum and other minerals, of airfields and a great road-building programme. Some minorities have fared worse, having been the victims of mass deportations to unknown destinations— Chechen-Ingushes from near Tiflis, the Turks from the Crimea, the Greeks from the Black Sea, the descendants of Catherine's German colonists from the Volga and many others. The old Tsarist imperialism, condemned as such by Karl Marx and the large Soviet Encyclopaedia, is now represented as the inevitable and benevolent transition from the feudal to a capitalist epoch; Shamil the Circasian, hitherto described as a " great Democrat," has now become the tool of British, Turkish and Persian Imperialism, Sheik Mansur and the Buryat Mongols' hero, Ghiser Khan, have become " feudal Lords." All the Republics must in their literature, drama and films write off the whole of their pre-Russian history, and count the revolution as the dawn of all, and Tsarist Russia as its necessary preliminary. Stalin's brilliant invention of " soviet patriotism," like the " Union Republic Ministry," has provided a simple formula for submerging local patriotism without substituting any obvious obedience to a master race.

The same technique of Imperialism through the agency of puppet governments has been applied in all the European Satellite Countries. Since the Second World War the whole economic life of this great area has been transformed to fit into Soviet requirements. The pre-War pattern of the exchange of primary products (grain and timber, etc.) for Western machinery and textiles has been destroyed by high-pressure industrialization inside the network of the Soviet trade orbit; in the case of Czechoslovakia which was already an Industrial State, its Prime Minister said in 1952 that whereas in 1948 their trade with the West exceeded seventy per cent of their total exports and imports, " this year it is the other way round." This diversion into the Soviet orbit had already occurred before the imposition in 1950 of strategic controls by the NATO countries of exports of certain war materials, controls which in 1954 were largely reduced in consequence of propaganda for " East–West trade." The main object of this propaganda had been to secure these reductions, rather than to restore East–West trade to its pre-War level, which in fact the " Molotov plan " was designed to destroy. The Soviet system has also been thoroughly applied in social, health, and labour legislation (which in the Satellite Countries had been previously developing on Western lines) and to the Party Control of art, literature and religion.

THE MESSIANIC MYTH OF HOLY RUSSIA

Imperialism wears the Mantle of the Panslav Elijahs

This substitution of Communism and Soviet patriotism for the master-race idea, is one obvious explanation of the strange fallacy so widely prevalent that Soviet Russia is not an imperial and colonizing Power. If President Roosevelt could say, " Of one thing I am certain, Stalin is not an imperialist "; if General Eisenhower could say that both the United States and Russia " were free from the stigma of colonial Empire-building by force " (which, as Mr. Chester Wilmot said, meant that politically " both peoples were free from original sin "); if *The Times* could infer in 1953 from Mr. Toynbee's Reith lectures that Communism " in Asia and elsewhere offers freedom from the political and economic ascendancy of the Western powers " (implying that the Soviet Communist Empire is not an " Empire "), is it then surprising that throughout the illiterate peoples of Asia and Africa the Russian claim to be the champion of racial equality and the freedom of colonial peoples from economic exploitation, should be widely accepted as gospel?

This strange unhistorical myth that the Russians are not a colonizing imperial power has, however, a much older academic background, for it is rooted in the delusion that the Russians are the spiritual people *par excellence*, with a mystical Messianic destiny. I had hoped to reserve this subject for a later stage when the outline of the surface events has been sketched, but it profoundly affects the actual contemporary reaction to the problem of Soviet Russia. This legend was built up by the Russian Panslavists in the nineteenth century and by their philosophical fellow-travellers in the West, especially in Germany. Dostoievsky said the Russian people were " the only God-bearing people, the only people called on to renew the world and to save it in the name of a new God." He said they know Christ and have always carried him in their hearts—he did not claim that they knew the Christian doctrine, but that they had assimilated its essence—" It is possible to know many things unconsciously." Chaadaev in 1840 said, " We are the cherished children of the East: are we not its natural heirs? " Danilevsky thirty years later scolded Europe for her selfish hostility to Russia; Europe was declining, Russia about to blossom out. " The Russian genius stands at the antipodes of the European genius, Russia by becoming European fell into a trap." It was Dostoievsky again who said that if they would devote themselves to the organization of " our Asia," they would see a great natural renaissance in Russia. He protested constantly against the influence of the European nations, " incurable liars," who engaged in " an animal struggle in which finally they will founder." (We do not know whether this mystical evangelist was himself lying or not when he confessed to having raped a small girl.)

The Panslavists' assumption of moral and spiritual superiority was warmly endorsed by the Western philosophic fellow-travellers who have had a great influence. Walter Schubart in 1938 said the next century belonged to the Slavs; the "promethean West" had deprived mankind of its soul, and Russia's mission was to return this soul to humanity. "The coming Russia is that refreshing wine which will revitalize the dried-up life stream of today's humanity." The Western soul was egoist, competitive, conquering, the Russian soul was fraternal, co-operative, Christian-pacifist; the youth of Weimar Germany applauded Ernst Curtius when he told them that "the large and human soul of the Russian nation seemed like the spring in which Germany and Europe would be renewed. It is not Goethe nor even Nietzsche but Dostoievsky who is the great literary hero of the young men of Germany." Goethe, Leibnitz, Schopenhauer, Herder, Von Humboldt, Von Hartmann, and many others were claimed as prophets of the eventual decay of Western culture and the conquering synthesis of Russian and Eastern culture. This chorus of self-congratulation has had an hypnotic effect and very few have realized that the same Panslavist "mystics" largely based their gospel on what are in fact the greatest weaknesses of the Russian character. They boasted that the Russian substituted his mystical intuition for the Western logic and sense of causality. Chaadaev said the syllogism of the West was unknown to them, that there was nothing general in their heads, everything was floating and incomplete. If an idea was accepted, it must be absolutely right and be carried to its extreme limit. Dostoievsky said, "We are all nihilists," and prophesied that the good seed would perhaps not arise for two centuries and that "meanwhile terrible things are reserved for us and our children." There at least he was right.

When the émigré Russian Orthodox faculties of theology and philosophy were founded in Paris in the 1920's, their programme described the Western Church as an imperialism that killed liberty, charity, and human thought, and the great Russian exiled philosopher Berdyaev said "they [the Orthodox] prefer Gengis Khan to St. Vladimir," and that "they were seeking to create a united front with all the non-Christian religions of the East against the Christian creeds of the West."

An outstanding feature has always been the attempt to combine the preaching of universal brotherhood, as the great Russian idea, with violent hatred of the culture, history and tradition of the West. Dostoievsky himself, illustrating the lack of logic of which he boasted, combined his hatred of the West with the characteristic statement that "to become truly and completely a Russian means perhaps to become the brother of all men . . . to welcome in that soul all their brethren with an equal love and also perhaps to pronounce the final word in the grand general harmony and the fraternal concord of all races in the evangelical law of Christ." The Soviet rulers rightly regard Dostoievsky's Russian, whether as typical or as an ideal, as quite out of keeping with their own technological enthusiasm, and Bogomolov, an Under-Secretary, once told me that the West would never understand the new Russian till they could forget Dostoievsky. The same combination of fraternal evangelism with the most violent hate-inspired intolerance was peculiarly evident in the case of Tolstoy. The great attraction of his novels lies precisely in his lack of the sense of causality, his lack of orderly composition; they are like a cinema, with no perspective, all the scenes of equal importance. Suddenly converted at the age of 55, he was overwhelmed by the conviction that he had lived "empty of all faith," and his sensual and worldly egotism turned over-night into a mystical egotism, rejecting society, tradition and science. His intolerant hatred vented itself on all non-manual workers, on the Russian and the Western clergy equally, on all medicine because it would not be necessary in a manual-working and agricultural society. He rejected history—"Of what use is it to know what happened a thousand years ago?" Tolstoy believed that "love one another" meant to sink your individuality in the "group soul"; and while preaching that manual labour would bring Utopia, he nevertheless believed that Schopenhauer, Von Hartmann and the Buddhists were perfectly right, humanity must annihilate itself to get rid of suffering.

Tolstoy was one of the greatest novelists of all time, but in his later period one can only conclude with G. K. Chesterton that he " combined in a chaos of contradictions an inhuman puritan and a presumptuous savage." In all the Panslavists' ravings one recurrent note is the appeal to the East. When Lenin said they would overcome the West by way of the East, he was speaking in terms of an established tradition; just as when he prophesied bloody clashes before the attainment of the World Revolution, he was echoing Tiushev's prediction that " Russian Scythianism would reduce the whole world to ashes in a hurricane of flames, storm and tempest, for a new gospel has come into the world." Dostoievsky's pessimism about the fate of the Russian intelligentsia was echoed by others; Herzen, the great nineteenth-century exile, predicted in 1850 that " the death of the old world will carry us away also." A note of pessimism is linked with the feeling of being uprooted, homeless, of belonging neither to the East nor to the West. Chaadaev compared his people to illegitimate children; " We adopt only ready-made ideas . . . we grow but we do not ripen." One is tempted to agree with Turgeniev's summary that " We are still in the gaseous period "; yet Oswald Spengler, joining in the fellow-travellers' chorus, suggested that the ninth great culture might be Russian.

Unhappily, the contradictions and self-criticisms of the Panslavs and their European admirers have been largely unheeded, and what has stuck has been the great propaganda build-up of alleged mystical, self-sacrificing, fraternal Russia. It is a great moral asset for the Soviet Empire, simultaneously appealing to the peoples of the East, and creating doubt and self-questioning amongst the free peoples of the West. The Panslav thesis has lately reappeared with the almost official authority of Professor Toynbee and the B.B.C. In the first of his Reith lectures, Professor Toynbee argued that Russia, like the rest of the world, has been " hit and hard hit by the West," and that Russia's lasting losses as a result of the Tartar conquest were due not to the Tartar conquest but to her Western neighbours. Since then Russia had been invaded by Western armies five times, and it was not till 1945 that Russia recaptured the last piece of these huge territories taken from her by Western powers. Professor Toynbee says these Western conquests were " one of the hard facts of Russian life that moved the Russians to submit to the yoke of a new native power at Moscow which, at the price of autocracy, imposed on Russia the political unity that she now had to have if she was to survive. This Moscovite Russian political tradition has perhaps always been as disagreeable for the Russians themselves . . . but unfortunately the Russians have learnt to put up with it . . . no doubt because they have felt it to be a lesser evil than the alternative fate of being conquered by aggressive neighbours." In six pages Professor Toynbee refers thirteen times to Communism being of Western origin, frequently adding that it is a Christian heresy; and insists that Russia has now this " Western spiritual weapon in her hands " which " nothing in the Russian tradition could have led them to invent for themselves."

This thesis of Russia turning a Western spiritual weapon against the West is a cardinal point in Professor Toynbee's argument, and leads to the conclusion that " it looks as if, in the encounter between Russia and the West, the spiritual initiative, though not the technological lead, has now passed, at any rate for the moment, from the Western to the Russian side." Now this authoritative statement that the Russians have accepted the Stalinist Police State as being a lesser evil than the alternative fate of being conquered by aggressive neighbours, has one outstanding significant feature to which I saw no attention drawn in the extensive press comment upon the lectures. One presumes Professor Toynbee really means that the Western nations have renounced their Christian heritage, concentrating exclusively on their technological values; and that the Russian materialist creed is really a spiritual one. But on the face of it his defence of the Russians seems identical with the official defence given by Stalin and all his propagandists to the Russian people when they ask why the State is not withering away.

It may or may not be inwardly accepted by the Russian people, but I am totally at a loss to understand how it can be reconciled with the main facts of Russian history. By what magic did the supposedly weak inoffensive pacifist Tsars extend their Empire in three centuries from the Grand Duchy of Moscow to an area extending from the Vistula to Vladivostok and from the Arctic Sea to the borders of Afghanistan? How had it happened that in 1921 *Pravda* could estimate the non-Russian national minorities as being nearly equal in numbers to the Great Russians themselves? Why does the area now controlled by Moscow extend from the Elbe to Vladivostok and include Germans, Poles, Czechoslovaks, Hungarians and so on? And can the reconquest in 1945 of the Baltic peoples and the Poles and the Western Ukrainians be fairly described as the recovery of the huge territories taken from Russia by Western Powers in the thirteenth and fourteenth centuries? I had always thought it was generally accepted that no other government had over a period of centuries pursued such a systematic consistent policy of aggrandizement and expansion as the Russian governments have done. Was not the Russian Bear with his designs on Constantinople and India the perpetual bogy even of proud secure Victorian England? And is there any Court or dynasty in history of which the domestic annals have been marked by so many scenes of revolting cruelty and hideous corruption as the Russian Court from Ivan the Terrible to Rasputin?

The picture is further distorted by Professor Toynbee's insistence that the Russians now have the spiritual initiative because they have taken over a Western Christian heresy, Marxism, which he says nothing in the Russian tradition could have led them to invent for themselves. Surely one of the salient characteristics of the whole Panslav tradition was precisely their repudiation of Western capitalism, their exaltation of the holy poverty and spiritual grandeur of the Russian mujik, and above all their exaltation of the revolutionary, messianic idea which fits in so perfectly with the equally messianic apocalyptic theories of Karl Marx? The distinguished rabbis from whom Karl Marx was descended must surely have turned in their graves when Professor Toynbee insisted that Marxism was a " Christian " heresy. On the contrary, Marx's religious faith in the great cataclysmic revolution which would abruptly establish a classless world was sheer emotional messianism, which had been so completely contradicted by the course of events since his death that only an unhistorically-minded people like the Russians could have accepted it as gospel truth in the 1920's. Though it might be an over-simplification, it would be easier to prove that Marxism was not a " Christian " heresy, that it could only in a relative and geographical sense be called a " Western " heresy, and that its basic idea that economic motives and changes are the sole ultimate determining facts in human history is definitely an un-Western and un-European idea, except as a philosophic reflexion of nineteenth-century Industrialism. And it would be easier still to show that there was everything in the Russian tradition to prepare them for its ready acceptance.

There are still two further reasons for which it is necessary for the Soviet Government to maintain the whole Marx-Stalin doctrine. First, it is essential that the Soviet state should continue to be officially atheist (a fact emphasized by *Pravda* in June, 1954). The total exploitation of the individual for the benefit of the community, in actual fact for the building up of the Soviet Empire, can only be rationally justified and accepted if it is accepted that the individual personality has no moral rights against the community. The gigantic technological development inside the Soviet Empire simply could not have taken place had the Soviet régime recognized the right of every individual citizen to " life, liberty and the pursuit of happiness." The present position of religion in the U.S.S.R. is a compromise, an application of tactics to the internal situation. For the Party and the new governing class the profession of atheism is indispensable. For the unthinking, unambitious masses, it is permissible to attend the services of the Orthodox Church. This compromise was established when it was thought that the Church had been sufficiently conditioned by the early persecutions during which 200 out of 250 bishops had disappeared; but the Orthodox Church, inherited from Byzantium, had always been a Russian State Church, relying on the secular arm because it lacked the missionary spirit, and its ideal of holiness had been the hermit, isolated from the world of men. At present the compromise works; but there is an inherent fundamental antagonism between Christianity (and Mohammedanism also), and the basic postulates of the Soviet system.

Finally, if the Soviet doctrine was to be abandoned as a whole the Soviet Empire would lose its great and unprecedented asset, the support of its fifth column in all the free countries. Soviet patriotism is " patriotism of a higher type," for being identified with the Soviet ideal it can be adopted by Communists of all nations. " One cannot call oneself a Marxist," said Stalin, " unless one openly and devotedly supports the first proletarian dictatorship." This was repeated by Zhdanov in 1947 and 1948, and the Soviet Government has working for it in every country an active minority of fanatical adherents and a far larger number of fellow-travellers and woolly sympathizers. Throughout recorded history, no government has possessed this incalculable asset.

All these lines of enquiry, which for lack of space I have only briefly outlined, seem to me to converge on one central conclusion. That conclusion is that the basic Soviet structure is one indivisible and interlocking whole, because the Soviet colonial Empire, the new industrial production, and the personal security of the governors themselves, all three essentially depend on the maintenance of the Police State and the theory of the conflict of two opposed worlds leading fatally and inevitably to the World Revolution. If it were admitted that the individual has a value independently of the community, if indeed any inalienable moral rights in the individual were recognized, any genuine recognition of freedom of discussion and of association, the whole fabric would be quickly and fatally undermined. Within the limits of the doctrine, many tactical gestures are possible.[1] Foreign diplomatists

[1] Since this was written, the abrupt resignation of the Chairman of Ministers, Malenkov, on February 8, 1955, has provided a salutary correction to much loose thinking. A baseless legend had grown up which represented him as personally identified, even under Stalin, with a real liberal " reforming " programme at home and in foreign relations. Both his own record and the circumstances of his resignation strongly suggest that he had never been more than the Agent of the real triumvirate, Khrushchev, Molotov and Marshal Bulganin. While his resignation may have been precipitated by his disagreeing (this is speculation) with the draft of Molotov's speech on foreign affairs, it had probably been decided to make Malenkov a scapegoat for the continued failure to solve the agricultural crisis. The two main points emerged that the Stalinist group were still in power and that the succession to Stalin and the rivalry between the Party and the Army were still undecided; the issue had been narrowed by the elimination of Beria.

may be given relatively more freedom of travel. Visas may be given more freely as in the 1930's. A partial amnesty may be given to ordinary criminals. Foreign Communists might be encouraged as in the 1930's to join in Popular Front Governments. But only within the limits of the doctrine. If at any point a basic change in the doctrine was effected—and it certainly could happen—its repercussions must inevitably be felt throughout the whole system and if they were not checked, the system could not long survive. There can be no question of individual changes of heart or attitude, for the members of the governing class have been conditioned by their whole training never to approach any question with an empirical personal attitude, but always in terms of their doctrine, that doctrine of which Stalin said, it is their "compass" and "that there can be no doubt that as long as we remain faithful to this doctrine, as long as we possess this compass, we shall be successful in our work."

The general Western reaction during the first months following the death of Stalin showed conclusively that very few indeed were willing to face up to this conclusion. Instead there was an orgy of wishful thinking mixed with wild guesses about the personal views and motives of this or that Kremlin personality. It is not surprising. The whole system, and the mentality and mental approach which it has created in those who control it, is utterly alien to the Western mind, and it is human nature to reject unconsciously and automatically that which is utterly alien. In many periods of the past, the Western mind would have been more capable of understanding the problem with which it was confronted, but, in the present age the habit of approaching all questions, if they cannot be postponed, with an empirical, opportunist attitude, seeking always for compromise and the line of least resistance, has become almost a second nature.

It required the Berlin conference, a year after Stalin's death, during which, according to a Belgian paper, two million words were spoken (with the net result of agreement to have a meeting at Geneva to discuss Indo-China and Korea), to make it evident except to wishful thinkers that the situation was

essentially the same that it had been the year before.   Changes
there had been, but these were changes in the feelings of the
satellite people, especially in Eastern Germany, not changes in
Soviet Policy—for the Berlin Conference had proved to any
objective mind that the Soviet Government under Molotov
had no more intention than it had under Stalin, of relaxing its
hold on East Germany unless it thereby achieved its prime
objects, and that its primary objects still were to check the
formation of a European Defence Community and to disrupt
the embryonic Atlantic Community.

Both these main objectives were pursued with marked
success in the Summer of 1954 through the medium of the
Geneva Conference, which had two different aspects.   Its
direct ostensible purpose was a settlement in Korea and
Indo-China.   Its indirect, but for Soviet world policy far
more important, aspect was the effect on Anglo-American
relations and on the ratification of the European Defence
Community treaty.   The effect on Anglo-American relations
was extremely bad.   On June 16th, when the Conference had
been running since April, *The Times* commented that " when
the whole Western Alliance had been nearly thrown into
disarray by Anglo-American disputes over Asian policy in the
past few weeks, it is obviously essential that steps should be
taken without delay to bring the two countries together in their
policies."   In other words, the U.S. and British Governments
had been compelled by public opinion to embark on a Far
Eastern Conference not only without having reached preliminary understanding as to what they wanted, but with a
serious division of opinion which became a public dispute after
the conference had started.   Whatever the local results in
the Far East had been, this Anglo-American friction was a
success for the major objective of Soviet policy, as was the
postponement once more of the E.D.C.   What exactly were the
direct local results in the Far East?   As regard Korea, admitted
failure.   In Indo-China, there was agreement to a cease-fire
and to a programme for settlement.   Under the programme a
country of 22 millions which the West had hoped to defend was
partitioned on a line which left 12 millions—including
well over one million Christians—under Communist rule

together with important centres like Hanoi and the mineral resources of Tongking. Elections in Vietnam and the neutralization of Laos and Cambodia were to be supervised by a Commission composed of Canada, Poland and India, the last-mentioned having a casting vote; even assuming the effectiveness and impartiality of the Commission as a whole, the chances of the remainder of Vietnam, and of Laos and Cambodia, passing also under Communist control are rated high by the local experts.

The agreement is a *fait accompli*, but it has raised a question for future guidance which a surprisingly large part of the public comment has ignored: could not the same local results have been obtained by direct negotiation between those chiefly concerned? The agreement registered on the one hand the military results to date and on the other hand the prudent decision of the Chinese and Soviet Governments to consolidate the existing gains as a base for political advance and to avoid the danger of provoking the United States further at this stage. These considerations would have been equally effective without a conference, and an agreement without a conference would have avoided the Anglo-American controversy, the association (and possible loss of prestige) of the British and American Governments with the terms of the cease-fire, and the demoralization of the wishful thinkers by the false impression that the agreement was a great achievement of conference diplomacy rather than the acknowledgment of hard facts. The Geneva Conference, or the misrepresentation of it, stirred a fresh orgy of wishful thinking, and the false impression was skilfully exploited by Soviet diplomacy to revive with an air of novelty its old Berlin Conference proposals for the withdrawal of occupation forces from Germany and an all-German Government before having elections in Germany. The agreement reached had nothing to do with moderation or compromise; whether in straight negotiation or conference debate Communist governments are moved solely by calculations of power politics, and the conference merely provided opportunities for moral successes in a wider field than the limited area affected by the agreement. Incidentally, but for the delay between the Berlin and Geneva conferences, the unexpectedly powerful offensive against Dien Bien Phu might never have been staged.[1]

TARDY REACTION TO THE SOVIET CHALLENGE

The Atlantic Community is born

I suggested that a future historian of what I called the surface events at this moment would select amongst the outstanding factors first the unique character of the Soviet Empire and secondly the growth of the Atlantic Community.

The birth and early years of the North Atlantic Treaty Organization constitute the first response by the West to the challenge of Communist Russia.   It was not a ready response; it is deeply unfortunate that it did not begin three years sooner. Its necessity should already have been obvious, at the latest, when Zhdanov in creating the Cominform announced to the world that the Socialist Camp as a result of the war was far stronger and the other " camp " correspondingly weaker, and that the " contradictions " which would lead to the World Revolution were now having full play.

The fortunate veto on the reception of Marshall Aid by the satellites was followed by the *coup d'état* in Czechoslovakia and this liquidation of a fellow-travelling Socialist Government, highly respected in the West, was the first red light which no amount of wishful thinking could obscure.   Perhaps even more effective was the systematic sabotage of the United Nations Organization in which so many, undeterred by the fate of the League of Nations, had put all their hopes.

Between February, 1946 and March, 1953, of 56 Recommendations in the Supreme Council supported by seven votes, 55 were rejected by the veto of the Soviet Government.   Of

---

[1] The same kind of considerations arose when the Security Council intervened to promote a cease-fire for the evacuation of the islands to Formosa. *The Times* in its leading article of February 4, 1955, said: " The opinion has been expressed in these columns more than once that the United Nations approach being public was not the most promising way.   There was always the danger that any public discussions would put a cease-fire further off because each side would have to stand on questions of principle and raise claims of sovereignty over Formosa or over the Mainland of China, and the warning has more than once been given that China was never likely to acknowledge any cease-fire that was formal or official; to do so would in her eyes prejudice her claims to Formosa."

the special bodies created by UNO 11 were boycotted from their inception, 34 at various times, by the Soviet Union. The North Atlantic Treaty of 1948 was not, in itself, a defensive alliance against Soviet Russia or any other Power. It is an arrangement between certain states—now with the addition of Greece and Turkey 14 in all, for collective defence against attack on any one of them from any quarter; and by its second article it is also a joint undertaking to strengthen their free institutions and promote their stability, well-being and economic collaboration. This article is a main obstacle to the admission of Russia as a member. It is a great experiment in joint planning for peace or war, and it is the first real and practical experiment in international collaboration. Although circumstances have led to the main emphasis being placed on mutual defence against the Soviet threat which had brought it into existence, the North Atlantic Treaty does cover four obvious objectives for any British Government: the co-operation of the members of the British Commonwealth, co-operation with the United States, the unity and recovery of Western Europe and the economic security of the United Kingdom (which it is no longer possible to combine with any attempt at military security without Allies).

The Atlantic Union has, so far, made no attempt to create any armed force comparable to that possessed by the Soviet Union even without its satellites. The target of 50 divisions set at Lisbon in 1952—compared to the minimum number of 175 Soviet divisions—was intended as a deterrent, and it is still admittedly a target and not a reality. Apart from the actual provision of ground and air troops, which has in fact so far served its deterrent purpose, the administrative and moral achievements of the NATO are far more striking than is commonly realized. It has built up a permanent inter-national team, in the Secretariats and the permanent repre-sentatives, for which there has been no precedent in times of peace. Not only are the representatives of 14 governments working together as one unit; 14 nations have agreed to communicate their defence estimates to an international staff and the North Atlantic Council. In the previous period this would certainly have been regarded as an infringement of national independence.   The local military bases are jointly financed on an International budget and some 30 committees and boards are at work.   These military bases, maintained in peace by one Government on the territory of another, are one of the most important results technically and morally of the Atlantic Organization.   Technically, because the complexity of modern weapons and equipment has made the old practice of " preparing for the last war " and relying on there being sufficient time for preparation after war has started, obviously suicidal.   Morally, because the establishment of military bases is a categorical assurance that the establishing power will be completely involved from zero hour, and it is equally a definite warning to the potential enemy of the same fact.   It is highly probable—I would almost think certain—that there would have been no war in 1914 (and therefore still less in 1939) had there been American bases in Britain and British bases in Belgium.

The European Defence Community, incorporating a German contingent, was the natural corollary of the Atlantic Union. The plain surface reason was military necessity; the NATO countries are unable to place a sufficiently deterrent force in the field without over-straining their economies.   The more profound reason belongs properly to the later stage in my argument;   at this point I would only say that a unique opportunity exists, such as has not presented itself for centuries, of dealing with a German Government, which, thanks to the shock of the war and the temporary elimination of East Germany, does represent the Christian, European tradition which has always been present in Germany but which has so often been overridden by the pagan primitive teutonic tradition which found such an apt instrument in the military monarchy of Prussia.   To obstruct its formation has been a prime motive of Soviet policy;   and the decision of the British Government, announced by Sir Anthony Eden at the London meeting in October, 1954, to maintain a standing Army and Air Force permanently in Europe, may prove the most important event since the formation of the Atlantic Union, and indeed in modern history.   Some may still regret that a unique historic opportunity for a great European Commonwealth, presented by the simultaneous holding of authority by Adenauer, Schuman, and De Gasperi has been lost. These three Christian statesmen represented a European tradition which, as I submit in the Second Part of this book, has been struggling against heavy odds since the disruption of the Roman Empire; the fact that they were simultaneously leading their three countries was a coincidence which may not recur. Nevertheless, if the Act of London is carried into effect, a European defence system will have been formed with Britain and West Germany collaborating; a great historical event from which there can be no return. Less spectacular, but also of high significance, was the arrival in August, 1952, of the Coal and Steel Community, a great step towards the integration of Western Europe.

Chapter Two

INTERNATIONAL RELATIONS IN THE "CENTURY OF THE COMMON MAN"

I N the preceding chapter I have tried to present the Soviet challenge as a whole; as a unique force representing simultaneously a State with modern equipment controlling the whole Euro-Asiatic plain and building the world's second largest navy; as an Empire organized and guided in accordance with a philosophy, and a philosophy which is of its nature exclusive, aggressive, and Atheist-Materialist; as a camouflaged imperialism of which the real character is misunderstood by vast masses outside it; and finally as the inheritor both of Tsarist Imperialism and mystical Panslavist Messianism. Secondly, I have outlined the political and military (rather than doctrinal) answer of the free nations—the North Atlantic Union, the attempted European Defence Community, the rearming of West Germany combined with the British military pledge within the framework of the Brussels Treaty. This story, even in outline, has indicated the influence on Western policy of diversionary and irrational factors, of the persistence of wishful thinking and reluctance to face obvious facts; influences which have resulted in alarmingly slow reactions and difficulty in getting necessary things done. The next stage is to discuss the manner and method—in addition to the content or substance—of the Western response to the Soviet challenge, beginning at the most external and surface level with the men and machinery of international life.

This enquiry—the subject of Part One—will raise many thorny problems: the influence of mass opinion and national passion on the conduct of foreign affairs; the side-tracking of diplomacy during the age of conferences and the substitution of shams and unrealistic slogans for principles. It must involve consideration of Britain's place in World Affairs; of the consequences of her threefold break from national tradition in adopting Free Trade, in the conduct of the 1914 War, and in the decision, without any serious consideration, to impose throughout the Colonial Empire copies of the British Parliamentary System at the moment when its historic basis is threatened in Britain itself, and without studying the results of the contrary policy adopted by the other Colonial Powers. I realize that in these chapters I risk appearing as an Iconoclast shooting left and right. My case is that owing to deeper causes—the subject of Part Two—our public opinion has tended to become vague, uncritical and irresponsible, and its expression in national policy, in consequence, floundering, confused and vacillating.

The lamentable slowness of the Western peoples and governments in realizing the true nature of the Soviet menace and in laying the foundations of the Atlantic Union is not dissimilar to the slowness of the same people in realizing the nature of the Nazi menace between 1932 and 1939, if indeed, judging by the practical test of rearmament, they ever realized it at all until the war was on them. There is a further parallel in the period immediately after the First World War. As Sir Harold Nicolson has pointed out, Lloyd George had realized by January, 1919, that the fantastic reparations demanded from Germany, even if they could be collected, would damage our own economy, but it took the House of Commons eighteen months to reach the same conclusion, and French opinion five years, involving meanwhile the ruin of the German middle classes. This contributed very greatly to the eventual supremacy of Hitler, by completing the upheaval caused by the war which released the primitive mass instincts to which he appealed. Any enquiry into the deeper causes of this slowness and delay raises the question of the impact of democratic control over foreign policy. By democratic control I mean the persistent active influence of mass opinion, as opposed to occasional fits of excitement over special issues. This active influence is a novelty in modern Europe; we must go back for an analogy to the ancient Greek city states, and even there the analogy is only partial, for the citizens of those states were for the most part leisurely slave owners, who were able to spend much of their time engaging in endless discussions.

Until the twentieth century, this influence of mass opinion was only occasional. When exerted, whether in the Greek city states or in modern Europe, it was normally in favour of war-like action. Mr. Henderson in his *Crimean War and Diplomacy* quotes Lord Clarendon writing as Secretary of State on July 5th, 1853, " Our pacific policy is at variance with public opinion, so it cannot long be persisted in." A few other examples out of many spring to mind at once. The wave of hysteria over Jenkins' ear; the French Revolution launching the twenty-year cycle of wars for freedom; the great outcry against the Prince Consort, who, rumour alleged, was incarcerated in the Tower of London, because he was known to oppose the Crimean War. Then there was the war stampede of the French in 1870, graphically described by the British Ambassador in Paris in his despatches, when Bismarck doctored the Ems telegram with just that intention[1]; the Press outcry in Paris and London against the Hoare-Laval proposals, which Mussolini had actually instructed Grandi in London to accept at the moment when the latter heard of Sir Samuel Hoare's resignation. Unfortunately, to make matters worse, this ferocity of mass opinion has been apt to be exerted only on specific issues, for in general when no specific object of hatred is presented to it, mass opinion is in favour of a vague pacifism and as much disarmament as it can get. When confronted in peace times with the competing claims of social welfare and military security, the mass influence is likely to be exerted in favour of the former. However, throughout the nineteenth century while the great urban masses were growing,

[1] The immediate origin of the Franco-German War in 1870 was connected with a complicated and confused crisis caused by the acceptance of an offer of the Spanish Crown by Prince Leopold of Hohenzollern-Sigmaringen, secretly encouraged by Bismarck. In the end the candidature had in fact been withdrawn with the acquiescence of the King of Prussia when Bismarck published a telegram from his Sovereign to himself which described a friendly interview with the French Ambassador. Bismarck without altering a word rearranged the text and made omissions, so that it gave the impression that the King had answered a challenge with a humiliating rebuff. He succeeded in provoking a wave of hysteria in which the French Government ordered general mobilization and then declared war, without allies and isolated by a series of follies described by Gladstone as " almost without a parallel," and which were due to the weakness of the new " Liberal Empire " régime under the pressure of a Chauvinist Press and public opinion.

their interest in foreign affairs was spasmodic and at long intervals. Canning and Palmerston both welcomed public opinion in this sphere but they were thinking in terms of the educated middle class who studied their *Times* with solemn assiduity. They did not realize how even a fairly educated electorate would come to be mobilized and exploited, as Bismarck, the first thorough manipulator of the Press, was able to do. During the nineteenth century, foreign policy was ultimately controlled by the educated middle classes, was greatly influenced by what Professor Mowat has called the " Monarchs' international," and was carried out by the Ministries for Foreign Affairs and the old Diplomatic Corps: its guiding principle was the doctrine of the balance of power, sometimes called the European system or the concert of Europe.

The strain of the 1914–18 War, and ignorance of the events which had led up to it, were responsible for an extraordinary forgetfulness of the outstanding fact that from the Congress of Vienna in 1815 until the outbreak of war in 1914 Europe as a whole had known a century of peace, which had been broken only by the remote Russo-Turkish and Crimean wars, by the relatively small campaigns for the unification of Italy, and the brief localized Austro-Prussian and Franco-German wars of 1866 and 1870. These campaigns, although already fought with modern national armies, cost so relatively little in men, money or civilian property, that the damage was repaired within a few years not only in the victor state but in the defeated one, and John Stuart Mill could plausibly argue that a war only effected in a year what would anyhow be replaced in a normal decade of industry and rebuilding; the daily life of the Western peoples was practically unaffected by *any* of these wars.

The reality of this century of peace and the unprecedented progress and prosperity which accompanied it, were obscured, in the period starting with 1918, by the wide currency of an elementary confusion between foreign policy and diplomatic negotiation; by an ill-informed attribution of the 1914 War to the diplomatic body, and by the wishful thinking engendered by the League of Nations (without the co-operation of the

United States) and the misleading slogan of collective security, which had no meaning after the natural failure to give it teeth in the Geneva Protocol in 1924, but which served to discredit the old and tested principle of the balance of power. This principle, in the mind of nineteenth-century statesmen of all views from Castlereagh and Metternich to Gladstone, simply meant the protection of the independence of small countries, and was the only practical alternative to imperialism. In so far as any individuals can be held responsible for the 1914 War, the chief blame must attach to the General Staffs, particularly the Austro–Hungarian Chief of Staff, Field-Marshal Conrad, who seems from 1906 onwards to have deliberately worked for a preventive war against Serbia and ultimately Russia. Bismarck, who said that he had found General Staffs very useful when he wanted to overcome his sovereign's reluctance to make war, but a nuisance when he did not want war, was himself over-ridden at times by the German General Staff, for example when they insisted on keeping Metz after the Franco–German war. The British people, without knowing it, were really fast-bound by General Staff and Admiralty undertakings to their French opposite numbers, which they had been building up since 1905, first without their Governments' authority and then with their general authorization but with no knowledge of the details.

This activity of the General Staffs unfortunately coincided with (or resulted from) a sudden deterioration in the character of the European monarchs, who as a group, throughout the nineteenth century, had worked in the interests of peace on the whole. Francis Joseph of Austria had become senile, Nicholas the Second, though desperately anxious to avoid war with Germany, was invertebrate, and Kaiser Wilhelm, rightly described by Queen Victoria as a " hot-headed, conceited, and wrong-headed young man, devoid of all feeling," was swept off his feet after his promise of support to Austria, itself the result of his fury and regret at having neglected to renew Bismarck's Russo-German agreements. Even the Kaiser did, too late, try to avoid war.

The popular delusion that the old diplomacy had been a cause of the Great War arose from a confusion of thought expressed in President Wilson's famous formula, " Open covenants, openly arrived at." This contained two propositions. The first was the legitimate though debatable one that treaties should be published as soon as concluded. It is debatable, because if for example Bismarck had explained his far-reaching policies to his neighbours and had published all his engagements, he would probably not have created the German Empire; and the same applies for example to Richelieu or Cavour. I think myself, on balance, that it would have been better for humanity if all three had failed, and that the requirements under Article 18 of the old League Covenant that all Treaties must be registered with the League Secretariat was about the only good result of the Versailles Conference. The secrecy of the old Treaties and engagements was, however, the responsibility entirely of the politicians, and in no way that of the diplomatists.

The second proposition, that covenants should be " openly arrived at," was a strange decision on the part of the representative of a nation of businessmen, for what businessman would conduct all his business in the full glare of publicity? Open diplomacy is a contradiction in terms; if it is open it is not diplomacy. The primary business of diplomacy is to achieve results, by moderation, tact, and compromise when possible. The ambassador can and should influence the course of events by his reports to his Government and by his personal relations with the people with whom he is negotiating, but the broad lines of foreign policy should be settled by the governments. When the actual negotiation is carried out under a running fire of press comment and parliamentary discussion, every compromise is likely to involve loss of face by one party or the other, people strike attitudes from which they feel unable to depart, and this is an aspect which becomes far more important when the negotiation is carried on by a conference among politicians, to which I will refer later. The memoirs of ex-Ambassadors of the pre-1914 period like Jules Cambon or Jusserand, and the published State papers, including for instance Sir Eyre Crowe's memorandum of 1907, afford convincing proof that the old diplomatists, far from encouraging war, had consistently warned the governments concerned of the dangers into which they were running. In the nineteenth century, the diplomatists, backed by Foreign Ministers who both had leisure to think and were in the habit of frequently meeting each other, not in spectacular conferences, but during holiday visits to spas and watering places, with rare exceptions played a major part in the conservation of the great peace of the nineteenth century.

While diplomacy of some sort has existed from early times, and there have been permanent Ambassadors and Ministers since the break-up of the European family of nations four centuries ago, the diplomatic body as a professional career service, with its own code of rules and conventions, was really a creation of the early nineteenth century, and it is easy to prove if one had space for illustrations, that to these men as a class is due very much of the credit. They spoke the same language (literally in the shape of French), they shared a common code of behaviour, a common training, and because they got to know each other well both at their posts and when they met again in other appointments, they developed a kind of common opinion about Ministers of Foreign Affairs and Ambassadors who were tricky and unreliable. This common opinion, like the unwritten law of the fo'c'sle at sea, acted as a salutary check. Above all, their whole technique and professional pride lay in getting negotiations to run smoothly and politely; they usually developed a rather objective, sceptical outlook, and their professional tendency and their temperament made them therefore as a class definite workers for peaceful solutions. It is of equal importance that if you spend a lifetime in discussing with people of other countries, you acquire the habit of seeing the two sides which exist in so many questions, and this tended to create a sense of balance and measure in forming judgements and above all an ingrained suspicion of all one-sided points of view. This, and the supreme need for patience, was what Talleyrand had in mind in his famous advice, " Above all not too much zeal." So on the whole the diplomatists acted quietly behind the scenes as a brake on the feverish nationalism released by the French Revolution, and on all the unreasoned fanaticism, self-righteousness, and popular hysteria which it engendered and

which Hitler and the Nazis so fatally exploited. Without
going so far as Count D'Ormesson in speaking of them as the
most civilized portion of mankind, one can fairly say that the
diplomatist represented in a real sense the old cultural unity
of Europe. Every profession has its " occupational maladies,"
and in the case of the old diplomatic body there was a tendency
among the less efficient members to undue solemnity and the
use of conventional clichés, as in the case of the diplomatic
hack in Marcel Proust (" *C'est bien dans la manière du Ballplatz
avec son eternel double-jeu*! ")—but these were harmless manner-
isms such as exist in all professional bodies, and were more than
offset by the relative absence of hypocrisy, intellectual dis-
honesty or ruthless personal ambition.

The value of this professional *esprit de corps* stands out now in
the contrast between the shrunken body of representatives of the
free countries, and the large separate block which represents
the Soviet Empire and its satellites. Once when we invited in
Ankara our Soviet colleagues to a reception for Turkish and
diplomatic friends, two of them sought out a member of my
staff whose family had belonged to the English colony in
Tsarist Russia and who had lived there as a child, and asked
her, " What is the national celebration for which this party is
being given? " They were amazed to hear that it was just a
friendly social gathering. At the official parties, at which
alone the Communist representatives could meet the representatives of the free states, the two diplomatic blocks tended
to keep apart and limit their intercourse with their colleagues
from the other camp to a formal exchange of " Bonjours."
Unfortunately, this is not a passing accident or due to any
personal incompatibilities; it is the result of a system which
regards mankind as irreconcilably divided into two hostile
camps, and which makes the representatives of the Soviet
camp terrified of being suspected by their chiefs of being
contaminated. It has led to negotiation being regarded as a
kind of warfare, a matter of scoring points against the adversary
and collecting scalps. If Clausewitz thought that war was
policy carried on by other means, so do the totalitarians regard
peaceful negotiation as warfare carried on by other means, in
fact " Cold War." This is the exact reverse of the old

diplomatic tradition, which assumed that negotiation must be a process of give and take, and that the only lasting agreements could be those which were genuinely accepted by both parties and left behind the minimum of resentment and no desire for revenge at the first opportunity. The personal knowledge of foreigners and their reactions was of special advantage to the governments of an insular country like Great Britain. Count Mensdorf, the Austrian Ambassador who stayed so long and was so popular in London before 1914, said that British politicians almost without exception had no clear idea about foreign conditions, and that they were " more ignorant, inexact and amateurish than we believed." Clemenceau told King Edward VII at Marienbad, " Some of your public men are appallingly ignorant." Sir Harold Nicolson has summarized the characteristics of British politicians in connection with foreign affairs as ignorance of foreign psychology (rather than of foreign conditions), unbounded optimism, dislike of facing unpleasant possibilities in advance, and a thirst for comforting agreements.

Agreements abound in pitfalls for the amateur, for a vague, ambiguous provision in a treaty or agreement can easily be the source of far greater dangers in the future than if agreement had not been reached at all. This brings us to one of the cardinal virtues of a diplomatic training, that it develops like a second nature the habit of precise wording in documents, without of course subjecting them to the extreme niceties exacted by courts of law in private litigation. Publicity not only makes concession on either side more difficult, but it may also easily excite public opinion by the ventilation of grievances and claims. The then head of the Swedish Foreign Office told me many years ago that the separation of Norway and Sweden might very easily have ended in war if at the time there had been a League of Nations with all the attendant publicity, and recrimination before an international forum, and I venture to record as illustrations in this connection two small personal experiences which happen to remain in my mind. When I was in Buenos Aires in the middle of the last war, and the conservative Argentine Government were being incessantly attacked by the Opposition for their neutrality, I had to present for the record one of our periodical protests about Argentine encroachments in the Falkland Islands area, and the Minister for Foreign Affairs could have obtained considerable credit and spiked the guns of his adversaries by making an incident out of it. Instead, I was able to obtain agreement that it was in the best interests of both parties that he should accept the protest as an academic one necessary to maintain our dossier in the event of an arbitration of the questions at issue. Some years later, when I was in Moscow, an English officer crash-landed in the Soviet Eastern zone of Germany and attempts on the part of the military authorities in Berlin to secure his release had failed. I was able to convince the Soviet Acting Minister for Foreign Affairs that His Majesty's Government really were precluded by tradition and principle from exchanging a Russian " defector " for the officer concerned, and as the matter had not yet got into the press, the Soviet Government decided to return the officer. These are merely examples which could of course be paralleled in the experience of most diplomatists.

The crusade against " secret " diplomacy fell on particularly fertile soil in Britain as it fitted in with two national traditions, mistrust of foreigners and mistrust of professionals. British diplomatists in those days usually spent their whole careers abroad, and they were regarded as professionals who played a tortuous game beyond the comprehension of the plain man. When Torcy established in France in 1712 his short-lived Académie Politique for the training of diplomatists, Addison had immense fun with it in the *Spectator*, giving the qualifications of the various professors as the " opening and shutting of letters, political grimaces, indirect answers, cyphers, casuistry and etiquette." In the United States, this inherited mistrust was exacerbated by a complex about Machiavellian British diplomacy, and contempt for their own professional service, expressed by one Congressman who, when the State Department Appropriation was under discussion, referred to them as those " white-spat boys with the English accent."

It is to the credit of the English Governments throughout the nineteenth century, dominated as they were by a coalition of the great landowners, the great industrialists, and the middle classes, that they left so much responsibility to the British diplomatic body, recruited though it was mostly from the landed gentry, much in the same way as there was general agreement to leave the running of the small professional army to officers recruited from a restricted class.

In stating the historical fact that a similar social background and personal means did create an international body of independent balanced and moderate men of the world with a common convention of international good manners and a common desire to reduce friction, I do not suggest that an efficient diplomatic body can only exist if it is recruited from a leisured class. The essential qualities of common sense, good manners, understanding of foreign mentalities, and clear precise expression, can be ensured by a rigorous selection and training with these qualifications in view. The difficulty will lie in securing and retaining the personnel potentially endowed with these qualifications if the Heads of Missions are treated by democratic governments as glorified postmen and their responsibility in the delicate art of negotiation confined to routine matters, and if all important relations are directly handled by politicians at public conferences under batteries of television cameras. The tendency to side-track the career diplomatist was accelerated by the creation of a great number of new Embassies. Until well into my own time, the Ambassadors (corresponding to the new First Grade) became on appointment automatically Privy Counsellors; on the initiative of Sir Warren Fisher, this rule (which had already been departed from when the first Ambassador to Moscow was appointed) was abolished. It is doubtful whether in future any Ambassador will feel free to take such a responsibility as, for example, when Sir Horace Rumbold as High Commissioner at Constantinople in September, 1922, refused to deliver an ultimatum to Ataturk, thereby averting a war without allies and enabling the Convention of Mudania to be made a fortnight later; or as Prince Schwarzenberg in November, 1850, disregarded his instructions from Vienna in order to avert an Austro-Prussian war.

The general conclusion would seem to be that foreign policy in the sense of the general objective should be open, but that the diplomatic negotiation by which it is carried out must remain secret. Though the Monarchs' International suffered from an unfortunate eclipse during the years immediately preceding the 1914 War, its services to peace throughout the nineteenth century were very important. They had and still have the immense advantage in diplomacy of continuity and long experience. It was very clear even in my own limited experience; the former Crown Prince of Sweden, King Albert of Belgium, and King George VI during the half dozen audiences which I had with His Majesty, spoke like permanent officials with an objectivity and deep knowledge in striking contrast to a democratic politician like Cordell Hull. Secondly, being usually cousins, in fact as well as on official documents, of each other (for example, Queen Alexandra, the Empress Feodorovna, and King George of Greece were all children of the same Danish King), they were able to talk and write privately in complete confidence with each other even at moments of national crisis. Throughout at least the eighty years following the Congress of Vienna countless examples proved that they were on the whole a peaceful and stabilizing influence. This was true in Germany and Austria as is shown by the tricks and subterfuges used by Bismarck against his own Emperor, including a press campaign which he staged in 1879 to overcome his opposition to the Austro-German Alliance; and the Austrian Chief of Staff Conrad found the strongest opposition to his bellicose schemes in the heir-apparent, Francis Ferdinand, whose murder at Sarajevo precipitated the war.

I refer mainly to the hereditary monarchs. The Emperor Napoleon III was a typical romantic in contrast to the eighteenth-century mentality of Louis XVIII and Louis Philippe; an ex-conspirator himself, he combined the woolly sentimental liberalism of his period with the old French passion for *la gloire*. To strengthen his personal position he crusaded against the 1815 Treaties which had guaranteed France, and hastened the rise of Prussia and the decline of France by attacking Austria in Italy in 1859 and 1866, a reversion to the anachronistic and discredited policy to which the French monarchy had put an end with the reversal of alliances in 1756. The Prince Consort, unable to stop the Crimean war, intervened decisively to avert the risk of war with the United States, and Queen Victoria and the Emperor Alexander II intervened in 1875 to avert the risk of a preventive war by Germany on France. The personal decline, through age or temperament, of the European monarchs in the period just before the 1914 War, synchronized with the extreme constitutional scrupulousness of King George V in England, and the same period witnessed a marked decline in the nineteenth-century custom of personal contacts between Prime Ministers and Ministers for Foreign Affairs with their opposite numbers. In that leisured and more cosmopolitan age sovereigns, statesmen, and ambassadors as already mentioned, constantly met each other casually on holiday visits at Spa, Baden, Marienbad, Homburg, Biarritz; my old chief Sir Lancelot Carnegie told me of his being Secretary on duty with his Ambassador at Homburg for six weeks on end, during which the Ambassador met more notabilities than if he had been in Berlin during the same dead season. Anyone who does not see the significance of these meetings in a friendly holiday atmosphere can have had little experience of affairs. By the end of the nineteenth century, this habit had largely died out with the new generation of politicians: Sir Edward Grey had practically no personal knowledge of his opposite numbers in Europe, and was so reserved that a leading German businessman, Herr Ballin of Hamburg, honestly believed that Britain would not join in a war.

The unfortunate result of these factors was an enormous increase in the influence of the General Staffs, during a critical period. Bismarck's disputes with his General Staff were always when he was in favour of moderation, as when after Sadova they wanted to march into Vienna, and after 1871 when they successfully insisted on keeping Metz. I have referred to the prolonged conflict between Field-Marshal Conrad and the Archduke Francis Ferdinand, and to the fact that the British Government found itself in 1914 bound by the undertakings of British and French General Staffs and Admiralties. Doctor Eyck, in a striking paper read to the Royal Historical Society some years ago, showed how the German General Staff (who had been responsible originally for the invasion of Belgium) were throughout the 1914 War the evil

genius both of the German monarchy and of the German
people. Hindenburg and Ludendorf over-ruled the Chancellor
Bethmann-Hollweg in insisting on the unrestricted submarine
warfare which the Chancellor was certain would bring in the
United States; when in March, 1917, Bethmann-Hollweg
announced in the Prussian Chamber of Deputies the decision
to give universal suffrage in Prussia, and did so by proclamation
on July 11th, the Generals forced his resignation two days later
and the electoral reform was postponed. They sabotaged the
Reichstag's peace resolution of July, 1917, and when Pope
Benedict XV in his note of August 1st raised publicly the
question of the total evacuation of Belgium, they insisted
against the wishes of the Kaiser on a long-term occupation,
the annexation of Liége, and a Belgian-German union.

It was Ludendorf who sent Lenin into Russia, who insisted
on the Brest-Litovsk Treaty being a dictated peace, and who,
when asked by Prince Max of Baden what would happen if his
1918 offensive failed, observed " Then Germany must perish."
Indifferent to the obvious exhaustion and impending collapse
of Austria, he resisted almost to the last all talk of renouncing
annexations East or West, and to maintain his position concealed the actual facts of the military situation from the
Emperor and the German people. When President Wilson
on October 23rd distinguished between the German people
and the " monarchical autocrat," Ludendorf prevented the
Kaiser from abdicating as Prince Max of Baden urged him to
do, and thereby threw away the last chance of saving the
German monarchy.

It would be encouraging, if one could say that the policy of
the General Staffs could have been corrected, if public opinion
had had a larger influence. Unfortunately the facts show that
my earlier references to mass opinion apply often to the press
as well. Professor Mowat's summing up is that " the record
of the press in great international crises is not very encouraging.
In July, 1914, the statesmen and diplomatists were as a whole
more conciliatory, more serious than the independent journals."

Moreover, this was written in 1935. Since the period of
the First World War it is common knowledge that a large
section of the press, both as a guide and interpreter of public

opinion, has either deteriorated or come into existence in a worse form. More than forty years ago, a satirical poem contained the lines " Hail gifted Harmsworth, thou who first divined the lowest common factor of the mind! " Recently, however, a senior member of the staff of a journal with a very great circulation, remarked to me that whereas the old Harmsworth press of half a century back had discovered that the new mass electorate wanted their foreign news in abbreviated tabloid form with simple headlines, the newer press had discovered that the mass did not want foreign news at all, but wished for escape from news!

THE INFLUENCE OF DEMOCRACY ON THE CONDUCT OF WAR AND THE MAKING OF PEACE

I do not recollect having seen attention drawn to the fact that during the 1914–1918 War the numerous abortive peace initiatives were almost always of completely undemocratic origin, and even in the case of President Wilson, purely personal. Pope Benedict XV on August 1st, 1917, asked: " Is Europe, so glorious and flourishing, to rush as though carried by universal folly, to the abyss and work its own suicide? " and he proposed permanent arbitration and the reduction of armaments, the independence of Belgium, the reciprocal renunciation of war costs, and the settlement of territorial claims in consideration of the immense advantage of lasting peace with disarmament. During the same year Prince Sixte of Bourbon Parma, on behalf of the new Emperor Charles of Austria, offered to support the restitution to France of Alsace Lorraine, the restoration of Belgian and Serbian independence, and even of the Trentino to Italy. In November of that year Lord Lansdowne, an ex-Viceroy of India and ex-Secretary of State, who had made the Anglo-Japanese alliance and the Entente Conventions, published in the *Daily Telegraph* his letter which *The Times*, then in the power of Lord Northcliffe, had refused to publish. In it he said: " We are not going to lose this war, but its prolongation will spell ruin for the civilized world and an infinite addition to the load of human suffering." In May, 1918, Lansdowne was preparing a new letter at the same time as the Germans were

endeavouring to start peace talks going at The Hague under
cover of discussions of prisoners-of-war matters; both these
facts became known to Lord Northcliffe who forestalled
Lansdowne's new initiative by a sensational leader in the *Daily
Mail* of June 18th, 1918, and the letter was never published.

I was on leave from France in England about that time
and can well remember the universal consternation caused by
Lansdowne's first letter. Looking back from our experience
of the Second World War, itself a consequence of the prolongation of the First War with its destruction of the German
monarchy and middle classes, and reflecting on the hundreds
of thousands of lives and thousands of millions of pounds
which continuation of the war cost our country alone after
the publication of the first letter, it seems the most elementary
common sense. Most people would now agree that the
actual earlier proposals of Pope Benedict XV were in themselves justified by events. The main point is that, with the
exception of unreasoning sentimentalists who discredited their
peace propaganda by their advocacy of " Conscientious
objection " to fighting, there was practically no popular
support for the initiatives of the distinguished personages.

In two other ways democracy and nationalism were responsible for the prolongation of both wars. As Jules Cambon
pointed out, in proportion as democracy makes war more
totalitarian, it makes it more difficult to stop. When war was
fought primarily for dynastic or commercial reasons with small
professional armies, they could still be fought in accordance
with the rules of the game, with a survival of the chivalrous
spirit and without working up a panic of hatred in the civilian
populations; neither was it necessary for the whole population
to be drawn into war industries in one way or another. One
obvious consequence, therefore, of democratic or total war is
that both sides draw the logical conclusion that the civilian
population has no claim to immunity. This lesson, already
acted on in the German submarine campaign during the
First World War, was finally sanctioned when it was decided
in London during the Second War to instruct Bomber Command to focus operations on " the morale of the enemy civil
population in particular of the industrial workers," in other

words to use the R.A.F. for the weakening of civilian morale by
direct and deliberate destruction of whole residential districts.[1]
The results in one city[2] will stick in the memory of anyone who
has read the late Lali Horstmann's *Nothing for Tears*; this
decision by the most humane of governments may well rank
among the decisive moments of history. A less obvious consequence is that when a whole nation is at war, the machine
cannot be halted and switched on again like a small professional
army. When in 1914 the German Government asked the
Russian Government to stop the partial mobilization they had
begun, it was practically impossible to set the machine in
reverse, and throughout the First World War Sir Henry
Wilson and the General Staff were always haunted by the
fear that the inception of any kind of negotiations or even
" peace talk " would make it impossible to get the war going
again. The mass hatred and prejudices raised by the First
World War survived it and made it impossible to effect a
permanent peace, while at the end of the Second War they
made it impossible to achieve any peace treaty at all![3]

" THE WILSONIAN EPOCH ": CONFERENCES AND WORLD ASSEMBLIES

All these considerations were totally disregarded by public
opinion at the end of the 1914 War, and the old diplomacy
which had contributed so much to the hundred years' peace

[1] Of course the decision was influenced by the fact that during 1942 and 1943
we had no other spectacular means of intervention to encourage the Russians
and our own civilian population. I am not arguing for or against the decision
in the circumstances, but it is important to note that it was a reversal of our
announced policy of 1939 and that it set the seal of our approval on the logical
conclusion of totalitarian war. This conclusion had not been previously
accepted even by the Germans, who professed, e.g., in the bombing of Rotter-
dam and London in 1940, to be using air-bombardment only as a military
weapon, in preparation for an imminent invasion.

[2] A writer in the *Quarterly Review* (October, 1953) states that in Germany
3,600,000 houses were destroyed, $7\frac{1}{2}$ million persons made homeless, and
305,000 civilians killed in air-raids; in Russia, 6 million buildings were
destroyed, 25 millions left homeless, 6 million civilians killed; and in Britain,
60,000 were killed in air-raids.

[3] I am referring to the years immediately following the war; the responsibility rested later on the Soviet Government.

and had given warning to the respective Governments of the dangers ahead (interesting examples can be found in the works of Cambon, Jusserand, and de Chambrun), just as it did during the years preceding the Second World War, was made the scapegoat. " The war to end war " had not even achieved a real peace treaty, but had inaugurated instead the epoch in which we are still living, the epoch on the one hand of an interminable series of theatrical spectacular " conferences," and on the other of attempts to maintain peace through the medium of world assemblies. This the writers of the 1930's called the " Wilsonian Epoch," and it is strange that even so experienced and balanced a judge as Monsieur Jusserand could write sincerely in 1934, " that humanity is progressing cannot be doubted "; and he said this in direct reference to the 1914 German Imperial gospel of force, inequality among nations, and the formula that necessity knows no law. Yet he wrote those words at the very moment when Germany was already dominated by Hitler, the hysterical demoniac psychopath who incarnated and led the terrifying upsurge, already noted long before by acute observers like C. G. Jung, of the ruthless lust for power and destruction released in Germany from the depths of the collective unconscious by the First World War, by its disastrous end, and by the decade of chaos which followed Versailles. The leaders of public opinion who inaugurated the Wilsonian epoch had been forced to notice the fatal results which had followed from the unlimited nationalism of the nineteenth century, but with a muddled mental hangover from the nineteenth century, they increased the evil at Versailles by hastening the break up of the Austro-Hungarian Empire, which had held together many " races " as a prosperous and civilized group of semi-autonomous cultures, and by unifying Germany in sweeping away all the old local monarchies which had acted as a brake on the egemony of Prussia. (Incidentally, Austria and the South German Princes had shared with Italy in the creation of the now fashionable Baroque art, which, though some of its admirers may go too far, was the last original culture devised in Europe.) It is often alleged that the break-up of Austria-Hungary was inevitable. This assumption ignores the fact that the Magyars had once been themselves " oppressed " by Austria as they in turn oppressed the Slavs, and that the murdered Archduke Francis Ferdinand's programme for associating the Slavs—converting the Dual Empire into a Triple Empire—was not essentially more unworkable than Tri-lingual Switzerland or indeed the Austro–Hungarian Dual Monarchy. The hatred felt for him by the Slav Nationalists was itself a proof that they feared the success of his project; and the assumption that it could not have succeeded is based not on the circumstances, but only on the fallacy that whatever has actually happened could not have taken any other course. There is no certainty that the Allies could not have succeeded in checking the centrifugal tendencies if they had tried, instead of actively encouraging them. We know that the Hungarians clung for many years to the hope of restoring the Habsburgs.

While thus greatly aggravating the evil of nationalism, they sought a remedy in the creation of a world assembly, and for the next twenty years international relations had to be made to fit nominally into what was called " the framework of the League of Nations." The League of Nations was built on sand, the shifting sand of unreality. It was unreal to suppose that over fifty nations, scattered all over the world, could have any common interests so concrete and positive as to induce them all to make real common sacrifices for the protection of one. It was unreal to give equal voting rights to the smallest republic in Central America with the United States or Great Britain. It was inevitable that such a loose collection of states should sort itself out in regional pressure-groups, Latin-American or Arab or those following French policy in Europe, and that these pressure groups should tend to follow the power which could be most useful to themselves. Such slender chance as the League possessed of effective action was destroyed when the attempt to give it teeth by the Geneva Protocol was (probably rightly) eliminated. Of course the League could do some effective work in non-controversial fields such as health or labour, but in the great issues of the period it acted as a will-o'-the-wisp, leading the peoples of the victorious alliance to substitute the essentially unreal formula of " collective security " for their own military security and the old and for so long successful principle of the balance of power.   There is always a day of reckoning for those who put their trust in wishful thinking and comforting formulas, and in the case of the League the day of reckoning started when its members voted for half-hearted sanctions against Italy in the hope of stopping the Italian occupation of Abyssinia. The United States were outside the League, and the leading powers in it had no intention of fighting, nor had they the means to do so.   France, torn by domestic factions, bled by the loss of millions of young men whom the fallen birth rate had not replaced, had acquired a defensive mentality, pinned her faith on the Maginot Line, and had allowed her Air Force to become hopelessly obsolescent.   The British Air Force, so formidable a few years later, still was largely in the blueprint stage; the British Fleet had ammunition for twenty minutes' fighting, the British Expeditionary Force even four years later, was relatively to its opponent inferior in equipment and fire-power to what the Expeditionary Force of 1914 had been relatively to the German Army of 1914.

Above all the country had been subjected for a number of years to a wave of unreasoning woolly pacifism, and by one of those inconsistencies so frequent in popular thinking, the decision itself to embark on sanctions had been largely the result of the Fulham by-election which had been won by the Opposition with a majority of 18,000 on the sole issue of " war-mongering."   No one, therefore, was prepared to give the sanctions teeth by applying them to the supply of oil; Mussolini called the bluff, and the net result was that, while the conquest of Abyssinia was not impeded, the fascist régime in Italy was solidified (as King Fuad of Egypt insisted to me)[1] and took the fatal decision to link up with Nazi Germany.   From time to time during the first years of the war while I was Minister in Berne, I had occasions to visit what remained of the League, consisting mainly of the Secretary General, and I will never forget the impression made on me as I walked through the vast empty halls of the League's Palace, which during twenty years had buzzed with such futile activity, the great permanent

[1] King Fuad was a very astute politician who had known Italy well and was said to have a considerable part of his large fortune invested there.

secretariat frequently reinforced by swarms of visiting politicians and experts with their satellite army of press reporters and photographers.

At the first opportunity, the League conception was revived with a notable change. It was agreed that the principle of giving equal voting rights to all states had been a failure, and the Security Council was created with the right of veto. The United Nations Charter adopted at San Francisco on June 26th, 1945, was a better document than the original Charter of the League, and in the more civilized world of the nineteenth century it might well have succeeded in its object. The fatal flaw was the admission to the Security Council, with the right of veto, of a great power which had objectives completely in contrast to those of the other members. The objects of the United Nations as laid down in the Charter were in sum to maintain international peace and security and by collective measures to remove threats to peace; to develop friendly international relations based on the principle of equal rights, to achieve international co-operation in solving problems of an economic or social character, and to promote respect for human rights and for fundamental freedoms. The objects laid down in the Soviet doctrine were very different. Stalin in his *Problems of Leninism* had quoted with approval the master's statement that " The existence of the Soviet Republic side by side with Imperialist States is unthinkable. One or the other must triumph in the end. Before that, a series of frightful collisions between the Soviet republic and the bourgeois States will be inevitable." In the fifth volume of the 1947 edition of his works, Stalin said that " The tasks of the Party in foreign policy are first to utilize every contradiction and conflict among the surrounding capitalist groups and governments for the purpose of disintegrating Imperialism, secondly to spare no means to assist the proletarian revolutions in the West, thirdly to spare no means to strengthen the national liberation movement in the East, and fourthly to strengthen the Red Army." The Soviet Professor Nicholai Rubenstein writing in *Problems of Philosophy* in 1952 said that " Soviet diplomacy is always on the defensive actively against the enemies of the land of socialism . . . extremely flexible, Soviet diplomacy remains loyal to the principles of communism, and to the general Party line . . . finding weak spots and cracks in the enemy's camp, it strikes effectively, always keeping the initiative."

The two sets of quotations reveal a fundamental contradiction in objectives, for while the declared object of UNO is to solve economic and social problems by international co-operation, it is equally the declared object of the Soviet revolution to foster by every means the internal contradictions among the non-Soviet powers with the object of hastening their disintegration and destruction. As regards promoting respect for human rights and fundamental freedoms, the entire Soviet edifice is built precisely upon the negation of human rights and fundamental freedoms. It is instructive to compare the above quotations from the basic doctrines with the late Mr. Vyshinsky's statement on September 18th, 1947, that the policy of the Soviet Union in regard to the United Nations "is a policy of strengthening the organization, broadening and strengthening international co-operation, of steady consistent observance of the Charter and of fulfilment of its principles." The factual commentary on this statement has been made in connection with the challenge that produced NATO but must be again amplified. Not merely were 55 resolutions of the Security Council turned down by the Soviet veto, but 11 special bodies created by UNO were boycotted from the start and 34 others occasionally. Not only have special UNO bodies been boycotted, but apparently competitive organizations have been set up, notably the famous Soviet controlled " World Peace Council." The above quotation from Mr. Vyshinsky is a further reminder of how necessary it is to consider all statements addressed by Soviet officials to foreign audiences in relation to the terms of the basic doctrine. Mr. Attlee explained to the House of Commons in 1946 that it had been understood that the veto would be used " only in the last resort, in extreme cases when the great powers themselves might be involved in conflict. It was never conceived as a device to be used constantly whenever a particular power was not in full agreement with the others." When, however, the 55 vetoes during a certain period by the Soviet

Government are analysed it is found that the veto has been used always to prevent the discussion of problems in which the Soviet Union or any of her satellite countries are involved, and to prevent the admission of a dozen states as members, including Portugal, Ireland, Italy, Austria, Finland and Ceylon.

This matter of the admission of new states suggests a further difficulty of World Assemblies, although its drawbacks can be argued pro and con. I mean the natural tendency of such organizations to freeze, or ossify as it were, existing situations; a point to which Jules Cambon and others drew attention in the early days of the League. Presumably the League or the United Nations would during the nineteenth century have tried to stop the integration of the Grand Duchy of Tuscany, the Papal States and Naples into united Italy, since they would all have been member states, just as the League felt it a duty to protect Abyssinia as a member state, and sought to stereotype the frontiers drawn in 1919. So also for some years past we have had the odd spectacle of a former Generalissimo of China, now ruling over a relatively small island, sitting in the Security Council with a right of veto. I am not discussing the question of whether the Government which has been recognized by Her Majesty's Government as the *de facto* Chinese Government, ought to be in the Security Council; but it seems unreal that General Chiang Kai-shek should be there. That other weakness of the League of Nations, namely the formation of rival pressure groups, has appeared in a much more obvious form in the United Nations, a natural result of the greatly increased influence of the United States in Latin America, of the greatly increased assertiveness of the so-called " Arab " States and their preoccupation with their antagonism to Israel, and the entry of new important Asiatic members such as India. The unrealism inherent in all World-Parliaments is illustrated by the fact that the Caribbean-Central American Republics have ten votes to Western Europe's eight!

The other new factor which the Wilsonian epoch introduced in substitution for the old diplomatic system, was the vogue for frequent theatrical international conferences. These have become so much a part of our way of life in the last 34 years that even when a " high-level " conference has been admittedly a failure, it is often described as having fulfilled a useful purpose by clearing the air, clarifying the respective points of view, or merely as having been necessary in order to satisfy public opinion that " every avenue had been explored and no stone left unturned." The latter point is unfortunately true; but this fact, while justifying the governments, is discreditable to the public opinion which insists on the conferences. For a conference which does not achieve any solid results is apt to raise exaggerated hopes with a corresponding reaction, and to have some results prejudicial to whichever parties concerned are the most vulnerable to public opinion and therefore the most influenced by the desire for results of some kind; and it involves a serious waste of time and energy by Ministers and their officials. In the days when Queen Victoria read all the more important despatches (written out by hand in the different posts of the world), the serious international problems were few and well known, only a few governments really mattered, or were even interested, in questions of high policy, and the main lines of foreign policy were apt to remain fairly constant over long periods of years and to be changed only after mature consideration. Today serious and complicated issues arise almost daily in every part of the world; but in addition to this the volume of normal business of all kinds has vastly increased, especially through multiplying international bodies composed of government delegations. The frenzied tempo of work in the important Foreign Offices has therefore created a serious problem, in that the permanent officials, and the Ministers with their Parliamentary and other activities as well, have literally no time for quiet reflection. The loss of time involved in an unsuccessful conference is therefore a serious matter, as is also the using up of energy. For to the long sessions of the Delegates round the conference table must be added the many hours of private discussion, the bargaining with members of other delegations, the preparation of memoranda and the drafting of enormous telegrams to send home.

The conclusion would seem to be that public opinion, instead of incessantly demanding new conferences, should insist that conferences should only be undertaken, as they were in the nineteenth century and as in the case of the London Conference in October, 1954, when there was some real prospect of success. The first condition for a successful conference is surely that all the parties should desire a real and permanent settlement, and that they should mean by this a settlement which would be definite, honest and workable. In practice the satisfaction of these objects really involves, first, a broad preliminary basic agreement; secondly, a real desire on both sides for such an agreement; thirdly, in order that no desire for revenge and sense of injustice should remain, the weaker side must be given a fair hearing; fourthly, that the negotiations should be carried on in confidence, free from publicity and the attacks of pressure groups; fifthly, patience, and sixthly, that the terms of agreement when reached should be set down in a precise and unambiguous form. The traditional view was that until these conditions were fairly sure, it was best to leave negotiations to be carried on through the diplomatic channels; conferences therefore were relatively few and far between, and a classic illustration is the Congress of Berlin of 1878, which only began after the British and Russian Governments had agreed on their minimum compromise terms. During the period of almost non-stop conferences inaugurated in 1919 the London Conference of 1925 accepted the Dawes Reparation Plan because Ramsay MacDonald and Herriot had agreed beforehand, and the Locarno Pact of 1925 followed on long secret negotiations between Stresemann and Briand and Lord D'Abernon. The London meeting in October, 1954, referred to earlier, was a success because the Soviet Union was not a party to it and there was a general desire to meet the French objections to the defunct EDC. The Berlin Conference earlier in the year was bound to fail because the fundamental objects of the Western Powers and the Soviet Union in regard to Germany were completely opposed.

During the period between the wars these temporary successes stood out in melancholy contrast with the interminable naval disarmament conferences at Geneva or the abortive world economic conference of 1933, staged in the quite unreal hope of inducing the United States Government

to wash out the British debt, but which failed spectacularly at
the very outset to achieve its nominal object of securing the
reduction of the United States tariff.   Its only result was to
cause a marked deterioration in Anglo-American relations.
Taken as a whole, the conferences between the two wars did
nothing to stop the coming of the Second World War, and
achieved no temporary results which could not have been
equally effected through ordinary diplomatic channels, but
did from time to time seriously prejudice international relations,
both Anglo-American and still more Anglo-French relations.
The annals of that period are full of personal incidents, such
as Lord Snowden's description of some French financial
proposals as " grotesque and ridiculous."   This happened
even when the amateurs had the best intentions, as when the
whole of France seethed with anger when Monsieur Briand
made himself ridiculous playing golf very badly with Mr.
Lloyd-George (" like a clown ") during the usual crisis.[1]
If the British and French Governments were divided and
morally paralysed at the crucial moment when Hitler, still
unready and bluffing, marched into the Rhineland, one of the
reasons was certainly not that there had been too few high-
level conferences.   Since the Second World War, the primary
conditions for successful conferences have been far more lacking.

At Yalta and Potsdam in 1945 there was no fundamental
agreement about anything, and in addition the parties concerned used words without attaching the same meaning to
them, while the Palais Rose conference has become a proverbial
joke.[2]   The situation has become much worse since 1945 in
respect to one of the other conditions, namely, negotiation free
from publicity and pressure.   Although the conferences
between the two wars were usually conducted in the glare of
journalistic publicity, it was still admitted as regards day-to-day

---

[1] The details of the crisis are unimportant in this connection.   The point is
that one cannot imagine a nineteenth-century politician or ambassador com-
promising political issues by such a childish episode, whereas Lloyd-George
had staged the game in an innocent insular belief that it would ease the pre-
vailing tension!

[2] A conference of Ministers' deputies sat in the Palais Rose in Paris in 1949
for several months without being able to produce even the *agenda* for a Four-
Power meeting.

progress and results, if any, that the actual discussions were better kept as confidential as possible. With the prominent rôle assigned to the United States by history since the Second World War, the tremendous power of the American press has come into play and even the discussions are no longer inviolable. The primary objection to publicity, even in the form of daily communiqués, was pointed out in a speech by Sir Austen Chamberlain, that Ministers representing their Governments could not withdraw from declarations which had been made public, so that compromise, which should be the essence of all negotiation, became impossible. Not only is compromise without loss of face made almost impossible; Ministers are under a constant temptation to strike attitudes and gain applause; and instead of discussing with each other, to address set speeches at the invisible millions. This is linked with the danger of constant intervention by newspapers and demonstrating pressure-groups. Patience was one of the cardinal virtues insisted on in all the old books on diplomacy; a classic illustration was when Napoleon at Dresden in June, 1813, losing his temper with Metternich, kicked his hat round the room as Sir Winston Churchill kicked the headmaster's hat at his Preparatory School—but with the important difference that the headmaster was not present whereas Metternich was, and that great diplomatist drew the correct conclusion that Napoleon's enemies could now safely offer him terms which he would refuse and thus give the Austrian Emperor an excuse to desert him. It seems obvious that it is a virtue much more difficult to practise in the atmosphere of a modern conference, with its interminable hours and often physically over-heated atmosphere, by overworked people who are under an imperious claim to get back as soon as they can to the work which is piling up at home.

If a real agreement is reached it is essential that it should be set down in precise and unambiguous terms; one must repeat that an ambiguous loosely-worded treaty can cause in the future far more harm than no treaty at all. It has been admitted that the Old Diplomacy sometimes tended to excessive reliance on formality and conventional usage, but one of the characteristics of a well-trained diplomatist is certainly the habit of expressing what he wishes to say in clear and unambiguous language.[1]   (I said " what he wishes to say " for there are inevitably occasions, when he should reply politely without either truth or falsehood.)   While this habit of precise language is a necessary result of a good diplomatic training, it is by no means necessary to success in party politics, which are ruled by a completely different convention.   No one expects a government to stick literally or even in substance to its previous declarations when in opposition and consistency even over a short term is regarded as the weakness of static minds.   Even sixty years ago, when Parliament was a real governing body and a serious debating society, Lord Salisbury preferred foreign affairs because they were " sincere," whereas, as Lady Gwendolyn Cecil says in her biography, " in home politics phrases ruled."   Therefore when the spectacular publicity-ridden type of conference becomes the vehicle for the settlement of all important international issues, the inevitable tendency is to try to achieve quick results by finding soothing formulas which leave the future to look after itself.   Another danger of this type of conference is that its success or failure may easily become entangled with the political status and future of the individual Ministers taking part.   The disarmament conference of 1932, for example, was hampered by the fall of Laval on a franchise reform bill, by a German presidential election and a Prussian general election, by a general election in France and a presidential election in the United States!

In discussing the slowness of Western opinion to realize the position from which NATO arose, I quoted as an analogous case the long time-lag after which Western opinion came to understand the German reparations question.   The whole business of Versailles in 1919 offers a most instructive parallel with the Congress of Vienna in 1815.   In 1815 France had been as thoroughly defeated as Germany in 1918, but the representative of defeated France, Prince Talleyrand, was

[1] A Foreign Office White Paper has severely criticized the loose amateurish drafting of a Report on the Foreign Service by the House of Commons Select Committee on Estimates, which apart from major errors and " a number of other statements and conclusions which are incorrect or unjustified," managed to give the newspapers the unintended impression that the Foreign Service was costing nearly six times the maximum possible figure!

received by the Congress of Vienna as an equal, and as the Comte de Chambrun has pointed out, the decisions of the Congress broadly followed the instructions which Talleyrand had himself drawn up for the French delegation to the Congress. During his long career which began under Louis XVI, Talleyrand changed sides but never changed his principles, which can be summarized as the restoration of the historic frontiers of France, the maintenance of legitimate governments, of national rights and non-intervention. At the height of Napoleon's power he was (and almost he alone) never taken in by the glamour of military conquests and consistently tried to apply the brake. In 1815 he stood for legitimacy; in 1830 when Belgium revolted from Holland, he stood in London for national rights and non-intervention. The statesmen at Vienna desired above all a long period of peace and stability, and they welcomed in the representative of the defeated enemy a helpful colleague. The result was a settlement which broadly lasted through the hundred years of progress and prosperity in Europe to which there is no real parallel in history since the Roman Empire.

At the democratic Paris peace conference in 1919, the defeated Germans were only invited (and to Versailles, not to the previous discussions in Paris) to receive the draft Treaty on May 7th and were told to offer their written comments in nine days. There was no discussion, the Allies answered in writing on June 16th giving the Germans five days in which to agree. The Versailles Treaty makers, under the influence of a public opinion still obsessed with war hysteria, represented for example by the memorial of the Members of Parliament to Lloyd-George, dictated a peace which was neither honest nor definite nor workable nor made the slightest effort to secure the co-operation of the losing side. It was dishonest because the Allies declared that the disarmament articles (159 to 213) were the first step towards a general reduction and limitation of arms, and their failure to do so was not unreasonably claimed by the Germans to be a breach of the treaty and therefore releasing them from their own obligations of part five, and this was one of the most successful points of Hitler's propaganda. It was not a definite settlement since the reparation and economic clauses could only be enforceable by continuous military pressure. Reparations were assessed at £6,600 million, and war pensions and separation allowances were included in the damages for civilians. It led logically and inevitably to the German default, the occupation of the Ruhr, the fatal estrangement between England and France, the ruin of the last stable elements in Germany—the middle classes—and so completed the necessary conditions for the rise of Hitler. President Wilson, who, as Sir Harold Nicolson has described, himself pushed all the conclusions through by an unparalleled exercise of secret diplomacy, was himself repudiated by the United States, so that the League of Nations came into existence without America; and this would have been most unlikely to happen had he been content to be represented, and himself remained at home in close touch with the Senate and public opinion.

No objective historian can really dispute the conclusion that the Paris negotiations were directed for the most part by a public opinion inspired by sheer hatred, and not by a sincere desire for a lasting peace. These two related points, of public pressure and the influence of hatred, reveal one of the main dangers and weaknesses of democratic foreign policy; for the need for private discussion free from public pressure is much greater under really democratic conditions than was the case even a hundred years ago. The only effective pressure then came usually from the middle classes; towards the end of the century, it began to be replaced by the pressure of mass public opinion, and the mass opinion was no longer that of still semi-agricultural societies, but of the vast urban masses, uprooted from their background of local tradition and custom. The characteristics of mass-psychology belong properly to the underlying currents and therefore to a later stage in my argument, but some reference to them is essential to any discussion of public and semi-public diplomacy. A mass of people sometimes is merely the aggregate of the individuals composing it, but even seen from this angle, it is liable to be misinformed about foreign affairs, for international relations have become so complicated that they must be followed regularly, and with some historical background, for any responsible judgement to be possible. No one acquainted with the really popular press will maintain that these conditions exist, and I quoted earlier the opinion of an experienced journalist to the effect that the daily interest in foreign news has actually diminished. When, for instance, on the occasion of international conferences, the interest springs to life, the news is apt to be reported as though they were sporting contests, " Dulles taunts Molotov," etc. When, however, a mass of people becomes excited, it ceases to be an aggregate of sensible individuals and becomes a unit with its own personality and laws. The moral or rational restraints of the ordinary decent individual are apt to be washed out and replaced by an upsurge of the primitive collective subconscious.

The automatic formation of this collective mass-psychology was first described many years ago by Gustav Lebon, whose illustrations included some curious testimonies from people who had taken an active part in the French Revolution and who said later that they could not believe in some of their own actions. It has now become a commonplace of psychological thinking, and it is no disparagement to individuals to say that mass opinion when excited is irrational and always more prone to hatred than to benevolence or moderation. So whenever mass opinion is stirred, if Brown makes an appeal for moderation and Smith makes an appeal for revenge and hate, it is highly probable that Smith's appeal will be the most effective.

Even if adequate information could be regularly provided at popular prices it would not normally be studied. I remember during the 1930's meeting in London one evening the famous French journalist " Pertinax," and his complaining that he had come specially to London in order to test public opinion on the international problem of the moment, only to find in all the evening papers one great headline, " Barbara in Ze Box! "[1] The increasingly sheltered and increasingly prosperous middle classes of the nineteenth century, basking in the sun of perpetual progress and evolutionary optimism, had no conception of the primitive and unconscious forces gathering strength behind the brilliant façade of progress, and even in

[1] The allusion was to one of the witnesses in a court case which, though of no public importance, had tickled the popular sense of humour.

the two decades following the First World War, remained so blind to these underlying forces that they were able to regard Hitler and his National Socialism as a right-wing conservative movement. The Communists, and indeed the Left-Wing elements in general, reiterated the same false view of Hitler, and still do so.

The essence of the foregoing may be stated briefly as follows. Throughout most of the long peace following the Vienna Conference, only the middle classes, in Europe as in England, were normally interested in foreign affairs, and the governments which represented them were chiefly interested in maintaining peace and the balance of power, and were much influenced and checked by the free-masonry of the monarchs' international and the old diplomatic corps. International conferences were only held at intervals to formulate decisions already basically agreed; they were conducted in confidence and were relatively little influenced by popular pressure. Since the 1914 War, the principle of the balance of power and of states with common interests working together was replaced by the idea of a World Assembly and the unreal formula of collective security; and the old methods of diplomacy were replaced in the most important matters by an endless series of spectacular conferences, for the most part inadequately prepared and since the Second World War practically conducted in public. In foreign affairs democratic opinion is necessarily apt to be uninformed, and is easier to mobilize either in the sense of xenophobia (" 'Ere's a foreigner. Let's 'eave 'alf a brick at 'im! ") or of reckless and unreasoning pacifism, i.e. for one or other extreme. Frequently the two contradictory attitudes are mixed up, as when the loss of a by-election through a " war-monger " stunt directly influenced the launching of the sanctions campaign against Italy or when the Labour Party recently " voted in one week in favour of the rearmament of Germany and the disarmament of England." A successful conference is one which results in a definite, clear, and workable agreement which the parties are certain that later governments will have the will and the power to enforce and which (if there is a losing side) the losers accept as natural and tolerable.

The Wishful-thinker's Paradise, 1918–19?

Any negative criticism, especially of the recent past, is apt to provoke comments about wisdom after the event. Apart from the merely personal fact that I had at the time little confidence in the post-1918 catchwords, the comment is unjust, for in politics as in one's own life, the analysis of past mistakes though not an infallible guide is one of the safest guides we have. This is particularly true in dealing with the thirty years following 1918. Few periods of history are so marked by the influence of shams and slogans or demonstrate more vividly their disastrous results; and though realism has made important gains in recent years, the lessons to be learned are still very much in point. The Victorians, though their economic and political optimism rested on false assumptions, were not bemused by woolly formulas. Their theories were most reasonable in themselves, and the surface facts of the time appeared to furnish abundant justification. There was a striking analogy with their scientific outlook—their knowledge of the nature and properties of " matter " appeared practically complete, just as did their doctrine of the ever-progressing evolution of mankind from simple to complex, from the monkey to the House of Commons, from primitive polytheism and devil worship to the most " broad-minded " bishop. All creation had been working slowly upwards to the England of 1900, after which only some minor adjustments would be needed. Their beliefs, whether in physics or politics, were thought out and based on classified facts; and if they are all gone with the wind, it is because a great many other facts were overlooked, and a great many on which they relied were not facts.

The period following the great disaster of the First World War was on the contrary distinguished by an unconscious urge to escape from facts, to trust to comforting slogans and hope for the best. English public opinion gambled its Army, Navy and Air Force on the League of Nations for fourteen years after their own government's natural refusal in 1925 to ratify the Geneva Protocol had made " Collective Security " a sham. The Locarno Pact was based on the sham that the Germany and France of the period were equally potential aggressors; this, combined with the vindictive unworkable Treaty of Versailles, estranged Britain and France and was the first step towards turning Mussolini towards Germany, and Belgium to strict neutrality. The principle followed for several centuries of working with those who had common interest to maintain the Balance of Power was obscured by nebulous phrases. When Hitler marched (then still unprepared to fight) into the Rhineland in 1936 there was no will to resist; British and French politicians, disabled by catchwords and a long period of mutual friction and recrimination, had no policy.

The estrangement of Britain and France during the League and Conferences' or Wilsonian Epoch should be contrasted with the procedure which resulted in the *Entente Cordiale* of 1904. I can just remember the Fashoda incident in 1898 when most people really thought war highly probable. French and British interests seemed opposed all over the world. When the chain of local agreements which were the basis of the *Entente* were announced, everyone was surprised to find how natural it seemed. Now this result had been achieved by half a dozen men—notably the Ambassador Paul Cambon and King Edward VII. Had they been left to the parliaments and semi-public conferences, with the old prejudices and recriminations actively interfering through the press and " public opinion," the negotiations could not have succeeded. Underlying the confusion of policy between the two Wars was the vogue of a completely emotional unconstructive pacifism both in Britain and France, the delayed reaction to the boredom of the trenches and the slaughter of the bull-headed offensives. Being emotional, this fashion had the paradoxical effect of weakening military security while simultaneously insisting on sanctions without teeth to stop the Italian invasion of Abyssinia. There never was a clearer case of policy and arms running in contrary directions instead of keeping step—most elementary of political axioms; neither British nor French public opinion was prepared to " follow through." Mussolini did accept the risk; the League was finished, and the Axis established.

Both the failure to stop Hitler in 1936 when it was still

possible, and the attempt to combine sanctions with Pacifism, were linked with a failure to understand the real character both of Nazism and Fascism. This subject does not properly belong to what I have called the surface of events, and must be explored at a later stage. Briefly the point here is that opinion in the parliamentary democracies let itself be led by Socialist propaganda into mixing up German Nazism and Italian Fascism and into labelling them both as a form of right-wing capitalist reaction. This was a major success of "popular front" propaganda. They were in fact quite distinct from each other except that neither of them was conservative or reactionary in the sense intended by their critics. Nazism was essentially a great dynamic movement of the common man, and especially the common young man, and drew its inspiration from the oldest pre-Christian and pre-Roman sources of German idealism. Hence it was essentially revolutionary, the instinctive enemy of the Christian Churches and of both the aristocratic and the best literary traditions of Germany. Hitler's rise to power was made easy by the breakdown of the German middle classes in the inflation which followed the Treaty of Versailles, and by the strong appeal of his propaganda against usury and financiers, and the régime was consolidated when he abolished unemployment by mobilizing the whole industrial machine for the preparation for war. That fact alone meant that he must some time have to choose between war and unemployment. Even if he had not been personally obsessed with lust for conquest and the conquest of the Eastern heartland—Russia (for Sir H. Mackinder's thesis had taken firm root in the geo-politics of Munich Nazism)—Nazism was a real German revolution, a retarded offshoot of tendencies stimulated by the French Revolution, and its militant character was obvious from 1933 onwards to any student of German history and psychology and long before to a profound observer like C. G. Jung.

The fascist régime was totally different—to start with it was Italian, and German and Italian history and psychology have nothing in common except in so far as one side of German life and character has represented the civilizing European influence of Rome. The strength of Italian Fascism was derived from

disillusionment with the very imperfect social and political
system resulting from Cavour's drastic way of unifying Italy,
with the temporary social chaos after the First Great War, and
the closing of the safety-valve of emigration to America.
Beginning as a movement to restore order, Fascism adopted a
theory of the organic State as an association of corporate
groups which it presides over for the common good, in opposition to the liberal view of society as an agglomeration of
atomic individuals; but to maintain himself in power Mussolini
denied both the political rights of the individual as a member
of the corporation, and the right of the corporations to lead
an independent life within the limit fixed by the fundamental
law of the State.   The Fascist Corporative System was a
marked contrast to the experiment of Professor Salazar in
Portugal.   Here the Employers' and Workers' organizations
are being encouraged to develop naturally, in the hope that
they will eventually combine.   Fascism adopted from Croce,
Gentile and others a version of Hegel's worship of the State as
a mystical Power in its own right, resulting in constant friction
with the Church, although its leaders, unlike the Nazis, did not
want a quarrel.   Above all, Fascism differed from Nazism in
that in its origin and general system it had no racial basis at
all, but on the contrary prided itself on being a champion of
Latinity and the heir to cosmopolitan Rome of the Caesars.

Even however when the benevolent theory was perverted
by personal ambition and corrupt vested interests in the party,
fascist Italy had no ambition for European war and if public
opinion in England and France had so wished, it should have
been possible to secure its neutrality.   The episode of the
belated commercial baits offered to Italy after the German
war had begun, was not consistent with the sanctions campaign;
for when the latter was launched the probability of a German
war was already generally admitted.   In October, 1935,
a realistic public opinion would have seen that we had two
alternatives: to stop the Abyssinian war even if it involved
going ourselves to war with Italy, or to regard the conquest of
Abyssinia as a lesser evil than the entry of Italy into the Nazi
orbit.   The half-way course actually followed was a classic
example of the confused public opinion of the period; its

first result was the occupation, fatal to Czechoslovakia, of Austria, which previously Mussolini had prevented by moving troops to the frontier.

The sacrifice of military security, which made any strong effective action against either Germany or Italy impossible, and which left Britain weaker in relation to her neighbours than in 1914, was not merely due to pacifist hysteria, but also to another unreality—the attempt to restore the gold standard with all its implications. Keynes, who had demonstrated the absurdity of the Versailles Treaty economic clauses, went straight to the point about the restoration of the gold standard, which he showed was meant to be linked, in the unspoken intention of its promoters, with a return towards the wage standards and cost of living of the golden age of Free Trade and *laissez-faire*, still regarded as normal. It was sincerely hoped to restore the British lead in world-trade, but it was unreal to hope that the trade unions would renounce what they had acquired during the war. On the very eve of the abandonment of the gold standard a few years later, it was firmly believed that this would lead to anarchy; and, although its abandonment, and the Ottawa Agreement in 1933, produced a substantial and too much forgotten economic and moral improvement and the growth of many new industries, the dominant deflationary influences behind the national Government maintained an effective brake on expenditure for military security. Economy for economy's sake where military security is concerned can be a tragic absurdity; a saving of one per cent on a peace-time estimate may cost in war many times as much and a loss in human life which cannot be expressed in cash. Economy which merely results in inefficient forces represents eventually a gigantic waste. Pacifist niggling at defence budgets (an annual event till the Second World War) is still more illogical—as Mr. Attlee has said, they considered an inefficient army was somehow less immoral than an efficient one.

The collapse at Munich was itself mere common sense in view of the respective military positions by that time; the real mistake was that the breathing space gained was not sufficiently used to make up in rearmament " for the years that the locusts had eaten," as Baldwin himself called them.   On the very day on which war broke out in 1939, the Treasury agreed to plans, submitted to it six months before, for a new anti-aircraft gun factory which would take nearly a year to get into operation. Obviously the year gained was vitally important for the production of Hurricanes and Spitfires; the point is that so much more use might have been made of it.

Chapter Three

THE PLACE OF BRITAIN IN WORLD AFFAIRS: 1954

*" That great city wherein all were made rich that had ships
at sea by reason of her prices "* (Apocalypse xviii.19)

I T is a relief to turn from the dangers of mass opinion, so much easier to analyse than to remedy, to certain speci-fically British problems which were largely created by our own action when the middle classes were in effective control, and which could be fundamentally changed for the better by changes in opinion.

The British Foreign Office, as a natural consequence of its tradition of dealing with situations as they arise, has always been reluctant to lay down broad lines of permanent policy in State papers of the kind in which the French Archives have been so rich over several centuries. It is probably to the fact that Sir Eyre Crowe (described by Lord Baldwin as the ablest servant of the Crown) had a German mother and had been educated in Dusseldorf and Berlin that we owe his famous memorandum to Sir E. Grey of January, 1907, which gives us the key to British policy during the seventy years preceding the Great Divide of the 1914 War. His argument in brief was as follows. To maintain British maritime preponderance, it must be used with the minimum of provocation and be identified with the primary interests, i.e., the trade and independence, of other nations. Commentators have tended to concentrate too much on the particular conclusion he drew from this major premise; namely, that opposition to dictator-ship by one Power was a law of Nature, that Germany by her efforts to estrange Britain from France was trying to dictate and must be met not by concessions but by firm defence of British interests such as had brought about the Anglo-French *rapprochement*. This conclusion embodied a short-term specific policy; but the major premise represented the basic policy of Victorian England, for it was the foreign policy appropriate to the whole economic and social structure of Victorian England. That structure—in some ways almost as much as the Soviet Union—was founded on a *theory*; of unlimited Free Trade and *Laissez-faire*. When Crowe wrote his memorandum, the theory was still supreme—Joseph Chamberlain's revolt had greatly contributed to the overwhelming defeat of the Conservative Party—and, as I well remember, it seemed unanswerable. As a pure theory, it perhaps still is unanswerable—but the facts of life had eaten away its foundations, and it is now clear that the logic of the classical Economists depended on a number of false assumptions, and on the neglect of certain social and security considerations; rejecting the truth that nations, like individuals, cannot govern their lives exclusively by financial considerations.

The first assumption was that British industrial and maritime supremacy had been *created* by the adoption in the 1840's of Free Trade. This claim was exaggerated. The period during which British industrial power was absolutely supreme had been at the end of four centuries of extreme protectionism consciously aimed at building up an all-round balanced production in which agriculture was regarded as an essential factor. The purely economic arguments were not weighed against social and national security considerations. The absolute increase in British trade distracted attention from the relatively faster increase in German and American expansion, and more important, the British food-supply became dependent, as Disraeli had predicted, on events in remote foreign countries over which Britain had no control. The long-term decline was masked by the gold discoveries in Australia and California, the world development of railways and other utilities by British capital and engineering, and the growth of invisible exports due to British Investment, Banking and Insurance. (The gold discoveries started a wave of industrial expansion from which British industry was the first beneficiary—for Britain controlled Australian and Californian trade, while British engineering—especially in railway construction—was ahead of the rest of the world.) The ultimate decline was masked again by a failure to realize that the new mass electorate must sooner or later insist on social changes which would increase the competitive cost and lower the efficiency of a production which had staked all on competitive cheapness; and it was masked by a complacent belief that there was an inherent superiority in the British character and the British climate. Herbert Spencer said in effect that one British labourer was worth two Italians, and we were assured that the Lancashire cotton industry was impregnable on account of the damp Lancashire climate, that German industry was " rotten with subsidies and State interference," American wealth was " all on paper " and so on. Though I could not answer the Free Trade arguments, I was much shaken by my historical reading, and especially by the unorthodox version of our history presented by a Harrow Master, Mr. Welsford (a disciple of the early German economist List), whose *Strength of England* and *Strength of Nations* attracted little notice because the orthodox school was so overwhelmingly strong. He was not, of course, a solitary voice; but of the small group of protectionist writers, he was the one who happened to impress me most.

The importance of Friedrich List (to whom Disraeli refers in his letters) was that Bismarck adopted his main principle, which List himself had drawn from English history. He advocated the building up of industry and agriculture together behind heavy protection regardless of the immediate short-term effects on the consumer's cost of living—a balanced economy aiming primarily at national *security*. I was puzzled, for instance, to find that despite the Lancashire climate, the India Company had not been allowed to sell its muslins and calicoes in England and that when the cotton industry was established at home its export was created by a bounty. I found that for centuries the English sheep farmers sent their wool to Flanders and that the English woollen industry was only created after Edward IV had decisively interfered with the export of wool and the import of woollen cloth. The same story is true of all the basic industries, including shipping which owed everything to seventeenth-century Navigation Acts, and the story has lately been brilliantly summarized in Mr. Leo Amery's *A Balanced Economy*. One must regretfully admit that it was not merely protection by

statute. Hurault de Maisse, French Ambassador in the last
years of Queen Elizabeth I, complained furiously in his
reports home that the English authorities deliberately made
business conditions intolerable for foreigners by vexatious
interferences and arbitrary holding-up of cargoes, by com-
mitting administrative abuses which were in effect more costly
than legal prohibitions, while themselves trading freely
(according to him) in France and elsewhere. In short, the
Free Trade régime did not create British industrial production;
it took it over and masked its slow relative decline by the
sacrifice of agriculture and the temporary accumulation of
inherited profits turned into paper investments all over the
world—of which the greater part has been lost through
the action of Nationalist governments. I fully appreciate the
immense achievement of the British Free Trade economy
during the nineteenth century—but it was an achievement
which in the long run benefited the rest of the world while
gradually making Britain vulnerable and completely blocking
preferential tariffs within the British Empire. There was a
fairly long period when the British Empire could have been
developed as an economic unit, which would have met the
argument that the British Isles, unlike Germany, had not
sufficient territory from which to feed an industrial population.
Britain invented international trade and developed North
and South American, Australian, and Indian and Japanese
industry; but there is a strong case for the belief that it was
an insecure foundation for British trade and that in the long
run the fruits were reaped by protected competitors—especially
Germany and the United States.

During the protectionist, mercantile period, British foreign
policy aimed at trade expansion, the Balance of Power in
Europe, and the independence of the Netherlands, but also at
securing these objectives as far as possible by alliances, use of
Naval power (which directly helped foreign trade) and a
minimum of direct military intervention. From Marlborough
to Wellington, the British Army, though often a deciding factor,
was never more than an element in coalition armies, its own
numbers bearing no relation to the size of the French Armies.
An English Ambassador could tell Frederick the Great that

" God is the only one of our Allies to whom we don't pay a subsidy in cash! "   The attempt of the French monarchy to be equally strong on land and sea—though apparently justified by the population and wealth of France—lost India and Canada for lack of reinforcements and finally bankrupted the monarchy itself; Britain, however, did not attempt to put a National Army in the field until 1915, and in 1944 repeated the experiment with a major Air Force as well—one can only say " Absit Omen."

This break with national tradition was to some extent inevitable on account of the great superiority over France which Germany had been able to build up before the two World Wars—but was its prolongation inevitable?   Were the results of the First World War, taken as a whole, better than would have been obtained by an old-style negotiated peace in 1917? The Second World War cost Britain £10,700 million in foreign capital and resources without counting home capital and production—of which £5,000 million were in Lend-Lease, £3,300 million in new sterling debt, £1,300 million by the realization of foreign investments and gold and dollar reserves. The loss of life was incalculable in money terms.   The question is, how much of this could have been saved if instead of Roosevelt's " unconditional surrender " formula, the Allied Governments had publicly offered to negotiate with any German Government which excluded Hitler and his gang?   Ernest Bevin, when criticized, as Secretary of State for Foreign Affairs, for the state of Germany, refused to take responsibility for the unconditional surrender policy imposed by Roosevelt to which he attributed the total collapse of all authority in Germany.

The Banker's and Investor's Paradise

During the Free Trade period—roughly 1846 to 1914— which may be summed up as the Banker's Paradise, to the Balance of Power in Europe and the independence of the Netherlands was added the protection of the route to India, the defence of Turkey, and Sir Eyre Crowe's principle of avoiding offence to customers.   This was in reality a reversal of the old policy of using national power to foster trade.

Under Free Trade the English national attitude did tend to become that of a nation of shopkeepers (which was not true when Napoleon said it); through the lack of a balanced economy at home, the World-trade of Britain became vulnerable all over the world and fear of fiscal retaliation engendered a climate of deference to foreigners' trade interests which would have been inconceivable in previous centuries. The customer is always right! For this was what Crowe's formula really meant and on his premises it was irrefutable. It meant also something more important, that a deliberate choice had been made to prefer wealth to security, as an examination of the other assumptions will also support.

The second assumption was that the industrial supremacy of Britain could not be undermined if foreign rivals refused to play the game of the division of labour and adopted an aggressive protectionism aimed at closing their own markets and underselling British exports in other markets—just as British Governments had done for four centuries. When from the 1870's onwards they began to do exactly this, the dogmas of the economists had acquired a religious force, and the wishful thinkers were able to marshall a great array of short-term but plausible facts. The prodigious expansion of Germany and the United States was held to be not due to protection but in spite of it. Living was cheaper and working hours were shorter in Britain. As one market was lost, another was opened by the then unrivalled enterprise and energy of the British pioneers. Above all, the great income from foreign investments and Banking and Insurance—the invisible exports —more than offset any deterioration in the terms of trade— and they seemed bound up with Free Trade.

This complacent optimism was linked with the third assumption, which was based on the failure to foresee the devastating effect of total democratic war, with scientific weapons, on accumulated wealth. I have quoted J. S. Mill's views on the temporary and transient effect of war on private property in his time. We now know that our two democratic " all-out " wars " to end war " have swept away in eight years the greater part of the foreign investments accumulated over a century and have led all the former purely primary producers (especially in South America) to embark on a reckless emotional crusade of industrial nationalism, wholly regardless of the principle of division of labour. They have so impoverished Britain that, first, she had to promise in return for the American loan of December, 1945, to work towards multilateral trading, lower tariffs and convertibility, and secondly, that she has had to get round these low tariff undertakings by quantitative and currency restrictions which interfere with trade far more than protectionist tariffs and are apt to be a greater source of international friction, as in the case of Dr. Schacht's similar policy in Germany.

The fourth assumption—perhaps the most dangerous—was that the Navy would always be able to ensure the flow of imports including food supplies. There is no need to dwell on this. Even in the 1914 War, the cutting of the lifeline by the German submarines came very near to success. If the Victorians had not foreseen the German submarine, still less did they foresee the power of the Russian submarine, which has inherited and developed the German legacy, Schnorkel and all. In the Second World War, the submarines were more efficient, and were reinforced in the Mediterranean by air power, with mines as a powerful auxiliary. The efficiency of all three is now still greater. One can hardly blame them for not foreseeing the exact nature of revolutionary inventions which might neutralize the protection of the sea lanes by the British fleet; but their fundamental assumption that the overseas line of communications could never be interrupted was a gamble on which to base a complete change in national policy (i.e., protectionism to Free Trade). A fifth assumption was that international relations would continue to be influenced by a certain degree of reason and moderation. The sheltered liberal-minded middle classes of the nineteenth century— especially in Britain—gave no thought to the ultimate effects of the gradual transfer of authority to the anonymous impersonal collective forces massed in the great urban agglomerations created by nineteenth-century Industrialism.

I have written at length on this controversial economic subject with reluctance, for I know how much there is to be said on the other side, and this book is not mainly concerned with economics. The motive for this seeming digression is that the British Free Trade movement was not purely an economic theory but part of a whole philosophy of life, held with religious fervour. In the mind of its leading apostles it was bound up with a theory of *laissez-faire* in industrial relations generally and with the optimistic Liberalism which believed that Humanity was entering the promised time, when

> Wars shall be no more,
> And lust, oppression, crime,
> Shall flee thy face before.

I think it was the belief in a Universal Peace, to be accelerated or preserved by Universal Free Trade (what Carlyle called the Calico Millennium) which made the sacrifice of British agriculture seem an unimportant risk. The argument is not that Free Trade is never the best policy, but that it is only an expedient which should be harmonized with National Security and therefore with a balanced economy.

Chapter Four

COLONIAL POLICY TAKES THE WRONG TURNING

Aɴ alternating series of posts at home and abroad impressed on me long ago a peculiar characteristic of the English brands of internationalism, pacifism, and anti-imperialism (that is, the repudiation of the control of other peoples). This common characteristic is that they really are, all three, manifestations of insularity and an unconscious national arrogance in its most extreme form. In the nineteenth century, the high priests and prophets of extreme liberalism assumed that all other countries must be happy to devote themselves for ever to supplying England with goods and raw materials and to providing a free market for English manufactured goods. Between the two World Wars the pacifists assumed that all the " lesser breeds without the Law " were only waiting for the English to set the example of disarmament and to assure them that " this House will not fight for King or Country." In the 30's a very rich lady married to a politician scolded me for speaking of " foreigners," taking it for granted that I must be using the word in a pejorative sense, and must therefore be an imperialist war-monger. In 1926 Mr. Bromley, of the Engine-drivers Union, speaking to me of his experiences as secretary of the Amsterdam Trade Union International, told me he had come to the conclusion that it was " the absence of the British spirit abroad which hit this internationalism so hard." How true. Paul Blouet (better known to readers of the 1890's as Max O'Rell) must have suffered from these innocent reactions as French master at St. Paul's school, for when, on top of a bus, an old lady asked him " if he was saved " he replied, " No, madame, I am a foreigner ! "

The anxiety to make dependent peoples adopt British parliamentary institutions with the utmost speed regardless of local circumstances and as a matter of principle is similarly

the expression of an unlimited belief in the universal efficacy
of British institutions, and a belief that these institutions are
all that is necessary to make people of all races and religions
act and think exactly like the inhabitants of this island, upon
whom they will be sure to model themselves. The revolt of
Asia against European control has been attributed to the moral
effect of the two suicidal European wars. As Napolean said,
" Every war in Europe is a civil war," and this is of course
important, since the European control, in Asia as in Africa,
rested so largely on prestige. When the British Raj in India
was at its strongest and most unquestioned, there were only
some 4,000 British civil servants, about 80,000 British troops,
and the British-officered Indian Army, although at the turn
of the century there were 294 millions speaking the many
languages of India; so that the Indian Empire quite obviously
did not rest merely or even mainly on force. Although there
are so many differences between Asia and Africa, the same is
broadly true of the European rule in the African continent.
But the effect on this mysterious element of prestige of the
spectacle of Europeans killing each other has surely been
exaggerated; after all, the British Empire in India started by
driving out the French Empire, both sides relying on Indian
troops and allies. The moral effect of the European war was
probably limited to the European-trained politically conscious
élite.

The first cause of the awakening of Eastern Nationalism has
been the deliberate European importation of the idea of
Nationalism, which was quite alien to Asia. Large areas of
the East are like a patchwork quilt of intermingled communities, and I understand that there was no native Indian
word for " nation " or indeed for " liberty " or " progress."
Professor René Grousset in Le reveil de l'Asie showed over
thirty years ago that Europe found China and India in the
same state (probably in a worse state) than in the time of
Marco Polo and the Moghuls, and created through Western
education the idea of Nationalism, and then the idea of Asiatic
solidarity. These ideas had, however, not penetrated below
the surface in South-East Asia until the dissolving influence of
the Japanese conquest was confirmed by the well-meant

encouragement of Eastern revolt by the United States. The influence of the United States in obstructing the return of the French and Dutch to Indo-China and Indonesia at the critical period and in encouraging Asiatic Nationalism everywhere is an historical fact. A recent American historian can still complain that " following World War Two Asians looked to the U.S. for leadership in their struggle against European Colonialism " but the U.S. " did not take an unequivocal stand and consequently the conclusion was drawn that the American people themselves had turned Imperialistic." In fact they had found that the alternative to " European Colonialism " was not a China and a South-East Asia co-operating with the China Lobby in Washington and seeking advice and sympathy, but a militant anti-American Communism. The U.S. attitude had encouraged revolt in Indo-China, but a few years later U.S. opinion was blaming the British for lack of co-operation in the defence of Indo-China.

Another main cause of the Asiatic revolt, as of unrest in Africa (both of which may lead eventually to the reclosing of Asia and Africa to European trade and investment), has been the more or less deliberate British renunciation, which has been specially important as Britain had the largest stake. Of course Asia and Africa are utterly different propositions, Asia being the home of so many civilizations and religions, while in Africa there has been no pretence of any civilization at all; but a common factor in both cases has been the British refusal to accept their responsibilities as natural and to concentrate on economic and moral welfare, but instead to insist on imposing peculiarly British institutions *en bloc*, parliamentary, judicial and educational. As often happens in our illogical history, two quite contradictory motives have been at work. On the one hand, specially in the last fifty years, there has been the loss of self-confidence by the governing people and especially by its own rulers. Since I laid stress on this point in my book *The Ruling Few*, I found that both Professor J. B. Bury and Professor Gilbert Murray had noted a similar process amongst the Greeks which they called loss of nerve. This self-confidence, the taking of one's authority for granted, has an immense psychic effect, and is obviously closely allied with the prestige which is its counterpart. On the other hand, the obstinate wilful thrusting of British political institutions on to every variety of people in Asia, and in Africa, is the third direct manifestation of British insular complacency which I had in mind.

It is sufficient to recall the circumstances of Macaulay's minute on Indian Education of February 2nd, 1835, which has been the subject of an interesting study by Mr. Elmer H. Cutts. The great Warren Hastings (very nearly ruined by the politicians as his reward for consolidating the Indian Empire) had bequeathed to his successors a programme of promoting Hindu and Moslem education on the lines of the best Hindu and Moslem scholarship and tradition, and of administration through their own Hindu or Moslem codes. An intelligent group of British orientalists who tried to carry on his work found themselves early in the nineteenth century the object of a ruthless and successful campaign backed by Lord William Bentinck, the Governor General, but inspired by the two typical British sects of the period: the Utilitarians and the Clapham Sect. J. S. Mill said " the great end " was " not to teach Hindu learning but useful learning," while Macaulay, who went out to India as a member of the supreme council of Bengal in 1834, had been brought up under the influence of William Wilberforce and the Anglo-Indian official Charles Grant. Macaulay's attitude is specially instructive as he represented both British utilitarianism and Anglican Evangelicalism. He asked why was it necessary to pay people " to learn Sanskrit or Arabic," since " on all subjects the state of the market is the decisive test," and he summed up native Hindu education as " false history, false astronomy, false medicine . . . in company with a false religion." He agreed with Bishop Middleton of Calcutta that the poor Indians, " in learning and reading English, will inevitably learn to think, and when the power of thinking is pretty generally diffused the cause will be gained "; and with Bishop Heber who in 1822 was ecstatic on finding the children of a " wealthy native," " dressed in jacket and trousers with round hats, shoes and stockings," and who recommended that Hindus must be taught above all English grammar, Hume's *History of England* and the use of the globes. All this pressure-group, backed by home influences which the unfortunate Anglo-Indian orientalists could not resist, assumed as axiomatic, that what Grant in 1817 called " the many millions of benighted heathens placed by the dispensation of divine Providence under British rule, particularly in British India," must be Anglicized; and, incredible though it may seem now, assumed that they really would become English in the process. It was admitted that it might take a very long time to turn all the many millions of Hindus, Moslems and others into complete little Englishmen, but Macaulay laid down the ideal as being " to form a class, who may be interpreters between us and the millions which we govern, a class of persons Indian in blood and colour, but English in tastes, opinions, morals and intellect." He therefore recommended the abolition of even the Arabic and Sanskrit colleges, and the supreme council made English the official language of instruction in Government-supported colleges. Whether or not one agrees with Macaulay's target of forming such an Indian class, " English in tastes, etc.," it is now clear that English rule was bound to be undermined in proportion as the target was approached. The final walk-out in the 1940's was really decided in 1835, and if the régime lasted as long as it did, this was due to the overwhelming sensation of relief created by the introduction of British order and peace, a feeling of relief which lasted among the common people for a century. Macaulay's error lay not so much in aiming at destroying the Hindu culture as in the naïve assumption that it could and would be replaced by English liberal utilitarianism—which incidentally we have since abandoned ourselves. If the English language had been imposed, as the Spanish was in South America, and Portuguese in Africa and Goa, as the vehicle of a living vital religious faith, the experiment might have succeeded; two centuries earlier Akbar the Great Moghul would probably have become a Christian if he could have kept his harem. The radical mistake was in believing that Indian Society could be transformed into a copy of Victorian England, itself a transitory phenomenon incapable of universal application. The British in Hanoverian and Victorian times believed like the Spaniards and Portuguese that as conquerors they had the right and the duty to impose their own religion on the conquered; but in fact the ideology they imposed was not Christianity. Modern Indian historians claim rightly that the new English Universities in India created a new India inspired by English Whig and radical philosophy; and the religion which was imparted *in practice* was the religion of Nationalism and Parliamentary Democracy—neither of which had any roots in Indian tradition.

What is so interesting, apart from the smug assumption of total superiority, is the contempt for the formative influences of history, geography, climate, all the accumulated weight of heredity and religion and the customs and character shaped by them. All these factors were not only disregarded but deliberately treated as not worth knowing or taking into consideration. The races and religious sects of India were lumped together like a lot of orphan children who had only to be taught English to become a slightly coloured equivalent of the domestic-servant class at home, and be equally part of the permanent order of Nature.

It may yet turn out that the creation of Macaulay's Anglicized Indian class and its inevitable replacement of its creators was an unintended stroke of genius, and the new India may well be in its own way successful. As regards Africa, however, where there was no civilization except tribal custom to build on, the conceited confidence in the universal applicability of the British Constitution seems certain to have results quite contrary to what had been intended. I think this applies particularly to English political institutions even more than other European or American ones. The latter are at least written constitutions with, in varying degrees, a balance of powers and checks on abuse of power either by Executives or Legislatures. The British Constitution and the whole political system reposes, not on a fundamental charter with checks and balances, but on an unwritten mutual confidence in the English character, which, one can only hope, will continue to be well founded in the era of the urban masses. I see a real analogy between the past working of English political institutions *in England*, and the national sporting sense; serious matters are treated as games because games are taken seriously. The fact remains that in Britain Parliament legally has totally unlimited power; that Parliament now virtually means the House of Commons, the House of Commons means the Ministers, and even the Ministers are coming to mean the Party leadership. Party discipline (eventually to be reinforced by full pay and pensions for long service) is so tight that a general election practically means the election of a government, not a debating chamber, for a period of years which it could prolong if it liked and during which there is no real restraint except their own common sense, tolerance and deference to the unwritten laws of the game—and to public opinion if sufficiently vocal and organized. One of the leading Conservative ministers has suggested that the vote should be taken first, and then " those who are interested in the subject could stay on and have a discussion! "

The insistence on thrusting British Parliamentary institutions on primitive and often heterogeneous African tribes, quite apart from questions of local unsuitability, reveals a failure to appreciate the grave decline in the efficiency of Parliamentary institutions in the United Kingdom itself. Professor Duverger in his well-known study of political parties has pointed out that the effective control of both the Legislature and the Executive by a governing majority *Party* has produced a régime " not so very different, in this respect, from the single Party System . . . in reality the Party alone exercises power." The individual member of the House of Commons is no longer responsible to his constituents but to the Party leadership, the important decisions are no longer made in parliamentary voting, but in the private Party meeting upstairs. Just as the member is no longer responsible to his constituents, but to the Party, so also the Government is no longer responsible to Parliament, but to the Party. The " Party " is coming to mean a small group, unknown to the Constitution, and the exact composition of which is unknown to the ordinary elector; and it is not identical with the Cabinet which is apparently no longer in practice collectively responsible for government policy. This transformation of the Constitution as known to Anson and Dicey, though it began with Joseph

Chamberlain and Sir John Gorst, is directly due, as Professor Duverger has pointed out, to organized democracy represented by the Labour Party, which cannot control its militant idealists unless it functions as a close oligarchy with block votes and a ruthless discipline. Just as in fighting Germany British Governments had to accept totalitarian dictator techniques, so also the Conservative Party, faced with organized Labour, has been compelled to adopt the Labour Party technique of oligarchic coercion. The British Parliamentary system, as expounded to us when I was at Oxford forty years ago, was perhaps mortally wounded when the historic Liberal Party, broken by Lloyd George, was pushed aside by the Labour Party in the early nineteen-twenties. To the suppression of the backbencher, and even of the Minister, must now be added the growing independence of the new irresponsible corporations—Coal Boards and Railway Boards. These new hybrids, though notoriously less amenable to the desires of either their customers or their employees than the old companies, are not under any effective State control, Ministerial or Parliamentary; but they affect the daily life of the law-abiding citizen far more than all the activities of a nineteenth-century Government put together. Finally, to all these curtailments of Parliamentary government must be added—and it is perhaps the most important of all—the ever-growing authority of the Bureaucracy which is using the vague powers conferred by statutes to become in practice a legislative and executive machine in its own right. In the United Kingdom the full façade of Parliamentary institutions is still maintained; but within ten years after the First World War, seven European States (without counting Russia or Kemalist Turkey) had rejected Parliamentary democracy in favour of some sort of Authoritarian régime, and Germany followed soon after. Today Parliamentary institutions maintain precarious and hotly criticized existence in Italy, France, West Germany, and seem to be firm only in Belgium, Holland, Scandinavia, Canada and the U.S.A. In the chain of Arab States throughout the Middle East Parliamentary institutions are constantly breaking down and order periodically has to be restored by military or civil dictatorship.

Now, just consider, quite objectively and purely on the merits of the case, the wisdom of imposing such a system, so insecure nowadays even in the hands of the most homogeneous, stabilized and politically adult nations in the world, on African territories. These territories are creations of administrative convenience representing no historical or national boundaries, and each is inhabited by a variety of races and cultures. What is similar among them is that a high proportion of the Africans have in some vital respects less in common with the modern British than the British have with their primitive predecessors who built Stonehenge. The African life as we found it was governed by traditional rules and taboos, emotional, mystical and dramatic; the tribal rules, initiation ceremonies and taboos were directly opposed to the sense of independence and personal responsibility. Apathy, lack of foresight, and the substitution of custom or attribution of witchcraft for independent thought, are outstanding characteristics. The suitability of giving English Parliamentary institutions (the fruit of seven centuries' development and far from a success as we have seen even in the most civilized European countries) to communities of this cultural type would appear at least arguable; but it seems to have become the recognized policy of all British Governments, on the assumption that there were no two sides to the question and no possible objections to the principle itself. Yet the possibility was surely at least worth considering that the principle might result in giving unlimited authority—such as is not even enjoyed by the United States Congress—to a very small minority of partially Anglicized natives who might have lost all their native tradition without acquiring the British political sense which is in essence instinctive and incommunicable. In short, British institutions torn out of their living historic framework and dumped in the Jungle could provide no safeguard against every sort of exploitation of the primitives by the Intelligentsia.

The risks have been obscured by the fact that the early experimental stages are being conducted under British official guidance and against the background of established British authority. This halfway house differs radically from its inevitable conclusion when the entire process will be free from all checks and restraints. Even this temporary restraint has been abandoned in the Sudan, where a heterogeneous people rescued in my lifetime from total anarchy and collapse have been given an elective two-Chamber legislature, Cabinet system, Westminster Parliamentary procedure, and where through the electoral defeat of the Umma Party (which had had five years' ministerial training) the whole system has passed straight into the hands of men without any political or administrative experience. The Sudan is a territory— it has never been a nation—the size of Europe without Russia, in which 120 languages are spoken. It is highly probable that in a few years Khartum will lose control of the outer provinces, and the future of the Gezira cotton plantations is very precarious. In the Gold Coast, Parliamentary candidates are restricted to those literate in English, with the result that in this primitive rural area, out of 267 candidates, there were only *fifteen* farmers and six chiefs. It is, however, clear that in the Gold Coast the opposition to Dr. Nkrumah is already adopting regional and tribal forms. Mrs. Huxley in *The Times* of February 11th, 1955, recalled that " in the Gold Coast so strong a separatist movement is developing in Ashanti that in your columns it was recently reported unsafe for leading members of the Central Convention People's Party to show themselves openly in Kumasi. The trouble in Uganda stemmed from a similar separatist emotion among the Baganda . . ." and why not, if we deliberately prepare to withdraw the only unifying principle, i.e. the rule of the British Crown? In a leading article on February 16th *The Times* pointed out that the separatist movement in Ashanti (which has a quarter of the population) and in Togoland and the Northern Territories, has come to a head since the disappearance from the Cabinet after the recent elections, of the Minority of European Ministers and the Governor.

In the case of Nigeria, we have a territory as large as the United Kingdom, France and Belgium but with more climatic diversity, and a population of 31 millions composed of many tribes who owe their superficial unity exclusively to British rule. During the last eight years we have tried to work *three*

Constitutions in Nigeria (1946, 1949, 1951) and yet another is scheduled for 1956! The Constitution-makers have had to admit the existence of three mutually opposed Regions—though each of these contains tribes which are likely to demand autonomy in their turn. The Constitution of 1951 proposed three Regional-elected Assemblies, three Regional Councils of Ministers, a Central Legislature and a Central Executive. It broke down in 1953—with 46 killed at Kano in a clash between North and South—and a conference in London reached a temporary agreement which in effect postponed the essential difficulties till 1956, when any Region will be able to claim complete self-government in all the subjects allotted to regional governments. The regional boundaries are artificial creations enclosing numerous tribes which may be expected in turn to claim self-government, and the Civil Service and judiciary must inevitably become regionalized as well. It seems clear that the Central Council of Ministers, presided over by the Governor-General, will eventually be composed of teams representing territorial groups; is such a government likely to function well? Why is public opinion indifferent to such reckless experimenting in a territory which had been one of the most successful achievements of British Colonial Administration?

In British Guiana it was speedily found that the " Progressive Party " was bent on using One-Party rule to destroy the new Constitution, and British troops had to be rushed in to restore order. The Commission of Enquiry reached the obvious conclusion that conditions for sound constitutional advance do not exist in British Guiana; but why was this ever in doubt?

There is a much darker side which seems to have been equally little taken into account. For some reason which is difficult to ascertain, the British public has only been partially informed of the nightmare horrors of bestiality and devil worship revealed by the Mau Mau campaign. Does anyone know how far similar forces are lurking beneath the surface in other areas? Once when I was one of several men talking after dinner we asked one of the party who was a member of the Government to tell us about the Mau Mau

initiation oath, which can only be read by a privileged few in
the House of Commons library. He began but immediately
stopped, saying the whole thing was too disgusting and awful
for repetition. The press has, however, been allowed to
publish some of the less sensational items, about expectant
mothers having the foetuses cut out and thrust into their
mouths, and British children of three and four having their
hands cut off and left to die; and Sir Philip Mitchell, Governor
of Kenya from 1944 to 1952, in a letter to the *Manchester
Guardian* on May 10th, 1954, refers to the taking of oaths as
including "copulation with goats, or with menstruating
prostitutes, cutting the throats of babies and drinking their
blood or the *other even more horrible* [my italics] practices of
the Mau Mau." Sir Philip's letter was in reply to a letter
by Professor Gluckman who had contended that the Mau Mau
ceremonies were not primitive but a degeneration resulting
from some consequences of contact with European culture.
As I will support later, Professor Gluckman's thesis that
Mau Mau practices are *not* primitive is in line with modern
anthropology, but Sir Philip is probably equally right in
denying that the blame for the degeneration can lie on the
British colonists. The question here is whether people whose
initiatory oaths (for whatever reason) are "limited" to
"blood, sex and excreta" are suitable candidates for Parliamentary self-government? If it is true, as is said to be the
case, that the Mau Mau are a small minority, the widespread
early success of their terrorism, and the large-scale (British)
military operations still in progress, do not suggest that the
humane majority would be able if self-governing to avoid
complete domination by the Mau Mau.

" SO MUCH OWED TO SO FEW "

Sir Winston Churchill's famous tribute to the R.A.F. was
equally deserved by the illustrious line of Administrators who
through several generations brought security and justice to so
many millions in Asia and Africa, working on the principle
laid down by one of the last, and greatest, Lord Cromer: " Our
primary duty is not to introduce a system which under the
specious cloak of free institutions, will enable a small minority

of natives to misgovern their countrymen, but to establish one which will enable the mass of the population to be governed according to the code of Christian morality." When one thinks of the African standard of life, of the great increase in well-being and population which modern agricultural technique would make possible, and when one thinks of the filthy moral customs and outlook bound up with degenerate religions in large areas, one should feel a great sense of shame at what is really a defeatist and cowardly action in rushing to get rid of our responsibilities by passing them on to tiny minorities of immature Intelligentsia.

Is it true to say that it is too late in most of the colonial territories to get back to a candid profession of the principle of benevolent enlightened paternalism? The experiments in autonomy so far indulged in can mean little to the great majority and there is not the slightest reason why the administrations should continue to permit the incessant abuse and irresponsible campaigns of lies and hatred in local " news "-papers, or encourage the wholesale alienation of the relatively intelligent and ambitious section of the youth by residence in the United Kingdom. This must in many cases inevitably produce the type of (in the Russian formula) " homeless cosmopolitan," without background and therefore without mental stability, without sympathy either with his primitive compatriots or his new models.

The Scribes and Pharisees of the myth of perpetual progress everywhere and all the time, ignorant also of the contrary policies followed by other European governments, dismiss all such observations as anachronistic fables by Blimp out of Kipling. My views are, however, supported by recent events and non-British examples, and they have as much right to a hearing as the clichés which were already faded in the nineteen-twenties. I hope moreover it is clear that this basic criticism of our recent colonial policy does *not* exclude the gradual devolution of economic and administrative authority to native elements, and that it is above all not a question of defending a " colour bar " for the advantage of white settlers; for the colour-bar in our sense of the word hardly exists in Belgian, French and Portuguese Africa. The objections are, first, to the reckless and indiscriminate encouragement of the growth of an Anglicized Intelligentsia mentally and morally uprooted, unstable and frustrated; secondly, to such Intelligentsia being treated as the natural political representatives of backward and racially divided majorities; and thirdly, to the imposition of purely British institutions without even effective safeguards embodied in fundamental instruments against the abuse of power and privilege by irresponsible demagogues lacking any tradition of political instinct and common sense. The charge is that our recent colonial policy, under a façade of generosity and progress, is a lazy evasion of responsibility; that having undermined the tribal organization in Africa, our policy is deliberately taking the risk of large populations lapsing into decadence by imposing nominal self-government (including the right to adopt Communism) without the preliminary discipline of civilization. New political institutions, in so far as they are necessary at all, should be helped to develop naturally out of the most responsible local elements, a principle which has indeed been occasionally attempted but sporadically and half-heartedly.

Even the ordinary European and American is influenced in all his actions by an immeasurable chain of ancestral influences and environments, which the African cannot share; but in the British universities, and many go abroad to attend universities, there is in addition an atmosphere of mental sophistication and scepticism which is far from successful in providing guidance, and a balanced stable world outlook and approach to life, even to the universities' own native intellectual *élite*. How much more difficult must it be for young Africans, just emerging from a Stone-Age Culture, to assimilate and profit by the best elements in our universities?

Apart from this aspect, it is clear from the recent report of " Political and Economic Planning " on " Students from the Colonies " that of the 8,000 colonial students now in Britain a great number return far less friendly than when they arrived. The conclusion that there can be no feeling of complacency about their education and treatment is an understatement, and a fundamental reason is said to be the discovery that " the fact of being a fellow-member of the Empire means nothing to the average Englishman . . . he knows little about it and cares less." It would seem common sense to limit the numbers to a select minority who can be suitably guided and looked after. An impressive contrast is offered in the recent opening of the "Lovanium" (god-child of the Belgian University of Louvain) at Kimuenza, near Leopoldville. On a site of 500 acres, at a healthy altitude of 500 metres, accommodation is being built for 600 students; seventeen natives and three Europeans are already in residence. (It is interesting that the majority prefer medicine, agriculture or pedagogy to administrative sciences.) The Agricultural Department will include a model farm; the Medical Department, the hospital for a new workers' city of 40,000 being built hard by. The university is open to all irrespective not only of colour, but of rank or means. Its diplomas will be recognized in Belgium, but the native students will acquire their knowledge free from the psychic dangers involved in being uprooted and adrift in a wholly alien environment. There are, of course, colleges in British Africa, e.g., Makerere, but the difference is that in 1954 there were only five Congo students in Belgian universities. When, on the other hand, special parties of Congo native technicians are sent to Belgium, they are received at the factories they visit as honoured guests and shown round by the directors in person. If the numbers of colonial students in Britain were greatly reduced, it would be possible for the British Council, the Victoria League and other institutions— and sympathetic individuals—to cope with the problem.

For this obsession with the virtue of English political institutions for Africans is in striking contrast with the policy adopted by the Belgians in their great and flourishing Congo, or that of the Portuguese in Angola and Mozambique, and the disregard for and lack of interest in these rival systems by our public opinion, which is responsible for our colonial policy, is shocking. The first maxim of Belgian policy is " good wages and no politics." No politics for the natives, *and* no politics for the European settlers. The latter are carefully selected, cannot be civil servants or employees, and number only 76,000 against 11,000,000 natives. The second maxim is that there is no colour-bar as it is understood in British Africa; Africans

and Europeans work side by side. The third maxim is that
the main official effort must be concentrated on increasing
the purchasing power and the economic resources of the
native; in Elisabethville alone 8,000 houses are owned by
Africans. The net result is that while there are no politics in
the Congo, there has also been practically no unrest, no
organized crime, not even strikes; and the successive annual
waves of young intelligentsia are automatically creamed off
into business administration and industry. The point of
particular importance in the foregoing is that the veto on
political agitation is applied equally to the European settlers;
the African " plain man " enjoys a position and prospects too
often confined under British rule to members of the political
cliques. Education (which even before the new university
was launched was admittedly much better up to matriculation
level than in neighbouring Northern Rhodesia) is related to
jobs; there are no educated unemployed, and there is no
arbitrary limit to the wages of coloured workers. All observers
are agreed on the more cheerful, happy and harmonious way
of life in the Congo, and the contrast is one between a realistic
paternalism and a lazy habit of incoherent drift into un-
representative oligarchy and industrial and racial warfare.

Portuguese Africa—which consists chiefly of Angola and
Mozambique—is both constitutionally and in fact an overseas part of Portugal (like Goa); all the inhabitants are
potentially Portuguese citizens, and in Angola out of a population of 4,000,000, there are 140,000 native Africans who are
Portuguese citizens. The Portuguese, like the French, have
never lost the Roman imperial idea of the gradual extension
of citizenship to all subject peoples as fast as they qualified
for it.

When the hopelessly corrupt and literally rotten Portuguese
parliamentary system was reaching its lowest point ten years
after the fall in 1910 of the monarchy, elected parliaments
started in the colonies. Angola adopted an organic charter,
and the direct result has been summarized by Professor
Livermore—" Indebtedness increased a hundredfold in a few
years, without any comparable gain in trade or public works
to offset this enormous liability, the service of which was

beyond the resources of the colony." (" The Portuguese Colonial Empire " in *Portugal and Brazil*.) Dr. Salazar consolidated the debts and with the help of a moratorium and ruthless economy balanced the Budget in 1931; but he also went to the root of the matter by his Colonial Act of 1930 and Organic Charter of the Empire of 1933. The new legislation boldly affirmed that the overseas Empire was united and inalienable, that it must be ruled by the Home Government, the colonial Governors and their Councils (composed of ex-officio, nominated and elected members) and the provincial Governors. Municipal government was organized on the same basis as in Portugal. Concessions formerly given to foreign companies were not renewed. While Portuguese citizenship was open to all who assimilate the Portuguese way of life, the Governors were required to preserve native customs so far as they did not conflict with morality and national sovereignty. The qualification for citizenship is not merely to speak and write the language of the metropolis, but to have really assimilated the Portuguese mentality and way of life; the colour-bar and the idea of eventual political independence simply do not exist. The resultant feeling of permanence and social stability, in marked contrast to British Africa, is illustrated by the fact that in Beira European settlers are expected when they build houses, to build for a hundred years; and visitors testify, as in the Congo, to the general impression of a more cheerful, optimistic, colourful life.

The French " Union " is inspired by the same Roman tradition, but further, does encourage political activity—but within the framework of the Union. There are twenty-three coloured African deputies in the National Assembly in Paris, and one has been Under-Secretary for the Colonies! While this appears preferable to imposing artificial constitutions, it is a hazardous experiment on which one can only reserve judgement, wait, and see.[1]

So in Africa south of the Sahara three alternatives are becoming clear. First, what may broadly be called the Roman way, though the Belgian practice differs from the

---

[1] French Northern Africa with its predominantly Arabic civilization is of course a more complicated problem than French Equatorial Africa.

French in its total exclusion of politics. Belgium, France and Portugal, however, all agree on the fundamental ideas of racial equality and giving total priority to social, economic and cultural development in close alignment with local conditions and actual mental and social development. Secondly, there is the recent British policy of giving priority to the imposition of British political institutions at top speed and in deliberate disregard of social, economic and mental conditions and of the practical consequences of oligarchic oppression and relapse into poverty and disorder worse than the primitive tribal organizations. The third course is the Dutch Calvinist solution of South Africa—segregation and permanent racial domination. Quite apart from Christian tradition, it is very doubtful if this is economically practicable, and the most recent information suggests that it is a theoretical programme which is making little real progress. It is characteristic that the domination of South Africa by the Transvaal Dutch, now so fiercely criticized by all liberal opinion, was the creation of the Liberal Government which restored South African independence. I do not say that was wrong, only that the Liberal Government did not foresee the inevitable result.

Of the three contrasting lines of development, that recently adopted by Britain and recently reasserted by the Labour Party (" Self-government for *all* colonies " and with a definite time-limit) seems to be the one which has the least support from history, psychology, or common sense. It is specially unfortunate that it should have developed just when we were getting away from the previous negative policy of leaving the colonies to drift along each on its own resources and revenue, with no controlled direction of its economic development and welfare. The fact that certain British colonies outside Africa —Cyprus for example—are excluded from complete self-government makes it still more inexplicable that self-government should be treated as a universal dogma in Africa or the Caribbean.

Chapter Five

THE LATEST AGE: NEW FACTORS AND
THE LINK WITH PART II

THE post-war period started in an atmosphere of hang-over from the unhappy inter-war period. Roosevelt dealt with Stalin on the two assumptions that he was very much like American politicians, and that British Imperialism was really worse than Soviet Russian; the long-dead League of Nations was replaced by the United Nations. No treaty with the vanquished could be even attempted, but the allied forces were hastily disbanded and the British Government disposed of the equipment of 25 divisions, some of it to Czecho-slovakia, and 50 jet planes were sold to Russia, thus saving their engineers several years' research.

With the North Atlantic Treaty in 1948 the tide began to turn and the beginnings of a realist approach to the new factors began to appear. A tentative appreciation of some of the main new factors with which we have to reckon suggests, first, that the balance of Power principle has been vindicated by experience, but that it must be global, and no longer merely European; indeed, for the moment the main weight of the attack has shifted to South-East Asia. Secondly, Britain is no longer capable of sustaining a major war single-handed even during the early stages, and can no longer provide for her own military security, single-handed, without undermining her already precarious economic security. Thirdly, we have to face the fact that the great Euro-Asiatic land-mass is now for the first time in the hands of a single government with enormous industrial and military resources, with a permanent strategy of world-revolution and a group of satellite states, and China; this combination means that no " world " association can be made to work. To these three factors the only answer is the North Atlantic Union which builds on all the favourable factors—partnership with the United States and the Common-wealth, partnership with West Europe, Greece and Turkey—

and gives Britain the only possible solution to the dilemma of how to combine military and economic security.

The fourth factor seems to be that, whatever may be the academic theory, or indeed the ideal solution, military security and the Welfare State can only be maintained by concentrating on a balanced economy and a great increase in production, and it is difficult to see how these are possible without a return to the principles which guided British governments from the Middle Ages to the reign of Queen Victoria. Temporary improvements in balances and terms of trade may obscure the long-term trend, but this without a great increase in production and a corresponding reduction of burdens, must surely be adverse. I appreciate, however, that this is a very complex and debatable matter.

Fifthly and sixthly, a reassessment of our strategic position is imposed by the loss of the Indian Empire and the new developments of air and submarine warfare. These new factors have changed the situation in the Mediterranean and the Middle East. Among their consequences must be included the loss of the Abadan oil refinery (a natural consequence of the loss of the Indian Army); that the Suez Canal, whatever its other uses may be, is no longer indispensable as the route to India; and that the Mediterranean route, which was only just tenable with very heavy losses in the last war, can be made too hot in another war. Obviously the problem of imperial communications needs rethinking out. Fortunately it has now been recognized that the convenience of holding the Suez Canal is not worth the pinning down of 80,000 troops while there is no strategic reserve in Britain, the discouragement of voluntary recruiting, and the danger of a hostile Egypt in the rear. What of the prestige argument—that each " scuttle " leads on to another? I have always laid great stress on the mystical importance of prestige, so apt like all imponderables to be underrated; but an obstinate refusal to face facts for the sake of prestige may defeat its own object. The only safe test is to stick to the merits of each case. If a strategic position is worth holding at all costs, and if one's physical resources and assurance of future support of public opinion (and we must now take American opinion into account as well) are such that the position can be held indefinitely, then

it should be held and the prestige argument is irrelevant. This, for example, is certainly the case in regard to Gibraltar, our only naval and air refuelling point and fortress on the 2,749 nautical miles' route from Plymouth to Freetown, and therefore as indispensable for the protection of the Atlantic West African route as it has been in the past for the Mediterranean route. (This conclusion does not exclude the eventual possibility of some agreement, if Spain became a member of the Atlantic Union, on the lines of the American bases leased from Great Britain, with no time-limit—but this is purely speculative.) If, however, a dispassionate analysis shows that the holding of a particular strategic position creates more problems than it solves and gives more trouble than it is worth, and if a substitute is possible even at the cost of some inconvenience, then the longer it is held, the worse it is for prestige when it has to be abandoned. The same question arose on a much larger scale from the withdrawal from India at the end of the war. One may hold that the handing over was too precipitate in that it involved some injustice to Moslem Pakistan, but this argument cuts both ways; hanging on to a position which has become in practice untenable is apt to lead to undue precipitation, and unnecessary sacrifices, when the inevitable happens. The British position in India had become untenable long before the withdrawal; morally from the time when the promise of Dominion status was made, and physically during the period in which the British element in the civil service was reduced below—and eventually far below—the level needed to control the administration effectively. There was a time when the Indian Princes, whose loyalty and good-will as a body was indisputable, could have been built up into a Federation under the British Crown; but the policy preferred was the steady expansion of the area of centralized bureaucracy. The situation had arisen in which clinging on had become a source of danger to our prestige, and whatever the long-term results may be for the common people in India, our prestige seems considerably higher in the sub-continent than it was in the last years of the moribund Raj.

A very delicate but indispensable adjustment has become necessary in regard to the position of Britain as a partly

European and partly Oceanic Power.   The fact must be faced that the tie-up between Britain and Europe has become very much more important and vital during the last fifty years and must be reconciled with the no less important Commonwealth link.   No one who was in England during the period of the V.1's and V.2's should still talk as if Britain was not a European Power.   Today a land army which controls the Channel Ports wields a threat unknown in the days of Napoleon or even Kaiser Wilhelm; yet public opinion rejected till the last moment the permanent maintenance of British troops in Europe, particularly on the ground that it might not be acceptable to some other members of the Commonwealth.   When a vital interest of this island is at stake, it is no longer realistic to invoke the possibility of Commonwealth disagreement as being in itself an unanswerable reason for jeopardizing it.   Perhaps a large factor in this exaggerated insistence is the subconscious feeling that the loss of India and our greater relative weakness can be compensated by constant over-insistence to the exclusion of all other considerations, on Britain's position as head of a great World Commonwealth; such exaggeration can become in psychological terms, a " compensation " for an inferiority complex.   The same feeling seems to be implied in the insistence on leaving the Commonwealth Relations office to co-ordinate foreign policy direct with the Dominions instead of allowing the real experts—namely the Secretary of State for Foreign Affairs and his advisers—to deal directly with the other members of the Commonwealth, involving delays and duplication which can be very serious.   The theory that the British, Australian, Canadian, South African and Indian Governments form a family bound to act as one political unit is an ideal which must be acted on with realism and common sense.   It would probably have become reality if the Empire had been channelled during the nineteenth century along the lines of Imperial Preference, but that opportunity seems irrevocably lost.

IS THE HYDROGEN BOMB A FACTOR MODIFYING OUR FOREIGN POLICY?

In the introduction to these comments and questions, I referred to the latest horrors of scientific warfare as one of the elements in the contemporary picture of surface events. I have not, however, listed the atom bomb or the hydrogen bomb among the new factors to be taken into account in forming our policies, and my reason is that none of the suggestions hitherto made for action in this connection seems likely to effect any result other than increasing our dangers. First, if these new weapons could be eliminated and we could revert to what are called " conventional arms," the Soviet Union would be much less vulnerable at home, and much stronger relatively in the field; and the Soviet Union, unlike the sentimental and neurotic Hitler, wants to avoid the risk of taking over ruins and being ruined itself in the process. The hydrogen bomb should therefore prove a deterrent to any major war. Secondly, it is impossible that any agreement, made on whatever level, could carry with it the certainty of elimination of the bomb; for this would involve such a system of inspection and supervision as would be completely incompatible with the whole Soviet structure. Actual experience of life in the Soviet Union very early induces an intuitive feeling that it would be impossible for the Soviet authorities to allow any sort of inspection at all without tearing up their system by the roots, and the more I got to know of the mechanics of their system, the stronger did this conviction grow. There seems no practical way in which we can diminish the menace of these atrocities except to increase their value as a deterrent by retaining the lead; but it would be folly to rely on it, or to discount in any way the importance of the other arms and the sea communications of Britain, for it is possible that neither side would take the initiative in using it.

If this rapid review of the world as I see it were to stop at this point, it could be plausibly criticized as being a series of negative, pessimistic and some of them admittedly debatable, propositions. The chief propositions are that we in this country sacrificed security to a Liberal philosophy of which the theory of Free Trade was a part; squandered our accumulated resources in attempting in 1914 a full-scale continental land war and unduly prolonging it; substituted an illusory system of continual conferences and world assemblies for that of diplomacy and co-operation with our proved friends;

followed policies which were not related to our military and
economic strength; have reacted sluggishly to changed
circumstances; adopted a false and unrealistic policy in relation to our overseas territories; and have by our mistakes
allowed the Soviet Union to fulfil Sir H. Mackinder's worst
predictions.   If it were left at that, the effect would be wholly
discouraging—granting, a critic could say, that your propositions are true, that such vast mistakes have been made in all
directions, then what is the use of discussing them?   These
propositions are, however, only an introduction to the second
part of the argument, which contains the real and main
thesis.   It is that such a chain of errors are the outward and
visible manifestation of a deep-rooted sickness of the *mind and
will*, a psychic cancer which is affecting the vitality of our
Western civilization as a whole, though taking different forms
in the peoples which belong to it.   The other major Western
Powers have made their own gigantic mistakes, now particularly obvious in the cases of France and Germany, which
fall more appropriately in later chapters; Britain, though very
vulnerable, is still in many ways more healthy than her
principal neighbours.

Common factors are the breakdown of rational standards of
judgement and of the traditions and instincts which formerly
acted as standards of judgement for the now up-rooted masses;
and as a result the invasion of herd-thinking, wishful thinking,
and wholly confused thinking.   In our own case the breakdown
both of rational judgement and inherited intuitive wisdom have
taken a special direction owing to the loss of confidence of the
" middle " classes and a curious sublimation of the unique
insularity of the English mind, which has been stressed as a
prime, if paradoxical, factor in the defeatist evasion of responsibility to subject peoples.   Both the common factors, however, and the specifically English ones, are all ultimately
derived from false *ideas* and their material consequences; and
these together form the " deeper currents " which the following
pages attempt to analyse.   I do so in the conviction that
false ideas can be replaced by true ideas, and that it is in fact
possible to " minister to a mind diseased."   For my contribution I claim a certain novelty only in one respect.   Our

accumulation of false ideas and consequent false tendencies has been attacked from many angles by many specialized students. My object is to bring together in a synthesis all these converging lines of attack, and by seeking a common denominator to suggest to " men of good will " the organic sources of our spiritual malady.   In saying that some of my propositions were debatable, I had in mind especially the views offered on questions of economic policy.   I am well aware that there is a strong case on either side in these matters, and I am always ready to change my views on them.   Whatever their merits may be, they are on an entirely different level to that of my main thesis and in no way essential to it.

General Elections and the ensuing changes of Governments, Budgets and Labour disputes, the vagaries of equities and gilt-edged—still more, dictatorships and revolutions—are important matters; but if we confine our attention to them, reading only the day's news, we cannot see the wood for the trees.   Current events cannot really be properly assessed unless they are seen against their background, as incidents in a long stream of happenings and influenced by ideas and beliefs which are sometimes dying survivals from the past, sometimes pregnant with future consequences which at the moment are not realized by the actors or the spectators.   These pages are an attempt—how inadequate no one can realize better than their author—to stimulate closer examination of some basic popular assumptions and formulas by testing their validity in the light of recent scholarship and against the background of the long-term massive social movements.

PART II
THE DEEPER CURRENTS

Chapter One

ON THE PRACTICAL IMPORTANCE
OF IDEAS

*" In the collective affairs of men bad doctrines are always
more deadly than bad actions "* (Professor R. H. Tawney)

THE distrust of general abstract ideas, innate in the
British character, has itself become an idea, and one
which has profoundly influenced British opinion. It
was carried over to the United States, although the American
Constitution is based on highly abstract speculative principles
derived from traditional Christian philosophy. When a
leading American newspaper applied for the reproduction
rights for one of two articles by myself, it explained that it did
not want the other one because in the first paragraph it
alluded to Hegel, and this would discourage its readers who
would say, " Who the hell was Hegel anyway? " Just as
Monsieur Jourdan talked prose without knowing it, so the
most practical and opportunist people are constantly acting
on, or being affected by, other people's ideas, and the name
of Hegel is a useful illustration, which can be summed up in
two propositions. First, the continuing Marx-Stalinist system
which has guided Russia for 35 years and vitally affects every
man, woman and child in the world, was not inevitable.
The Revolution of October, 1917, was a *coup d'état* secretly
prepared by " a tiny minority " (Mr. Deutscher's words) of
fanatical Marxists who succeeded through the ineptitude of
the Kerensky government and, subsequently, by Trotsky's
creation of the Red Army and his administrative and military
genius. Its success and eventual permanence verged on the
miraculous.

Secondly, the whole system which Lenin, Trotsky, and
finally Stalin, imposed on Russia was taken straight from
Marx, and Soviet policy cannot be understood without a

knowledge of Marx—which is one reason why few people
ever have understood it.[1]

The Marxist jargon is so boring that I dare not amplify the
complete dependence of Stalinism on Hegel, but will pass to a
simple illustration from more recent history.   In 1945 Russia
was on the top of the wave of success.   She had obtained
defence in depth on both Eastern and Western fronts.   Pro-
Russian governments controlled all the new states, including
Czechoslovakia.   There was a pathological mood of goodwill
and optimism in Britain, France and in the U.S.A.   With tact
and restraint, Russia could have easily established a world
hegemony before the wishful thinkers woke up.   Within three
years, she had thrown away this great asset and the North
Atlantic Union was in being.   Why?   Because the Kremlin
was wholly guided by the Marx-Stalin doctrine.   The
Capitalist Powers *could not* be well disposed; their professions
of goodwill must be bogus.   Constitutional Socialist governments could not be trusted; they were the worst enemies of
the revolution.   The capitalist " camp " was weakened,
therefore it was the moment for " strategy," the aggressive
line.   Finally, a friendly response to Western goodwill meant
personal contacts and Western cultural influences, and these
would mean contamination of Soviet citizens and a reaction
against the Police State.   These assumptions must not be
examined, for they all flowed from the doctrine.   And so
instead of playing up to the wishful thinkers, Soviet Russia
embarked on a ruthless pressure for direct control of the

---

[1] Hegel's " dialectic," or theory of progress through the conflict of opposites,
was the source of Marx's " dialectical philosophy," and materialist interpretation of history, just as Nazism and Fascism took Hegel's thesis that the State is
the Divine Idea as it exists on earth and that the individual only realizes himself
through membership of it.   History was for Hegel the progressive unfolding
of God (" Absolute spirit ") through the " dialectic," and the dialectic was his
theory of the struggle, and union, of opposites.   Marx's materialist interpretation of history was the application of Hegel's theory to the development of
society.   On the basis of Hegel's law of the transformation of " quantity " into
" quality " he argued that revolutions must be abrupt and violent; on the basis
of Hegel's " union of opposites " he argued that the bourgeoisie and the pro-
letariate are both interconnected and contradictory; on the basis of Hegel's
theory that the antithesis negates the thesis, and the synthesis negates the
antithesis, the Soviet doctrinaires have defended Lenin's " NEP " (as the
antithesis of early Bolshevism) and Stalinism as the synthesis of the two.

satellites, intervention in Greece and Persia, obstructive opposition to the Marshall Plan and the Austrian Treaty, the Berlin blockade, the creation of the Cominform. In a later chapter I will draw attention to the great influence of Hegel on late Victorian England, not of course directly on the mass of the people but on the *élite* of civil servants and parliamentarians and editors, especially those who had taken the Oxford School of " Greats " or the Scottish universities.

If the post-war history was controlled by Soviet doctrine, the course of the war was influenced, perhaps changed, by Nazi doctrine. In the first few months after the German attack on Russia 1,500,000 Russian soldiers had surrendered, and military opinion everywhere shared Hitler's belief that the invasion had practically succeeded. From that time on, the Russian surrenders became a trickle, the war became a holy war, and within another few months the eventual decision was virtually assured. The prime factor in this turn of the tide was the Nazi race-theory. The German Army had achieved everything expected of it when the German race theorists butted in. They treated the Russian prisoners as vermin, letting many die of starvation. They refused the offered co-operation of many thousands of General Vlassov's Russian volunteers, not using on the Russian front the few they accepted. They loosed the Gestapo on the Ukrainian and other minority nationalities who had welcomed the German Army as liberators. All this was the result of their obsession with the theory of their own " racial " superiority.

A third contemporary example is the incendiary effect all over Asia of the nineteenth-century European idea of Nationalism, in the Arab States, Indonesia, Indo-China for example. The American anti-colonialism, which, as we have seen, poured oil on the fire at a critical period, was itself inspired by the traditional American idea that it is morally wrong for one man to have political domination over another. In industry, the Fords and Carnegies fulfilled a national ideal, but in politics the ideal was equality, to the point that incorruptibility was regarded with distrust as suggesting lust for authority—whereas political corruption was merely an understandable human weakness. So it may be said that the present generation has witnessed three examples of the practical force of an Idea; the Hegelian idea at work in Russia, the Racial idea counteracting the victories of the German Army, the Nationalist idea turning Asia upside down and creating hostility to the West throughout that immense area.

Theories can also change the course of events by indirect action, without being accepted as conscious beliefs, by undermining accepted beliefs and attitudes; and so producing bewilderment and loss of confidence. This was the real contribution of the French eighteenth-century philosophers, who did not start the French Revolution and foresaw neither its course nor its ultimate effects, but did create a mental climate of scepticism and undermined the self-confidence of the privileged classes to which they belonged and who formed their reading public. A more topical illustration is the influence during the first quarter of this century of Bernard Shaw and H. G. Wells in sapping the morale of the English middle classes, creating a mood of doubt, shame and self-questioning both about their economic and social position at home and their right to govern other people abroad. They did not consciously accept their doctrines—for instance Shaw's equality of incomes or Wells' hatred of the English Public Schools; the influence was specially exerted by the younger writers whose outlook was formed by the two Masters. J. B. Priestley has told us how " Shaw, like Wells, dominated the world in which I grew up . . . his influence on people of my sort has been so immense, so all-pervading." Laurence Housman: " I regard Bernard Shaw . . . as the most devastating influence which has befallen my country from the nineties of the last century . . . by having so many of our pet notions reduced to absurdity our minds were changed for us." Sir William Haley calls Shaw " one of the few seminal and most incisive minds of our time," and Sir Gilbert Murray, speaking of Shaw's concentration on ideas, said he was chiefly actuated not by sympathy for human suffering but more by the absurdity of the institutions. Mr. Housman, Sir Osbert Sitwell, and Mr. Aldous Huxley have all compared Shaw to Voltaire; the comparison is apt in many ways, and not least in regard to Voltaire's admiration for the Prussian Military despot Frederick, and Shaw's admiration for Stalin.

Shaw and Wells did not preach identical doctrine like Belloc and Chesterton, but their influence worked in the same direction and they had certain significant traits in common. Both started as orthodox Fabians, both developed into preachers of Utopia, and both ended as pessimists, disbelieving in benevolent evolution, expecting imminent catastrophe, and proclaiming that the stupid human race had committed suicide and must be replaced by a more adaptable species. Wells as usual had no doubts; Shaw had a faint hope that people might learn sense by learning to live for 300 years.

Unfortunately they had achieved their mission before they reached these relatively salutary conclusions.   Wells' Utopia was in essence that of a schoolboy—a technologist's paradise like the inside of a submarine, where the *élite* would press buttons and pull levers, and in their abundant leisure (here he became more adolescent) flit from one free love to another. Shaw imagined a Utopia sparsely inhabited by teetotal vegetarians, free from jealousy or possessiveness, where no one would hurt a fly (once a few million human misfits had been liquidated).   In short, both Utopias were self-projections: Wells' was the least amiable, as he represented the worst side of the Victorian English lower middle-class attitude raised to the *n*th degree by his imaginative genius.   His ideals were largely negative, as he was obsessed by his passionate hatred for God, soldiers, priests, kings, aristocrats, gentlemen, the ancient Greeks and Romans and therefore of classical scholarship—the last three hatreds closely connected with his phobia about the English Public Schools.   Though Shaw's Utopia was more aesthetic than mechanized, both agreed that a superman and a superstate were necessary preliminaries. But their ideals did not matter; they did not launch pregnant philosophies, and what mattered was, as in the case of Voltaire, their joint influence through Shaw's mocking wit and Wells' vivid imagination, in creating a whole miasma of doubt and criticism in which the younger writers bathed.   Wells was perhaps the most effective, as he applied his gifts as a novelist to diffuse on a vast scale all the philosophic, scientific

and historical theories current in " advanced " circles in the
eighteen-eighties, giving them a new lease of life when the
specialists were already discarding them.

The great difficulty in tracing the history of ideas is that
they have to work through the conflicting currents of chance,
or the presence or absence at given times of great personalities,
of greed and self-sacrifice, of the soul's free will and the pressure
of biological facts.   H. A. L. Fisher was so impressed by these
cross-currents that he could see only one safe rule for the
historian, to " recognize in the development of human destinies
the play of the contingent and the unforeseen." He was
rightly reacting against the common academic tendency to
regard all events as inevitable, to classify the past in pre-
determined patterns; but it would be perhaps as great an
error to ignore the influence of ideas and beliefs on men's
actions, however much the ideas get retarded and distorted—
even transformed—when they get loose in the whirlpool of
accidents and personalities, and are subject to the selective
and modifying force of character and circumstances. Ideas,
like books, " have their fates," in a way a life of their own;
they vary greatly in their inherent force of appeal, their radius
of action, and the time-lag in their activity, though so long as
they are purely human speculations, they are all liable to
similar experiences. Some are, in form at least, original,
fertile, of universal appeal.   Some are (or derive their strength
from being) in effect rationalizations of primitive national
instincts and desires, like most German philosophies; others
are rationalizations of class interests and temporary economic
conditions, like Marxism or the English Utilitarians. Among
the experiences they are liable to undergo are that they can
lie dormant for long periods till the right conjunction of
circumstances brings them to the top; that they possess a
latent explosive force and can, like some rockets, erupt at
intervals in successive explosions; and that their eventual
repercussions and ramifications are hardly ever foreseen by
their originators.

Ideas can lie dormant for long periods, as even the obvious
general idea of evolution remained a matter of academic
discussion for many centuries until the attachment to it of

Darwin and Wallace's hypothesis of natural selection, when it swept the civilized world, and assumed despotic control for sixty years of every department of thought and research, sometimes with deplorable results.   Marx's doctrine, though it had remained the nominal official creed of the Continental Socialist Parties, had lost its vitality by 1917, as evidenced by the rare reprinting of his works and the line-up of the French and German socialists behind their governments in 1914.   It was rescued by the Revolution in Russia—which on Marxist principles should have been the last country to adopt it— revived and converted into a workable and missionary Faith by Lenin and Stalin who destroyed its democratic façade and gave it teeth with the Dictatorship of the Proletariat (i.e., Communist Party) and a régime of Privilege.

Ideas have a latent explosive force, and may have successive outbreaks in varying forms.   Thus the theological ideas of the German and Swiss reformers in the sixteenth century, coupled with the obscured forces they released, have had a major responsibility for a series of delayed-action explosions; the rise of modern capitalism (in the form it took), the Divine Right of Kings, the revival of pagan State-worship (typified in Hegel and the Prussian Monarchy), the religions of Nationalism, Marxism, and Nazism; the final form of the French Revolution; and the Romantic movement in art and letters (" Luther was the first great Romantic ").   Yet—and here we return to H. A. L. Fisher's creed—the whole movement might have come to nothing like the Albigensians, the Hussites and the Lollards, " if " . . . if Charles V had had his hands free, and still more if Richelieu a century later had not thrown his genius and the power of France behind Gustavus Adolphus, thus decisively tilting the balance of the Thirty Years' War against the forces of the Counter-Reformation headed by the Habsburgs.

Ideas develop and take forms which their originators seldom foresee and often quite contrary to their hopes.   Just as false assumptions led Columbus to discover America, so do examples abound in every age of the failure of the critical subversive elements to read the signs of the times and see where their ideas are leading. They do not often live to realize their own failure, as did

Shaw and Wells, the French Girondins, or Erasmus—who with his fellow humanists cleared the ground for Luther and ended by wailing, " *Ubicumque Lutheranismus regnat, ibi Litteratorum interitus.*"   Think of the French governing class sentimentalizing with Rousseau and sniggering with Voltaire (the churchgoer Madame Geoffrin saved the Encyclopaedia from bankruptcy);   the French nineteenth-century radicals persisting down to 1870 in the " philosophers' " cult of Prussia; the adoption of German philosophy by Victorian Oxford and Edinburgh.

Ideas do not necessarily cause revolutions, but when the factors of accident, circumstances, and personality combine to produce a revolution, the ideas of a minority come in to supply the driving force and the revolutionary fervour which so often turns them into imperialist movements. The Jacobins' slogan of fraternity soon turned into " Be my brother or I'll kill you! "—it has been well said that the Jacobins' ideology masked their imperialism while the Nazis' imperialism masked their ideology.

Ideas which merely rationalize instincts or existing interests develop and strengthen the tendencies which they justify. For three-quarters of the nineteenth century English legislation and administration were dominated by the teachings of the Utilitarians or " Philosophic radicals."   Their founder Jeremy Bentham, " the greatest social engineer in history," " guided the movement for social and political reform from his retreat in Westminster."   Sir Henry Maine said, " I don't know a single law reform since Bentham's day which cannot be traced to his influence."   Bentham wrote 7,000 pages of small type double column and 75,000 pages of manuscript but he condensed his doctrine into a few lines: " Nature has placed mankind under two sovereign Masters, pain and pleasure . . . they govern us in all we do."   Self-interest was the sole motive of human action;   moral obligation was a feeling resulting from the association of disagreeable or advantageous results with particular actions. Pleasures only differed from each other in quantity—Bentham made a " hedonic calculus " measuring pleasures and pains. He hated the past (especially and naturally Dr. Johnson!), advocated infanticide, Basic

English, and also homosexuality on the interesting ground that Christianity had often been infiltrated through female influence on princes, but never by a male favourite! His spiritual children included Ricardo, the two Mills, Sidgwick, and in practice Herbert Spencer. His greatest disciple, J. S. Mill, found the greatest happiness (i.e., utility) principle (that every man acts to obtain his happiness, and that actions are right in proportion as they produce happiness) a shaky foundation for morals. He illogically substituted the " general happiness," meaning the sum total of all individual desires, and slipped in a moral test by changing " preferable " to " higher " pleasures. To explain why men in fact often do right when happiness is not likely to result, he argued that if an action is condemned or approved often enough, men end by thinking it bad or good without thinking of the consequences. But to the end, Utilitarianism meant that self-interest and benevolence are identical because men desire other people's happiness in their own interest, that " useful " and " morally right " are identical, that pleasure is a measurable objective quantity and the only motive of action.

How did this inadequate, illogical and inhuman doctrine exert such vast influence on English thought and action? The clear answer is that the practical conclusions rationalized and justified the mood of the English governing classes during the Industrial Revolution. It gave a halo to unlimited greed and the " Iron laws " of *laissez-faire* economics (largely the product of this school) and at the same time provided the driving force for a wholesale sweeping away of all old laws, customs, corporate rights, and all privileges except those which in practice mere wealth automatically creates. In short, it was the ideal philosophy for the newly rich millowner. In the final outcome, the creed, like so many others, falsified the expectations of its votaries. The Utilitarians were the leading preachers of Parliamentary reform and looked forward (as J. S. Mill said of his father, " With an almost unbounded confidence ") to the day when everyone would vote and read newspapers—and vote as a philosophic radical. They seriously imagined that the new urban proletariats would see *laissez-faire* economics, " everyone for himself and the devil take·

the hindmost," from the same angle as they themselves saw the picture from their comfortable libraries, and would take the same view of "the greatest happiness of the greatest number." The idea of old-age pensions, for example, never occurred to them—or that they might be increased before each General Election!

Do institutions arise from ideas or vice versa? Many beside the Marxists would have it that ideas are themselves the product of their social and technological environment. My own feeling is that this is one of those questions to which the complexity of human nature will never allow a complete answer either way; I hope that the following chapters may help to throw some light on the constant interaction of ideas and institutions. The "practical" man may still say: "I am not interested in the ideas, only in their results; give me facts." The first answer is that such important facts as the Soviet Empire and its foreign activities are literally unintelligible without reference to the ideas on which its directors act and that President Roosevelt's total ignorance of those ideas, or even that Stalin had any ideas, was largely responsible for Russia's overwhelming diplomatic successes at Yalta and Potsdam. A second and more general answer is that all presentations of facts, whether in a textbook or a newspaper, are selections, from a great number of facts, of what the writer *thinks* are the significant ones: in other words, every presentation of facts, whether it be a Chairman's annual report or a report from "our Correspondent" in Washington, a travel-book or a history, is and must be an arrangement of selected facts to present a point of view, and behind that point of view is an idea, however incapable a particular reporter might be of formulating and defending it. Of course, factual reporting is a reality and one constantly practised: but the more complicated the subject, the more selective it must be.

The purpose of this introduction has been to suggest that a descriptive survey of the contemporary scene must be supplemented by a consideration of the deeper currents at work, and that such consideration carries us inevitably into the realm of theories, beliefs, and the prejudices which so often pass themselves off as ideas.

Chapter Two

ON THE OLD PERSPECTIVE IN HISTORY

" Their works are vain " (Isaiah xli.29).

DESPITE the achievements in historical writing of some supreme literary artists like Thucydides and Tacitus, or Philippe de Commynes, More, Bacon or Clarendon, history is largely the creation of the last two centuries, and it is stamped with the character of that period. While the general public, fascinated by physical science, is broadly aware that materialist mechanical explanations of the universe, determinism and the Atomic Theory, are no longer dogmas and that " the Scientific Universe is once more full of mystery," we are still using the simplifying language of our grandfathers in regard to the highly complex history of mankind. It is the language, not of the eighteenth or early nineteenth century, but of the second half of the nineteenth. The first characteristic mark of that period was the invasion of all departments of the study of mankind by the dogma of universal endless upward progress, physical, mental and moral. Over seventy years ago Beatrice Webb was already noting as a commonplace that " the Creeds " had been generally replaced by the Religion of Progress. It was a dogma, because any inconvenient facts which did not fit into the general scheme were denied or shelved on that express ground. Its success was made easier by the fact that apart from legal and political history, the human studies—psychology, sociology, comparative religion—were created or reborn during the period, and therefore built up by men who had no doubts whatever that the dogma must offer the key to all human problems.

Its success was further helped by the extraordinary security and wellbeing of the Western middle classes in the Victorian Age. One must go back to the middle period of the Roman Empire—the age of the Antonines—to find any parallel to the sheltered life of our professional and business predecessors, and even then the highest classes who were near to the Emperors were a bad insurance risk and the standards both of comfort and freedom were lower for all.   This environment of law and order, absolute freedom, and increasing comfort, ease and prosperity, was assumed without any misgiving to be stable and permanent in a way that no one born in this century can really grasp; it was known to be new and unique, but no one dreamed it could be passing and temporary.   This period-optimism fitted and reinforced the basic assumption that the human story represents a gradual but constant and inevitable improvement of the species in every department of thought and life, moral, mental, physical.   The biological theory of evolution from simple to complex, lower to higher, amoeba to man, was applied to man, who was conceived as necessarily developing, since his first appearance, from reflexes and instincts to reason by infinite small variations, gradually evolving a soul or at least all the capacities which differentiate the species so radically from the other animals.

Some might admit a " spiral " or oscillations in progress; all agreed that there was an eternal law of evolutionary progress (except a rare eccentric like the Comte de Gobineau whose doctrine of degeneration of the pure Nordic race has been called " linear progress in reverse," and who silenced a critic with " On the contrary—men are obviously turning *into* monkeys! ")   With few exceptions, both philosophers and social scientists saw in history a progressive decrease of violence and physical laws, an increase of peace, freedom, justice, morality, intelligence; Tuesday better than Monday, Wednesday better than Tuesday.   Some postulated a law of acceleration, that the changes for the better grow faster.   No one seemed worried by the fact, which began to puzzle me as a boy, that the exponents of the dogma gave the most contradictory versions of how progress had worked.   There was as good authority for believing that development had been from patriarchy to matriarchy, from matriarchy to patriarchy, from sex-equality to sex-inequality and vice versa, from communism to private ownership and vice versa, from republic to monarchy and monarchy to republic; and that religion had started as animism, totemism, magic or from the murder and burial of the pater-familias, rudely called " the Old Man."

The key to all these contradictions was that everyone agreed that earlier institutions must be inferior to later ones, and consequently what you personally preferred must have been a later development. Thus while the various accounts of primitive religion were obviously contradictory, they all agreed in not even discussing the possibility that it was mono-theism; for belief in one supreme God was the highest form, therefore it must be the latest to evolve. It was the reverse of scientific method; the new social scientists started with a theory and arbitrarily accepted or rejected the facts to suit it. When the Abbé Breuil produced his reproductions of the palaeolithic cave drawings—as mature and competent as anything in their *genre* ever produced, an art which had suddenly appeared and then disappeared leaving no successor— his established colleagues at once announced their disbelief. Evidence so contradictory to official archaeology and anthropology must be wrong somewhere. Just as all debased forms of religion must be primitive, so must rude implements everywhere be older than better ones.

These two obsessions—a dogmatic theory of linear progress and a belief that the local temporary conditions of Europe in the nineteenth century were final and stable—converged to produce a false out-of-focus picture of humanity which has caused incalculable mischief. Intoxicated with optimism and pseudo-science, Western men ignored the permanent rôle of the non-rational subconscious elements; the psychology of the herd; the appeal of tyranny to the uprooted masses yearning for material stability and security, the power of inertia and routine when freedom is lost. They regarded as obsolete the tendency to sheer wickedness, the fear of evil powers leading to their propitiation, and disregarded the widespread evidence that when the fear of God is weakened, it has been so often replaced by the God of Fear. Emerson, with the typical armchair optimism of the eighteen-sixties, said patronizingly that he never could give much reality to evil, and Lord Keynes, referring to the Cambridge society of his friends at the beginning of the present century, said they did not know " that civilization was a thin and precarious crust erected by the personality and the will of a very few, only maintained by rules and conventions

skilfully put across and guilefully preserved." Evil was
associated with Nature, pestilences and earthquakes, and
primitive man shared in the cruelty of nature because he was
still half animal—but civilized man was envisaged as the
innocent victim of evil and advancing rapidly to its conquest.

The optimistic-progressive obsession led not only to forgetting the frequency of catastrophes; it ignored their possible
recurrence.   Marshall the economist took as the motto for his
standard text book " *Natura non facit per Saltum.*"   It seemed
true, on the facts of his period, but events were soon to justify
an older tag—" *Naturam expellas furca tamen usque recurret.*"
Concentrating on the Law of Progress, we disregarded the
evidences of its counterpart—the Law of Degeneration.   The
prevalence and frequent recurrence of arbitrary tyranny,
slavery, the mass extermination or deportation of whole
populations, the cult of evil with ritual human sacrifice (arising
in fact with *higher* stages of material civilization) were all
dismissed as primitive crudities which progress had eliminated
for ever.   Apart from moral degeneration, there have been so
many cases of material, artistic and intellectual retrogression
that they seem the normal pattern; the palaeolithic art, the
decline and submergence of post-Roman Britain, the luxurious
civilizations of Crete and Mycenae of which even the historic
memory had disappeared, and many others.   Just as the new
studies of sociology and comparative religion were deviated
and retarded for a generation by blind adherence to a dogma
borrowed from purely physical sciences, so also was the new
psychology hobbled to the dogmas of nineteenth-century
materialism; for Freud and Breuer when they began the
exploration of the unconscious were already soaked in the
clinical atmosphere of that century, of Haeckel and his school,
and Freud's vast influence in England as a pioneer has obscured
from the layman the revolutionary work of his successors.

All these subjects belong to a later stage of this argument, as
this chapter refers specially to the old perspective in general
history, the record of civilizations with written documentary
evidence.   Here, too, the assumption of continual moral
improvement has led to a superficial treatment of great revolutionary upheavals and a rationalization of the course they took.

It has been assumed, as a guide in arranging the facts, that the course actually taken by revolutions is an inevitable one; that their course and effects are always consciously willed by those who initiate and those who take part in them, and that the course and results represent always the will of a majority of the community concerned.   I referred earlier to the agreement of Mr. Deutscher—the greatest authority on Trotsky and his period in Russia—that the Soviet Revolution was the work of " a mere handful," who seized power after long, careful and secret preparation.   Turn to Kerensky's own evidence: in his book published in 1928 he tells how he left the nomination of local authorities and governors to electoral vote; how he refused the help of Kornilov's troops because " We had full confidence in the justice of our cause and were sure that the population would not tolerate acts of violence against the Government."   The members of the first Cabinet when it fell complained in a manifesto that the refusal of the Government to use " the old methods of restraint " had made their task of restoring order impossible.   Instead of rebuilding, they exhausted themselves and wasted their time in endless theoretical arguments with delegates of different groups, talking, talking.

The classic example, however—if also far more complicated than the Russian Revolution—is the French Revolution.   An immense literature has grown up around it, so large that even the admirable analyses made by Doctor C. P. Gooch and more recently by Professor Cobban could hardly do more than classify it, though this is very valuable; and no historical event has been more variously interpreted, or generated more mythology—unless perhaps the German Reformation.   For a century it was the happy hunting-ground of partisan literary historians; under the comb of modern research it has become the most valuable of guides to the study of the pathology of revolutions.   An attempt therefore to summarize the French Revolution in a few pages is a bold undertaking, but it is essential to the main purpose of this book.   By the contradictions between its causes and effects, the contradictions between its origins and course on the one hand, and on the other hand the historical myth about it; and by the immense influence of that myth or legend to this day, the French

Revolution provides convincing illustrations of the inadequacy of the oversimplified progressive formula with which, in its various forms, this book is specially concerned.

The popular legend, on both sides, saw the Revolution from 1789 to 1795 as a monolithic movement consciously aimed at the destruction of the Crown and the nobility, inspired by a Philosophy of revolt preached by the Voltairean group and Rousseau, and deriving its material force from the land hunger of starving peasants. The Terror was seen as an integral inevitable part of it, inherent from the start, just as Republicanism was. Taine, who hated it, attributed both the events of 1789 and the Terror to the same minority of abstract reasoners—" Several million savages impelled into action by a few thousand thinkers." Michelet, who raved about it, saw it as the triumph of Justice and the " People," inspired by Montesquieu, Voltaire and Rousseau; and painted the classic picture of a peasantry who had been growing more and more miserable, of a nobility all concentrated at Versailles. Carlyle —a Scots Presbyterian bathed in German romanticism—saw it as a single cataclysm sent to *punish* the sceptical philosophers and the feminist influence in French society, as a movement directed primarily against the Court extravagance, and in general as a Scottish-Hebrew moral revolt of 25 labouring millions against a " mouldering mass of sensuality and falsehood " and as " a huge bonfire of feudal lumber." His epic is still the basis of all Hollywood scenarios, but he differs from most of his French contemporaries in condemning the philosophers themselves. Roustan said the Revolution did not happen 25 years earlier because it needed that time for the philosophers to convert the French peasantry to their views. The only discordant voice was that of the profound political thinker Alexis de Tocqueville, who went to the sources and studied the provincial archives. He concluded that the essence of the Revolution was that it carried on and completed the work of the monarchy in centralizing the administration and establishing equality before the Law; and that the literary men had only advocated specific concrete reforms, not political upheaval, and had, therefore, only indirectly contributed by undermining authority.

Tocqueville was, as they say in the children's game of "find it," getting "hot," but another generation elapsed before his pioneer intuitions were expanded, with much else, by the researches of Aulard, Madelin, Funck-Brentano, Henri Sée, Gaxotte, Matthiez, Malet and others; some of whom, notably Aulard, were firm believers in the beneficent work of the Revolution. Albert Sorel dealt with the whole period from 1789 to 1815 as a part of European history, the Revolution in its international aspect, but his work was complementary to Tocqueville's in showing that the Revolutionary foreign policy was the direct heritage of the monarchy, just as Spenser Wilkinson, lecturing when I was at Oxford, showed Napoleon's debt to the generals of the Old Régime.

If we stick closely to the facts established by these workers and eliminate as far as possible all hypothesis and speculation, we get a decidedly different picture to set against the legend outlined above. First, the Revolution was not a continuous, logical monolithic movement, as Taine, Carlyle, Michelet thought; it is now recognized that there was no Republican party in 1789. Brissot and Condorcet were exceptions; the Constituent and Legislative assemblies were monarchist, and the records of even the Jacobin Club show that its atmosphere was monarchist also. Secondly, it began, not as a popular revolt against the Crown and the nobility, but as a revolt of the nobility and the "Parlements"—i.e., the privileged classes—against the Crown. The King's appeal to the Third Estate was the climax to a long and bitter struggle with the Parlements, close corporations of reactionary and entirely selfish lawyers, which had been brought to a head by the bankruptcy caused by the American War. The Court expenditure accounted for only one-ninth of the Budget, the loan expenses for one-third. His appeal failed through his lack of personality, and the unpopularity of the Austrian Queen, and the encouragement of the mob by the "monied interest," as Burke called it, and the aristocratic conspirators led by the Duke of Orleans. Thirdly, there was no direct connection with the literary movement. The philosophers did not preach Republicanism or attacks on property; they had demanded specific, and moderate, reforms. Since

Professor Cobban's bibliography, Mr. Gordon McNeill has shown that throughout 1789, 1790 and most of 1791, both the Emigrés and the Conservative minority in the National Assembly constantly invoked Rousseau in speeches and pamphlets—against the Revolution and the New Constitution, against hasty and violent changes, in defence of Church and private property, and of the monarchy. He had said that democracy required a small state where all the citizens knew each other, and was the opposite of representative government; that revolutions almost always delivered the people to " seducers who only aggravate their chains "; and had especially warned against the dangers of revolution in France. The *contrat Social* had not been republished between 1775 and 1790; Rousseau's reputation was as an educational and religious theorist—in *Emile* and the *Nouvelle Heloïse* for example, which led the majority in the Assembly to insist (successfully) on claiming him for their own. Here we come to the real point; the rôle of the philosophers had been to create a mental and moral climate of scepticism, to destroy the self-confidence of the governing classes and dissolve the force of tradition which had compensated for the weakness of the monarchy. The strongest points in the old régime had been the strength of the family and the immense variety of institutions and customs, the absence of an all-pervading central bureaucracy; pride in these had been, as Madelin stresses in what Doctor Gooch calls " the best modern history," discredited by purely destructive " writers who believed themselves to be thinkers." What they had produced was an " intellectual and moral crisis " (Gaxotte, Madelin, de Tocqueville) which made insoluble the otherwise manageable problem of the finances and the surviving vestiges of feudalism.

Fourthly, nine-tenths of the peasantry were in fact already proprietors (Henri Sée) and their growing prosperity has been demonstrated by Sée, Madelin and Funck-Brentano. Their grievances, as Arthur Young noted at the time—he equally noted the great rôle of the Parlements in blocking reform and creating a " revolutionary situation "—were the relics of feudal finance—corvées, gabelles, dues, tithes, militia service. Incidentally, the nobles were not all concentrated in Versailles;

there were 80,000 noble families! Arthur Young noted that many lived on their estates, and many biographies confirm this. The whole question of the origins of the Revolution has been transformed by the detailed study of the *cahiers*, the parish registers of 1789; for these show an exclusive concentration on concrete local grievances, and prove the total absence of abstract literary influence on the peasantry—which indeed would on the face of it be a psychological miracle.   Professor Madelin sums it up, that what nine-tenths of France really wanted was equality in justice and taxation and the abolition of feudal dues, and that all this had been achieved by August, 1789; and Professor Aulard, although writing as " a grateful son of the Revolution which has emancipated humanity and science," agrees that the opposition was not to the tyranny of the monarchy but to its weakness, and that the old privileged Parlements were the greatest barrier to reform and the instigators of a revolt in the provinces. Burke had also noted the evidence of the *cahiers*, but his pointer was not followed for nearly a century.

Fifthly, the Terror is now realized to have been not an integral and logical part of the movement of 1789, but an outbreak of panic and mob-hysteria fostered by the War.   The War itself was specially due, not to the Jacobins and Robespierre, who wished to avoid it, but to the Chauvinism of the Girondins, the explosive force generated by the Revolutionary spirit, and the old instinct for the Rhine and Alps frontiers (Sybel, Sorel, Bire); the Terror was the work less of Robespierre than of the great War Minister Carnot (the Trotsky of 1793); and it is highly typical of revolutionary pathology that the Girondins should have dug their own grave.

In sum, all the latest historians agree that the Revolution had a concrete twofold origin in (*a*) the struggle of a weak monarchy against the privileged classes, and (*b*) certain specific grievances of the under-privileged; that it was not republican in origin, but was transformed by the collapse of authority, the " climate " created by previous literary propaganda, and the impact of the War.   I would add two other factors; a temporary economic crisis and inflation due to bad finance and the effects of Vergennes' commercial Treaty with England (noted by Mr. Welsford), and the weakness of the

Church, to which too little attention is paid. The French Church with its Court-appointed bishops, including Talleyrand, had the additional weakness that the more serious members had been infected by Jansenism, which had killed the spiritual fervour of the mass of layfolk at its source.

The contrast between these origins and the ulterior consequences of the Revolution as it finally developed, is astounding. In Germany, it swept away the Holy Roman Empire, and with it more than seventy of the lay and clerical principalities, the Circles and Diet, the Imperial Knights, the Court of Appeal, all but six of the Free Cities—thus clearing the way, morally and physically, for Bismarck and finally Hitler. In Italy the Habsburgs and Bourbons returned in 1815 as alien conquerors. By proclaiming the principle of social equality, it promoted everywhere first Republicanism, then Socialism in its original form of economic equality. Above all, it created the religion of Nationalism, first in Europe, destined a century and a half later to spread to Asia. Nationalism was contrary to the cosmopolitan ideology of the Revolution, but it directly followed from the example of the French nation in changing its régime, in proclaiming the sovereignty of the " People," in adopting military conscription and forcing the others to do the same in self-defence, and by the mere fact of its military occupation of its neighbours. Until then, states were still thought of as geographical areas with local authorities, almost as large private estates with dynastic landlords— not as tribal communities in which unpatriotic criticism was to be substituted (for attacks on religion) as the object of the new religious intolerance. Finally, it revived the almost extinct fire of religious war by creating the new warfare of bourgeois liberalism against the Christian Church, identifying the latter with monarchist and aristocratic reaction, a war which dominated Europe, but specially the Latin countries, for over a century. This great red-herring of anti-clericalism resulted from the accident that the French Church had been so weakened by literary attack from without and Jansenism or Court patronage from within that the men of 1790 took for granted that the Church would swallow the Civil Constitution for the Clergy and were amazed and then furious when it refused.

I submit then that from the mass of detail involved in this most complicated chapter of European history four broad conclusions emerge. Practically no one in 1789 foresaw the course events would take from 1790 onwards, and in 1793 no one foresaw the Napoleonic period. The whole shape of the Revolution was transformed three times in the space of ten years. Neither the Republic, the Terror, the Twenty Years' War, nor the Empire, were foreseen, still less consciously willed. Secondly, there was no conscious national revolt against the monarchy—it was the monarchy which launched the Revolution by appealing to the States-general for help against the diehards of privilege, especially the Parlements. Thirdly, if the actual course of events inside France was neither willed nor foreseen, still less were the ulterior effects intended—the legacy to the World of Nationalism, militarism (incarnate in the Prussian monarchy which finally broke France), Socialism and class-warfare ending in Communism (Marx and Engels were deeply influenced by the French Revolution) and the identification of bourgeois liberalism with the campaign to destroy the Christian Church. Perhaps the only result they did foresee and welcome was the immense stimulus given to the Romantic Movement in art and letters with its inherent attack on the family and its social traditions. Fourthly, the literary forerunners—the school of Voltaire and the school of Rousseau—did not create or guide the Revolution; they influenced it indirectly by their negative effect in discrediting national tradition, loosening social ligaments, sapping the confidence of the Court and the governing and middle classes, above all in creating an atmosphere of doubt, bewilderment and hysterical sentimentality. Hysterical sentimentality is the great adversary not only of the intelligence but of humane feeling; it is inexorably followed by a surge of bestial ferocity under the cloak of idealism. In varying forms —varied by the play of accident, personality and the fortunes of war—every revolution passes out of the control of its initiators; the Unconscious takes charge, and the most disciplined and determined of the minority groups imposes a doctrine which transforms the whole character of the movement and becomes the accepted ideology.

Chapter Three

THE NEW PERSPECTIVE IN HISTORY

ALTHOUGH in history, as in the other human sciences, the average layman is still thinking in nineteenth-century terms, our age is marked not only by a greatly increased interest in it, but also by a growing interest in the comparative history of different social systems and institutions. This is evident in England in the press headlines and leading articles about the views of Professor Toynbee or Bertrand Russell.[1] This has some unwelcome aspects, though they are unavoidable and I hope only temporary stages. Interest in criticism and analysis is apt to arise as a phase or symptom of a decadent civilization or culture, a failing in creative energy, just as unsuccessful novelists are said to become critics! Secondly, and more significant, the comparison of periods and systems easily breeds a mood of " relativism " which tends to create total scepticism, and a denial that there is any absolute truth. A relativist approach to history, what the Germans call *Historismus*, is, they claim, becoming a World-View (*Weltanschauung*) and a whole philosophy of life. Karl Mannheim said, " We seek to tell what the time is by the cosmic clock of History," first by isolating and tracing the various elements in a cultural process, then by linking them in an organic synthesis. He opposes this " dynamic historical philosophy " to the old " static philosophy of reason." Troeltsch says any historical narrative (unlike a mathematical proposition) reveals when and where it was written and the background of its author; that the historical picture each epoch makes reflects its local aspirations and values. The extreme form of relativism was reached with Spengler, who made his eight main cultures correspond to eight philosophies, eight religions, eight mathematical systems and so on.

---

[1] I appreciate that Bertrand Russell is not an historian; but his views on historical matters are freely expressed and must have far more readers than his mathematical logic.

Even if we do not agree that the material of history—i.e. the facts—are only relatively true, there is no doubt that the reinterpretation of facts and the reassessment of their importance and interconnection can amount to a completely new picture of a period.   When Macaulay and Belloc wrote of the English Revolution of 1688 both knew their subject, but the resulting pictures are radically different.   The mediaeval German adventures in Italy were quite differently viewed by the Prussian and Austrian schools.   Again, when Germany was on the crest of the wave, the imperialist school stressed the action of great historical forces, while the post-Hitler writers stress the element of chance, as shown by the failure of the bomb to kill Hitler.   Similarly, when Mommsen abused Cicero and boosted Augustus he was thinking of the Frankfurt liberals of 1848; when he was disillusioned by the Empire he took refuge in pure textual scholarship.   A further danger of relativism is the tendency to equalize contemporary cultures— the idea that all group or national cultures and values are equally valid and respectable and vary only in their differing degrees of technological or spiritual emphasis, seems to have inspired much of Professor Toynbee's work, despite the importance which he assigns to religion.

This relativist tendency in historical writing is, of course, closely linked with the typical philosophies of our period, in America, England and Western Europe, notably Pragmatism, Logical Positivism, and Existentialism, which really are all elaborate expansions of " What is Truth? said Jesting Pilate, and would not stay for an answer."   Here I am faced with a recurrent problem in this series of studies.   I am trying throughout to appeal to the ordinary educated layman (i.e., the man or woman who has no time to delve deeply into the subjects but is seriously interested in the question, Where do we go from here?).   Now philosophy and psychology cannot be simplified beyond a certain point—one must use some of the professionals' jargon and this is inevitably boring to the non-specialist; but if I omit it altogether how can he tell whether my conclusions about the practical implications of the doctrines are well founded?   If however the summary is over-simplified, it becomes a target for the specialist, with facile accusations of misrepresentation. I shall be very sorry if the following short digression into contemporary philosophy seems too tough for the ordinary educated reader, for its whole point is to bring out something that concerns him— namely that our three chief intellectual fashions—Pragmatism, Logical Positivism, and Existentialism[1]—are nothing more than elaborate statements of complete scepticism; that they amount in effect to a total rejection of all absolute standards in philosophy and morals. All three boil down to the funda- mental conclusion that, subject to commonsense avoidance of legal penalties, you can believe what you like and do what you like—and if one or other professor prefers to deny that this is what he really means, one can only ask him to try and prove what he does mean. All three are philosophies to end philosophy, to dress up negation with the familiar comforting appearances of positive doctrine; in fact, a typical doctrine for an age of crisis, lost confidence and bewilderment. All three schools, the American, the Anglo-Viennese, the French, express in varying forms the same central theme: that there is no absolute truth, no necessary axiomatic first principles, no objective certainty or objective values, and that we can select the beliefs that we feel suit us best and the morals which we think make most for " happiness," whatever that means. What distinguishes them from previous Atheist or sceptical or " agnostic " philosophies is the open and explicit rejection of the traditional rôle of reason and logic, the reduction of all intellectual and spiritual questions to the test of practical results, or to the analysis of language, or to individual feeling. As has always been the case, the serious side of all this is not the effect on the intellectuals themselves who usually lead a sheltered academic life, are kept busy and happy with their work, and are anyhow usually by Nature of a law-abiding and domesticated type. What matters is the effect on successive waves of students of this deliberate withdrawal of rational and moral guidance.

[1] I select these three—especially the first two—as the *typical* period philo- sophies and the ones which have mainly affected general opinion and education. There are other contemporary British, American and European philosophers; only I am not trying to write a History of Philosophy, but to illustrate a general thesis.

Pragmatism was taken up by William James in 1898 though the word was launched twenty years earlier, and it was developed by Professors Dewey in America, Schiller in England, Bergson in France. It was the application to philosophy and religion of the evolutionary scientists' working idea that a hypothesis is as good as a law if it works. So, as between two beliefs, the one which in practice is best for me, is the true one. There are no necessary truths—two plus two may make five outside our experience. God is a limited part of our Universe working out a history like ourselves in a " strung-along type of universe." If the hypothesis of God works out satisfactorily as a hypothesis, then it is true—though James really meant that the *belief* in God worked out satisfactorily. Professor Dewey developed what he called " Instrumentalism," that knowledge is indissolubly bound up with action, just as the Existentialists say " I exist only in so far as I act." Thus the basic feature of Pragmatism is the substitution of usefulness for reasoning as the test of truth, and of individual experience for logic and first principles. It is the consecration of scepticism under the forms of a doctrine.

Consider next the fashionable Oxford and Cambridge philosophy of Logical Positivism and logical analysis. Until the nineteenth century British philosophers, notably Hobbes, Locke and Hume, had been " empirical," i.e., had concentrated on individual things learned by the senses rather than on deduction of the Universe from principles. From Stirling's *Secret of Hegel* in 1865 to Bosanquet's *Philosophical Theory of the State* in 1899 the British universities were dominated by Hegel's idealist philosophy that the world and history are the development (through the " dialectic ") of absolute Spirit. Green, Bradley, Bosanquet and so on, through their influence on clever undergraduates (especially in Oxford " Greats ") influenced two generations of politicians and civil servants, and the practical effect was the growth of Socialist doctrine in the ruling few through Hegel's glorification of the State. The twentieth-century movement in English philosophy which has culminated in Logical Positivism and logical analysis (it cannot go any further) began as a reaction against the influence of Hegel. Already before 1914 the new realists (e.g., Prichard and Bertrand Russell) had rejected the use of abstract reasoning about the Universe and attacked the foundations of traditional logic. Bertrand Russell said that mathematics and logic were identical, and that logic included statements which were true, false and meaningless. Their work was the starting point for the " Vienna Circle " in the nineteen-twenties, most of whom ended in Oxford or Cambridge where Wittgenstein and Professor Ayer (now of London University) joined forces with Bertrand Russell and Professor Ryle (now Waynflete Professor at Oxford). The central features of Logical Positivism are that philosophy deals only with the analysis of language and logic, is useful only as a mental activity, should pose problems, not try to solve them. Its function is wholly critical, it deals not with the properties of things but with the way we speak of them. There are no necessary truths, even in natural science, only probable hypothesis. Morals are a branch of sociology, assertions of moral value are " emotive," neither true nor false but " strictly meaningless " and " not verifiable." This brings us to the parallel development of logico-positive ethics or morals, which provide a very important example of the practical effect of ideas. Hegelian dons in the nineteenth century had preached a high standard of professional honour and morals to the Cromers, Milners and Asquiths. The reaction began in 1903 with Professor G. E. Moore's *Principia Ethica*. He did not in principle deny moral values but his whole emphasis was on aesthetic and relative values, and the effect on his disciples was the substitution of moral analysis for ethical principles.

Now the point for the practical man is that Professor Moore's disciples were no less than the future loosely so-called " Bloomsbury Circle "—Keynes, Lytton Strachey, Leonard Woolf, Clive Bell, Desmond MacCarthy—need one stress their influence on the English educated public? Well, writing many years later, Keynes told us how Moore's effect (on them) " dominated everything else . . . our apprehension of good was exactly the same as our apprehension of green . . . we entirely repudiated a personal liability on us to obey general rules . . . customary morals, conventions and traditional wisdom. We were in the strict sense of the term immoralists."

Is it far-fetched to see a connection with Lytton Strachey's brilliant technique of " debunking " the heroes of legend (precisely contrary to Plutarch's idea of biography[1]) which has set the course for a stream of inferior imitators guying General Gordon as a drunken homosexual and so on? Moore's *Principia Ethica* was, however, only the herald. Through Field and Lowes Dickinson, his views developed into the so-called School of Oxford Moralists who also still accepted in theory the possibility of moral judgements but in practice concentrated on the analysis of the notions of " good " or " right," of which they arrived at a dozen interpretations, and ended in a game of casuistry about particular moral situations. As in revolutions, the more extreme party—the Logical Positivists in this case—won the day. Professor Ayer pointed out that as philosophy is concerned with the logical structure of language, and science is concerned with facts, exhortations to moral virtue are neither philosophy nor science, they are not propositions at all; and if two people disagree about a moral question, " there is plainly no sense in asking which of us is right." (*Language, Truth and Logic*; Chapter VI.) Ethics as a branch of knowledge " must be assigned to the science of psychology or sociology." As Professor Joad concluded in his *Critique of Logical Positivism*, there is no incentive, logical or psychological, to act on moral values which are "emotive" and have no objective character. In an attempt to save moral values, Professor Toulmin (*Place of Reason in Ethics*, 1950) has proposed as guides existing moral codes and current institutions as they make for greater happiness—" in the same kind of way as codes of standard practice in engineering "!

Lastly, we find the same repudiation of all first principles and objective standards in the current French fashion of Existentialism. Sartre, Jaspers, Heidegger, Marcel, Camus (and earlier Kierkegaard) all differ except that they concentrate on man and his personal problems and feelings, and are agreed in reaction against Marxism, Nazism, and the prophet of both, Hegel, and his insistence on man attaining true freedom through the State. Sartre is an atheist and, like

---

[1] " Virtuous deeds implant in those who search them out a great and zealous eagerness which leads to imitation."

Nietzsche, sees that an atheist should admit no absolute values. Man is free but responsible only to himself.   Existence precedes essence, i.e., there is no essential or common human nature. Camus, also atheist, says the sentiment of the absurd arises from the contrast between the world and the human mind with its longing for meaning.   Heidegger says God is an open question: Jaspers and Marcel infer God from the existence of fidelity, hope, the power of choice, but this is obviously also a subjective non-rational approach.   In short, Existentialism is really an attitude; it reacts against all forms of authority, concentrates on individual states of mind and the analysis of them and rejects or accepts God, or any objective standards, without rational discussion.[1]

We can now return to my first proposition that all this climate of sceptical " relativism " is an inevitable stage but one which our generation may be able to turn to good account if it chooses to do so.   It is unavoidable because it is the final end of all the previous wrong turnings and false philosophies, but it is also the necessary preliminary to the liberation of our thought, and especially of our historical outlook, from the narrow, one-sided dogmatism of the nineteenth century.   One of the reasons for which the Western world has lost its grip on fundamentals is its ignorance of its own background, and our history must be revalued and restated before we can make an objective appreciation of our present and future.   I suggest five main defects in our historical writing, which naturally are at their worst in the general text-books.   First, it is distorted by the biological analogy of unlimited one-line progress —the later always better than the earlier, all English history (for example) an inevitable progress upwards to Gladstone and Jowitt of Balliol.   Secondly, it has lacked all sense of continuity, of our close links with our mediaeval ancestors and through them with the pagan world of Greece and Rome.   A whole millennium of our history—including the age of Dante and St. Thomas Aquinas, St. Louis and King Edward the First, was for centuries just washed out as having no significance, and

[1] Up to a point, Existentialism is a healthy reaction against mass-tyranny and " Social engineering "—unfortunately it tends to the other extreme of complete anarchy.

our cultural life has been regarded as suddenly starting again after being suspended for a thousand years, under the title of " Modern History," with the later Renaissance and the disruption of European Unity.[1]   Thirdly, under the influence of biological analogy and materialist mechanical dogma, historians have concentrated on documentary evidence to the exclusion of the evidence of tradition, on whatever can be quantitatively measured and weighed, and on purely material factors—" race," environment, climate (" Monotheism is the religion of the desert," said Renan), laws and regulations, technology—minimizing the formative influence even of secular ideas and often disregarding religious beliefs entirely. This latter is a glaring defect, and is often unconscious, arising from sheer ignorance of what the beliefs really were and are, what they meant or mean to those who hold them.   Karl Marx who attributed all beliefs and institutions to technical changes and economic causes—they are merely the secondary " superstructure "—was only carrying *ad absurdum* the practical attitude of nearly all nineteenth-century—and after—historians.

Now as an unexpected consequence of the new " relativist " approach, this revaluation is already well on its way.   It is being made not by the historians in the accepted sense but by the various new schools of sociology, which now means the philosophy or interpretation of history in a wide sense, treating orthodox political history as only one factor in the whole social cultural complex.   The movement started with the attempt by Flinders Petrie and others to find patterns and curves in the

---

[1] Fortunately there is in progress for the last fifty years a slow but very welcome awakening of interest in mediaeval studies in academic circles, though some mediaevalists like the late G. G. Coulton have seemed mainly concerned to denigrate the subjects of their studies.   This revival of interest in Dante and Aquinas has, however, as yet made no real impression on the long accumulation of popular prejudice.   For the average non-specialist the word " mediaeval " is still the accepted synonym for barbarism, ignorance and oppression—an American Secretary of State wielding the immense world influence of Mr. Cordell Hull could refer a few years ago to the " archaic mediaeval Empire ideas " of the " British Colonial Empire " (which did not exist before the seventeenth century!).   In the press and in popular books the word is incessantly used as equivalent to the " Dark Ages " following the fall of Rome with the sixteenth-century Spanish Inquisition thrown in.

history of the Fine Arts, or in Economic History, and then developed, beginning with Danilevsky, into a comprehensive view of the whole story of man and all his activities divided into a series of culture cycles, each with a beginning, a middle and an end, and all showing similarities of growth and decay. Professor Toynbee is the only popular British " cycle " philosopher, and the only foreign one who has become well known in England is Oswald Spengler: but different versions have been elaborated by Danilevsky, Schubart, Northrop, Kroeber, Schweitzer and Sorokin—in fact practically all modern sociologists hold some kind of cyclist theory of history. It is a massive return to the outlook of the Greeks, Hindoos, and the Chinese alternating rhythm of the negative " Yin " and the positive " Yang." Now no two cycle-historians agree in their classifications and each can produce facts to show up the weaknesses and oversimplifications of the others. This, however, only illustrates that man is so complex that no single explanation can fit all the facts, and that even the best cannot resist the temptation, having formulated a law, to make troublesome facts fit into it. The two remarkable things about the whole school of modern sociologists are, first, their very substantial agreement on major points, and secondly, the new technique of team work, especially thanks to the vast financial resources of the American Universities and Research Funds. An illustration of the second point will give an idea of the new outlook. Professor Sorokin, the Russian exile who founded the Department of Sociology at Harvard, has through his team-workers classified nearly 50,000 pictures and sculptures to make graphs showing dominant art styles of different periods; 967 wars to check the connection between wars and particular régimes or economic conditions; 1,700 major social disturbances to check general theories about their causes; and has grouped into 50-year periods and ten categories 1,875 British individuals recorded in the *Encyclopaedia Britannica* from A.D. 950 to A.D. 1849 to show the relation of conduct and mentality and the relative importance, in different periods, of religion, business, science and so on. In the same way he has prepared tables showing the activity of invention and discovery at different periods in nine branches of Science, and a graph showing the fluctuation of philosophic influences from 580 B.C. to A.D. 1920, based on a 75-page catalogue of philosophers classified as mystics, sceptics, Empiricists and so on. (I am indebted for these details to F. R. Cowell's brilliant study of the Historical and Social Philosophy of Professor Sorokin.)

The work of these historians is so relevant to my subject that I devote Chapter Four to their theories and their application to our times, but my point here is that they *all* agree in totally rejecting all the single-line theories of a progressive evolution of Man. They all substitute a series of basic cultural systems (though allowing for the co-existence of unintegrated or disintegrated social groups), each of which they represent as a real interconnected system with its own meaning and unity and an internal motive power which directs the varying phases of the culture within the limits set by certain recurring themes. They condemn the " linear " theories as illogical because external forces are always at work stopping any continuous trend in one direction, and as an assumption contrary to the evidence of the facts. The emphasis is now on the analysis and results of the constant, recurring processes such as imitation and adaptation, migrations and diffusions, integration and its reverse, and on the interaction of these recurrent uniformities with the variable factors, from climate and sunspots to ideas, technology or urbanization. Finally, all agree that the great integrated cultural entities rise in a phase of predominantly spiritual values and creative intuition, and after an intermediate period of mixed values, enter a materialist, utilitarian phase, which sacrifices quality to quantity and substitutes technique for reason and intuition, and which has hitherto always ended in disintegration.

Now great though the differences are in the actual application of their theories, the sociologists have between them accumulated by their systematic comparative study of institutions and cultures, sufficient evidence to make the dogma of progress quite untenable; and I hope to show good reasons for saying that the more recent work in psychology and anthropology (particularly the comparative study of religions) strikingly reinforces this general trend.

Chapter Four

A BRIEF RUN WITH THE CYCLISTS

" The ungodly turn in circles " (St. Augustine)

MANY of the " cycle " historians are well worth reading apart from the value of their theories, for the wealth of illustrations they have amassed, notably Spengler and Professor Toynbee, or for their spiritual intuition as in the case of Berdyaev. Their conclusions are summarized and critically compared in Professor Sorokin's two large volumes on *Social Philosophies of an Age of Crisis*, and in his older *Contemporary Sociological Theories*. Here I can only hope to indicate by a few examples some of the points they have in common, and the sort of contradictions which suggest that no one theory can cover all the facts and all the complexity of human nature.

The general idea first occurred to students of the history of the arts—Flinders Petrie, Ligeti, Deorna, Bovet, Lalo, to name a few—who built theories of art-cycles on the basis of uniform sequences and curves in the artistic life of different civilizations. While there often is a broad similarity in the artistic life of two rising or two decaying civilizations, all these theories break down on points of fact, such as the maturity of early Chinese art and European palaeolithic art or the early appearance of great poetry, and on close examination the patterns do not in fact fit into uniform curves.

The pioneer of the complete culture-cycle theory was the Russian Danilevsky, who first formulated the idea of certain peoples forming creative civilizations which grow, flourish and decay from inner causes like an individual organism. Already in 1870 he preached that the " European " civilization was in decline and destined to be superseded by the Slavs. Oswald Spengler in his famous *Decline of the West* (1914–1917) said that cultures were living organisms each with its childhood, youth, manhood and old age, and " World history was their collective biography." The final end of each culture is to petrify into a mere civilization characterized by the loss of real values, cynical materialism, and ultimate disintegration. Each of his eight main cultures is based on its own " prime symbol " which determines its essential character; for example, his " Apollinian," e.g., classical Greco-Roman, had for prime symbol the " sensuously present individual body," the city State, the Doric temple, the nude statue—form, contour, relief; his " Faustian," i.e., Western, had " pure and limitless space " and " voluntarism "—Gothic cathedrals, Rembrandt, Hamlet, Faust, Beethoven; his " Magian," i.e., Arabic, " cavernous eternal vaulted space "—the dome and the cupola. External forces can accelerate, retard, or kill a culture, they cannot change its basic character or transform it into another. It goes through its life stages guided by " cosmic forces," must be understood by intuition, not explained by cause and effect. Professor Toynbee lists 26 civilizations (which are societies not states) of which he says 16 " are by now dead and buried." For him also, civilizations grow by inward self-determination, and are not due to race, geography, or technical progress but to the incessant challenge of an environment, neither too favourable nor unfavourable, to a creative minority which responds to the challenge. This minority responds by withdrawal and return, and is imitated by an internal proletarian majority and an external barbarian proletariat. A growing civilization has a dominant tendency —aesthetic with the Greeks, religious in India, machinist in the West. Breakdown means the failure to respond through failure in the creative power of the minority, followed by the revolt of the internal and external proletariats, loss of social unity and final disintegration—in a word, suicide.

The other social philosophers mentioned in the previous chapter are, with one exception, more impressionist than Spengler and Professor Toynbee. Thus Walter Schubart postulates a rhythmic alternation of four main prototypes— harmonious, heroic, ascetic (Hindu-Buddhist), Messianic. The latter epoch will favour the Russians: like Danilevsky and Spengler, he predicts " the next centuries belong to the Slavs." Berdyaev, like Spengler, says history must be a " direct intui- tional identification," no longer photographic. He found the

supreme types of integrated disciplined personality in the
monk and the knight; the humanist secular culture has used
up the fund of creative force accumulated under discipline,
and boundless self-confidence ends in complete disillusion.
The exception is Professor Sorokin, whose elaborate techniques
in graphs and charts were illustrated in the last chapter.
Professor Sorokin rejects the theory of human societies having
individual life-cycles like persons.   He substitutes the idea of a
succession of " culture supersystems " in which the prime
factor is the attitude to life of the particular society in any
given period, i.e., to what things does the society attach most
value?   Does it base its way of life mainly on religion, or on a
mixed religious and rational, intellectual approach, or does it
attach supreme importance to purely material considerations,
to the sensuous enjoyment of entirely material commodities?
When the values are predominantly spiritual, he classifies a
culture as " ideational "; when they mix spiritual and intellectual standards, the culture is " idealistic "; when the
outlook becomes predominantly materialist, the culture is
" sensate." These are ugly and difficult words, but the
Professor's guiding idea is clear enough and in his hands it
becomes a chart which fits a great many facts.   For him,
facts become elements in a culture system when they have a
" meaning-value "—to use his own quaint illustration, copulation is a mere biological phenomenon, rape and adultery are
cultural phenomena. Broadly speaking, he follows the
" cyclists " in seeing each historic culture as having a beginning,
a middle, and an end, but for their " spring " or " youth " he
substitutes his " ideational " or mainly spiritual and intuitional
phase; for their " maturity," he substitutes his " idealistic "
or mixed spiritual and rational basis; for their period of
decline or old age he substitutes the gradual transition to his
" sensate " or purely materialist age. Examples of the
ideational phase are the early Greek Society and the sixth to
twelfth centuries of our era, the period from the collapse of the
Roman Empire to the Middle Ages; of the idealistic phase,
examples are the great age of Classical Greece (fifth century
B.C.) and the flowering of the mediaeval culture of Europe;
while the transition to the " sensate " or materialist culture is

typified in the later Greco-Roman world and our own last four centuries, the secular period culminating in the " Machine Age."

This system of analysing and synthesizing societies on the basis of the cultural values to which they attach most importance has great practical advantages. It is flexible, comprehensive and avoids rigid biological analogies which are quite inappropriate to the elusive spirit of man. It allows particular cultures to have frequent revivals and no fixed limit of duration. It leaves scope for endless interaction of cultures by their diffusion and transmission. But—and here is the main point of this chapter—the overall picture of social history built up by Professor Sorokin is broadly the same as that of his predecessors and living co-workers; he criticizes their methods on points of fact, but the wide area of agreement in his other conclusions is the really significant feature.

A few examples of his criticism will also illustrate Professor Sorokin's own method. He argues that the differences of opinion about the composition of the closed, self-contained cycles prove that they are not real unities. Thus Spengler amalgamates into one " magian " culture at least seven different systems—Arabic, Islamic, Byzantine, Persian, Syrian, Jewish and Early Christian; whereas Professor Toynbee distinguished the Persian, Syriac, Arabic and Byzantine as separate civiliza-tions, and also the Babylonian, Hittite and Sumeric, which Danilevsky united as " Ancient Semitic." They do not agree on basic definitions. Thus the " cultures " of Danilevsky and Spengler, the " civilizations " of Professor Toynbee, are regarded by them as real unities identical with particular social groups; while Schubart, Berdyaev, Schweitzer dis-tinguish between a culture and a social group acting as its agent; and Northrop and Kroeber claim the co-existence of various systems inside one total culture (e.g., Modern Mexico). They seek to identify each civilization with one specific over-riding tendency regardless of its different periods. Thus for Professor Toynbee Hellenic civilization was predominantly aesthetic, Western European always machinist-technological; shelving the Greek genius for mathematics and pure reasoning and the intense spiritual and aesthetic activity of Western

Europe from the twelfth century to quite recent times. The closed-cycle theory inevitably involves arbitrary manipulation of periods. Thus Professor Toynbee takes the Peloponnesian War (431-403 B.C.) as the period of Hellenic breakdown. This implies on his principles that a period then set in of social disorders and mental decline; but Professor Sorokin's charts show 617 social disturbances in the sixth and fifth centuries B.C., and 579 in the two following centuries; and the same following period, which should have been one of mental decline, was in fact the age of Plato, Aristotle, Aristophanes and, much later still, of the Greek " Fathers " of the Church. Another fundamental criticism of the life-and-death closed-cycle theory is its necessary conclusion that because the *States* which figured in a bygone civilization no longer exist, therefore the *culture* has ceased to exist. Professor Toynbee says 16 of his 26 civilizations " are by now dead and buried," and that of the remaining 10, nine are in their last agonies and our own is in acute crisis. Professor Sorokin points out that the Greek culture (included in the first 16) is still a most vital element in ours; that Islam, included in the moribund nine, is expanding in Africa and elsewhere; and that many prehistoric techniques are flourishing—such as the use of fire, the wheel, domestic and farm animals, etcetera.

For Renaissance man the Greek and Roman classics were for two or three centuries more alive than his own literature—as G. M. Young wrote in 1908, public men read Livy or the *Politics* of Aristotle, not as Lord Cromer read the Greek Anthology, but as Theodore Roosevelt read Lord Cromer; and Montaigne could not speak a word of French (but only Latin) till he was six years old. In other words, the specific individual forms of a cultural system disappear, but its typical generic forms in religion, art, philosophy are virtually immortal. One other example of Professor Sorokin's critical method must suffice. He argues that Professor Toynbee's stress on the geographical factor (an environment neither too hard nor too easy) is opposed by the cases of many cultures and civilizations which have risen and disintegrated without any change in their environment; and he asks how the creative minority arises, to respond to the challenge of the environment, when

Professor Toynbee rejects the influence of racial and biological heredity?

The way is now clear to look at the significant points of agreement among the modern sociologists—without implying that they are necessarily right whenever they agree. First, all reject the nineteenth-century theory (or rather, dogma) of continuous one-line progress, as contrary to the evidence, and merely one form of development which is constantly being interrupted and deviated. Attention is directed to constant repeated features, to the search for causal uniformities between variable factors such as climate, heredity, urbanization, business, sunspots, philosophy; to tracing the nature and effects of inventions, imitation, isolation, adaptation and failure to adapt, conflict and migration. There is general agreement under different labels on the existence, in " the ocean of social-cultural phenomena," of some sort of vast unified cultural systems not identical with particular states, and side by side with loose, indefinite groupings which are either not yet integrated or have disintegrated and lapsed. The relatively few basic cultural systems which exist or have existed are or have been real coherent unities, each working out its own ultimate meaning by some mysterious self-directing process. Sorokin's originality lies in his attempt to replace the cycle of birth to death by a succession of cultural systems incessantly varying on recurring themes.

These broad points of agreement are masked by the different terminologies used and the very varying appreciations of the facts and their arrangement into periods and regions. When, however, we come to the historical description of the succeeding phases and their general character, and exclude the different opinions about their duration, their causes and effects, and their precise location, we find a very striking agreement among the social philosophers, representing half a dozen different countries, with whom this chapter is concerned. In describing, under various names, the beginning, the middle and the end of each culture cycle, civilization, or cultural system, they all agree that the early rising period of each one is a phase of creative intuition, of spiritual values, absolute not relative—in short, of a religious world-outlook. Purely utilitarian ethics are almost unknown, and physical science is in an early stage, and society is based on family and corporate relationships. Secondly, while there is much divergence about the middle or peak period, how long it has lasted and whether it has been revived in different forms, all agree that there is a final phase in every civilization, marked by complete secularism of art, ethics, law and general outlook; in which creative intuition decays, technical skill replaces genius, quantity is admired instead of quality; family and corporate relationships are replaced first by contract and finally by compulsion on the individual. All associate this phase with the growth of large cities, with their uprooted anonymous herds of floating individuals without property or tradition, and the elimination of creative middle-class minorities by irresponsible wealth and dictatorship. All agree that this last phase is masked by at least an attempt at religious revival (Spengler's " Second religiosity," Toynbee's " Universal Church " as bridge to a new civilization, Berdyaev's coming " New Mediaeval Culture," Schubart's " Messianic prototype "). All agree that no purely rational or empirical philosophy, no utilitarian calculation, can create a new civilization or culture to replace one which disintegrates; it can only arise from genuine religion, founded on intuition, and it must eventually ripen by a union of the intuitional, rational and sense values.

Finally, there is unanimous agreement that our own age, whatever name each one gives to it, is the end of a civilization or culture, and one of the greatest transitions in history; that it will be superseded somewhere by a new cultural centre based on spiritual, intuitional values. As we have seen, Spengler and others locate it in Russia; others, whose views belong to a later chapter, press the claims of India and China.

I hope it will be clear from my earlier chapters that as a believer in the transforming power of ideas and in man's immense reserves of spiritual energy, I do not accept these conclusions about the inevitable disintegration of our society. That there is a danger of it and that the nature of this danger is the supreme question far outweighing any of the political or economic problems I called the " surface " picture, is a different matter, and I have tried to summarize the views of a varied assortment of modern sociologists simply to bring out that there is a *prima facie* case for their pessimism. If there were no case, they could not all have reached the same conclusion. I now take my leave of the " cyclists," and hope to suggest as a pendant to their views, some converging lines of enquiry which reinforce their conclusion, not that our civilization is inevitably doomed, but that it is certainly in danger.

Chapter Five

WHY IS OUR CIVILIZATION SAID TO BE DISINTEGRATING?

" And all the earth . . . adored the Beast, saying, Who is like to the Beast ? And who shall be able to fight with him ? And there was given to him a mouth speaking great things and blasphemies " (Apocalypse xiii.3–4)

THE general agreement of the " cyclists " that our own " Western " civilization is the end of a cycle and that this is proved by its being in rapid disintegration might be thought to be merely the result of their general theory. If all civilizations hitherto have waxed, waned, and been liquidated, and if our own has already gone through all the usual phases, then it must also in its turn have entered on the inevitable phase of final breakdown.

In fact, however, their pessimism coincides with a wide trend of thought among modern writers who have not been identified with any circular theories. I have referred earlier to the complete final pessimism of two of the most influential apostles of modernity—Bernard Shaw and H. G. Wells—and to the final rejection of philosophy itself by the most modern schools of philosophy. This sceptical disillusionment has an interesting reflection in the reversal of the traditional optimism when modern writers try their hand at constructing a picture of a future Utopian society. The traditional Utopia is essentially a Christian heresy, for the pagans (with rare exceptions) looked back, not forward, to a golden age, and the great Asiatic religions have always been pessimistic to the core. The motive idea of our Utopians was that of imposing moral perfection and ideal justice through the compulsory institution of a new social order. They were heretical, not Christian, because they blamed the Creator instead of the defective human will, and ignored the warning that " My Kingdom is not of this World "; hence Utopian aspirations all too easily

148

have become identified in practice with ruthless destruction and terrorism, for it was found that to create a new world you must destroy the old world and to do this you must root out by terrorism all possible agents of counter-revolution. The Utopians did, however, believe that the process of destruction would be followed by a good time coming for all, and this we have seen was still the expectation of Shaw and Wells in their period of influence.

When the original and unconventional writers of the later generation apply their imagination to the future, we find on the contrary that they anticipate a very bad time coming. Obvious examples are two of the most brilliant satires since Swift—Aldous Huxley's *Brave New World* and George Orwell's *1984*—and these were the work of two young writers who had emancipated themselves from conventional attitudes and prejudices as far as human limitations allow. To the pessimism of the " cyclists " (who are *ipso facto* pessimists), of the dis-illusioned prophets like Shaw and Wells, and of the younger imaginative writers like Huxley and Orwell, one could add a volume of quotations, tending in the same direction, from more scientific and less ambitious students of society. Thus Mr. Isaiah Berlin of All Souls' College, Oxford, writing in *Foreign Affairs* some years ago, pointed to the novel and terrible fact that the Modern Totalitarian State seeks not merely to liquidate the individual who preaches unorthodox ideas, but the very faculty of thought, " to end the *idea* of ideas "; to destroy, by conditioning, man's supreme attribute, free-will. This insidious radical attack on private unpublished thought is a novelty, not found in the old forms of Tyranny. Thus Alexis Carrel, writing as a biologist, concludes that man has created a new environment to which he cannot adapt himself because it is in defiance of the Laws of Life. Man has concen-trated on the physical sciences, ignoring the sciences of human nature; and Carrel advocates a revolutionary attack on the very principles of industrial civilization. A special interest attaches to the analysis, long before Carrel, of Emile Durkheim, for he was a typical French savant of the Third Republic and his research in sociology pointed to conclusions so contrary to the orthodox mechanical atheistic philosophy which he shared with all his group that neither he nor they were willing to draw them.

In his classic study of *Suicide* (republished in England in
1952) he first demonstrated a " tremendous aggravation " in
the rate of suicide during the nineteenth century.   Durkheim
argued that this aggravation sprang from the special conditions
in which progress was taking place, that it was a symptom of
maladjustment and that a large factor was the increase of
pessimism as an effect of the maladjustment.   This was his
text for a general survey of social tendencies at the turn of
the century.   Even when suicides had increased 411 per cent,
as in Prussia, during the century, they remained exceptional,
but he rightly viewed them as a symptom of frustration affecting
vastly greater numbers; and his first conclusion was that they
were due not to economic poverty but to " an alarming poverty
of morality," not to greater difficulty in satisfying legitimate
needs but " because we no longer know the limits of legitimate
needs nor perceive the direction of our efforts."   His second
conclusion—in striking contrast to the official tradition of
the French Revolution—was that the ultimate cause was the
sweeping away of all the older social forms of organization.
The only collective form which had survived—and was rapidly
growing—was the State, which he argued, tended to absorb all
forms of social activity, and which, confronted by an unstable
flux of atomic individuals, was assuming functions for which it
was unsuited, thus becoming " as intrusive as it is impotent."
Individuals, discharging their social obligations only through
the State, lapsed inevitably into egoism and anarchy, tumbling
over one another without mutual relationships, like liquid
molecules with no central energy to retain and organize them.

His natural conclusion was to advocate the restoration of the
occupational and local groups swept away by the French
Revolution and the bourgeois liberal epoch, the restoration of
" a cluster of collective forces outside the State though subject
to its action," as had existed in Greek, Roman, and mediaeval
society.   The problem was how to bring this about, and here
the orthodox Professor encountered a still deeper current and
was baffled by his religious prejudices.   For the one obvious
institution which had not yet been wholly swept away, and one
" the prophylactic value of which is assured," was the family;
but now " it is barely formed when it begins to disperse," and

his statistics brought him up against a very inconvenient fact. This was that the strength of the family unit varied, not only as between countries but also inside countries, with the strength of religious feeling, but that this source of reform was hopeless because it " would mean the re-establishment of the most archaic religions." For his statistics revealed that the countries with the least suicide in Europe were Spain, Ireland and Italy, with 17, 21 and 37 cases per million respectively, as compared with 160 in secularized France and 260 in Lutheran Prussia; and he sadly concluded " that moral and intellectual superiority counts for nothing in its possible influence on suicide." He also found that stable family life while moderating suicide " rather stimulates murder " (!)—but he meant not premeditated murder or murder for gain, but " homicide "; the reason of course being that the stronger family feeling is, the more likely are the members to regard assaults on " the honour of the family " as sacrilege and to take the law into their own hands by recourse to the *crime passionnel*. Education as a remedy he equally rejected on the logical ground that being itself a reflection of society, it cannot be reformed until society itself is reformed. Durkheim was therefore driven to count on the State itself providing the remedies, for instance, by making marriage more indissoluble.[1] This has in fact been adopted by the Soviet State for reasons of policy, but only after the power of the State, which Durkheim already found excessive, had been carried to its extreme limit in every other respect. So he was finally left with conclusions which

---

[1] The history of divorce in our modern society illustrates how would-be " practical " people, by always disregarding logical conclusions and the " thin end of the wedge " argument, can prepare the way for consequences which they do not at all want. When divorce became legal in one country after another during the last hundred years, it was intended (in Britain or Scandinavia as much as in France or Belgium) to apply only to very hard and pathetic cases, perhaps two or three hundred in a year. The time came—already some time ago—when Denis Mackail could refer in a story to the mental cruelty of leaving the top off the Kolynos tube—and now, truth proving stranger than fiction, a divorce has been granted in a Scandinavian country because one of the parties had squeezed the tube in the middle instead of at the end! In one American state it is sufficient to drink black coffee if the other party objects . . . an analogous process will eventually operate if for example " progressive opinion " succeeds in getting " Euthanasia " legalized, or the compulsory limitation of the families of the poor.

presupposed a vast moral revolution which he could suggest no means of bringing about.

The general argument for regarding our civilization as being on the verge of dissolution—apart from the obvious immediate political dangers—and as bearing a close analogy to the last phase of bygone civilizations, can be broadly summarized. A healthy civilization rests on a rough balance and harmony between a number of essential interests—economic, social, political, intellectual, artistic, religious—all of which have their material and their spiritual side. When there is a fair balance, there is an integrated civilization, very much as individual personality is integrated by a sane balance of the animal and distinctively human, i.e., spiritual, faculties. When one interest gets out of control and crushes the others, the principle of unity is broken, there is disequilibrium and discord ending sooner or later in ruin. During the last few centuries, the economic purely material interest has been steadily increasing in our civilization at the expense of the others, and it has now become overwhelmingly predominant. This does not, in the mind of the sociologist, refer merely to single-minded desire for profit on the part of a small section as during the Industrial Revolution; it means a purely materialist, mechanical way of life and is entirely compatible with the most enthusiastic cult of the physical-welfare state and " the common man." The essential point of the loss of balance is not greed for higher wages or higher dividends (both legitimate in their proper limits) but the gradual substitution of the material values, mass and quantity, for the values and standards of quality. The most obvious material standards are size and speed; the most obvious examples of qualitative standards are those which in all creative periods have been the only standards in art, literature and spiritual life. The inherent tendency of a mass civilization with quantitative values is to crush the individual person into a common average type, to create a general level of mediocrity; to transform education into an instrument for training docile, passive servants of the bureaucracy, willing to accept the mass-produced hand-out in every field from philosophy to tinned food. The tyranny of a mass civilization is infinitely more crushing, all-pervasive and demoralizing than any of the merely political or religious despotisms of peasant or city-states, because besides being formless and impersonal, it poisons the very root of aspiration— the intelligence itself. In a mass civilization education, and consequently the organs of opinion, being based on the lowest common factors and standards of quantity, weakens and gradually atrophies the prime faculty of the intellect, that of abstracting, distinguishing, classifying values. The effect on poetry, from which humanity has derived so much inspiration and stimulus, is still worse; it seems already incredible that even a generation ago, the majority of those who went from an English Public School to a University had learned many thousands of words from the world's greatest poets and had a thorough grounding—often a great deal more—in the grammar and syntax of the expression of thought and feeling. Memory training and verse and prose composition in the classical languages have disappeared because the Public Schools can no longer set their own standards; the conditions for entering the universities are geared down to more quantitative standards.

Two characteristic features of mass civilization are that science, and such not strictly utilitarian learning as survives, becomes over-specialized and tends to become technique, and secondly that there is a growing divorce between reason—the controlling mind—and the arts. The fantastic aberrations of American teachers' training colleges, though they have provoked strong adverse reaction, cannot be disregarded as a symptom of the " progressive " revolt against the training of the intelligence, for this betrayal of educational values has come from the educationists themselves. Under the influence of Pragmatic " philosophies " the American training colleges adopted a theory—or rather an attitude—called " Progressive Education," which one of its pontiffs, Mr. Kirkpatrick, summed up in the formula, " You don't take something you want children to learn . . . you find out what they want to learn." In many American schools the lunatic fringe of progressive teachers abandoned work altogether in favour of canasta, playing at Indians, and " tuna-fish projects "; history teachers were advised that " if they have completely missed out on the Middle Ages, the teacher might help them to select a project on weapons so they could get to study the Middle Ages through crossbows." Granted that these are exaggerated cases, they are only exaggerations of a wide-spread hostility in high educational quarters to all sustained intellectual effort, all mental discipline, and most significantly of hostility to the gaining of any advantage by individual mental superiority. That this typical vice of mass civilization has infected England was blatantly demonstrated by the attempt to stop children under 16 from competing for a certificate, and in general by the fashion for " visual aids " and " work through play "—though there are welcome signs that in England educationists are concerned by the rejection of a quarter of the candidates for the regular Army as illiterate, and by the increasing percentage who leave our incredibly costly State schools with an inadequate knowledge of the alphabet.

The official adoption in the mass civilization of mediocrity[1] as the educational standard is aided by an economic factor which tends inexorably to depress the standard of the middle class which—and not the wealthy or the proletariat—has been in Europe and America the main source of all intellectual and artistic progress, and social progress as well.[2] The crushing taxation of the bureaucratic mass State is highly favourable

[1] I have an uneasy suspicion that this cult of mediocrity may be partly responsible for the application to candidates for the highest branches of the civil service of so-called " Intelligence " tests of the type which begin " Five men and five women are seated in a railway carriage." The samples which have come my way seem better calculated for the selection of " Smart Alecs " than for detecting potential high-grade civil servants or Ambassadors. The technique can be taught by special crammers, which is perhaps why Professor C. W. Valentine, editor of the *British Journal of Educational Psychology*, finds that schoolboys do better in these tests than the first-class honours graduates, and that children from the poorest homes easily beat the average children of well-educated parents. It is true that I am prejudiced by a life-long distaste for puzzles which have no ulterior significance, and the authorities might reply that the object of the new tests is precisely to eliminate those who might harbour dangerous thoughts. That is indeed what I suspect!

[2] At an Educational Conference in Leeds the Headmistress of the Putney County Secondary School, during a discussion of the problem presented to the Grammar School by the large influx since the Education Act, 1944, said " the characteristics of these homes " included " a declining sense of responsibility, the opinion that success could be attained easily, a tendency to denigrate culture, and an ignorant sense of self-importance. The Grammar School was not winning to its way of thinking the boys and girls from these homes." (*The Times*, February 14, 1955.)

to all those with a nose for money through their greatly increased opportunities for capital gains, just as it is, for a time at least, favourable to the large section of the proletariat whose rents, food, schooling, health and old age are heavily subsidized by other people some of whom have lower incomes. For the middle classes, traditionally the nursery of critical standards and new social values, are fighting a losing battle—in France and Germany already largely lost—against taxation, inflation and all the growing pressures of the mass State. As Mr. Mabane showed in the *Sunday Times*, a married man with two children who in 1938 was earning £400 a year must today earn £1,000 to get the equivalent; if he had £1,350 then, he needs £5,000 now. The professional and salaried men of these levels have, however, made no such increases and they are particularly hard hit because they lack the resources and the inside knowledge for capital gains and the various advantages accruing from the opportunities of business. Deprived in consequence of savings and domestic leisure, forced to choose between comparative sterility and their children's education, they are slowly but inevitably sinking—disregarded equally by the trade union bosses and multiple company directors who between them lay down the main directions for the bureaucracy to interpret.

I spoke of a growing divorce between the arts and the controlling mind, and finally between art and society itself; it will soon be an understatement. When the only recognized standards are those applied to what can be measured, size, speed, mechanism—spiritual values, quality values, which cannot be measured, and can only be appreciated by mental effort and intuition, must dissolve into a vague twilight in which the latest fashion is *ipso facto* right, and easy formulas and catchwords replace criticism. The cult of new " movements " in the arts is closely allied to the cult of change and speed, stunts and record-breaking—of action for the sake of action. Hence the divorce between art and reality; the artist, unable to fit into an environment which is hostile to style and form, and which rejects any absolute standard of beauty or truth, takes refuge in anti-social cliques and the cult of dissonance, inhuman distortion and monstrous aberration. There is a large element of truth in the Soviet condemnation of

" bourgeois decadent formalism " in the arts.   I develop this argument in a later chapter, for it specially concerns the Western standard of value.

As Durkheim foresaw, the nemesis of anarchy in art and thought is that the wandering disinherited individual turns for guidance and authority to the only authority left—the State. The State is essential to Society; yes, but so are air and water, and that is no reason for getting drowned or never living indoors. The State is a necessary evil, but when it becomes the sole and absolute authority, a pseudo-scientific bureaucratic dictatorship, ubiquitous and without appeal, its inherent vices are magnified and the natural restraints disappear.   A century ago, when the State was an infant compared to what it has become even in the " free democratic world," Hippolyte Taine wrote of it as " a bad head of a family, bad business man, bad farmer, a philanthropist without discernment, an incompetent director of fine arts, science and education, having no internal motor such as private interest, family affection, local patriotism, scientific curiosity, charitable instinct, or religious faith."   This was true then; it becomes more true as the anonymous soulless machine becomes more autonomous and more a law to itself. The State is a bad master.   I remember the case of an aged foreigner who had given loyal service for fifty years to an Embassy but being for technical reasons ineligible for a pension, was turned adrift with a gratuity which was from a third to a half of what local private firms consulted would have given to one of their employees. The State tends as it develops to adopt what Sir Andrew Clarke in his report on the Crichel Down case called " a most regrettable attitude of hostility " to outsiders and " a feeling of irritation that any members of the public should have the temerity to oppose or even question the acts or decisions of officials."[1]   Mr. Petrov,

[1] The Crichel Down estate had been requisitioned for military training: when no longer required, instead of being resold to the owners, it " was sold to the Commissioners of Crown lands for no other reason than that the Land Commissioners wanted to use it as an experiment in model farming . . . resolved to use any means, and not always fair, to pursue that object regardless of cost." The *Daily Telegraph* called it " a monstrous example of bureaucratic tyranny; " and *The Times* said the cruellest and most irresponsible maker of gibes against the arbitrary incompetence of bureaucracy could scarcely have invented Crichel Down.

the Soviet diplomatist in Australia, related how his Minister changed his name for him and the first he knew of it was from his passport—a classic example of contempt for the individual, even when a member of the hierarchy, in a totalitarian State. All this has—and it is the worst feature—nothing to do with the characters of the individual bureaucrats, in England at least most honest and decent; it is as a corporation that any Civil Service, with every increase in authority and numbers, develops by an inner law the character of an independent self-directed army with its own policies and an attitude of resentment and distrust to the outside layman. In the democratic countries, as Parliaments become assemblies of full-time professionals and the Party machines acquire complete control, the departments will only have to deal with their particular ministers who are becoming helpless agents of the " competent channels " and overwhelmed by the complexity and volume of affairs and the routine of the conveyor belt of files.

The War of 1914 was welcomed by nearly everyone in the countries of the victorious Allies as " making the world safe for democracy " because it destroyed the three Empires—the German Empire of Fichte and Hegel, the Austro-Hungarian Dual Empire which perhaps came nearest since the Roman Empire to being a liberal multi-national bureaucracy, and the Tsardom. No prophecy was more completely reversed by events; the three Empires were replaced by the Empire of Hitler and the Empire of Stalin; and what was killed was not Imperialism but the Liberal democracy of the nineteenth century. Socialist democracy, which looked a very promising successor in 1918, also received what may prove to have been a fatal blow. The Liberal bourgeois régime, first heir of the French Revolution, had provided a very agreeable civilized world to live in and an extraordinary appearance of stability and security; in reality it was fragile and transitory, a glass-house which could only survive so long as the inmates could avoid throwing stones at each other. The Liberal régime fitted perfectly the economic, social, intellectual state of Europe in the nineteenth century; it *was* the nineteenth century. It did not so much create internal peace and external security, commercial expansion and personal freedom; rather it was

the result of these factors, they were its prerequisites. Its
creed was based on certain fundamental errors of philosophy,
history and psychology; over-confidence in human benevolence
and reasonableness, excessive welcome to speculative ideas
without regard to their implications, a hopelessly inadequate
view of history as a process of continual improvement. Above
all it tended to judge all mankind, including all the social and
mental levels inside the liberal countries, by the standards of
the European educated middle classes. Standing for personal
liberties, Liberalism worked for equality, absolute parliamentary democracy, and reaped a harvest in the form of the
conflict of mass interests and economic groups and classes, of
perpetually changing governments (outside England), and
chronic instability and friction in international affairs. Though
the death of the Liberal spirit was specially obvious in Europe,
it was no accident that even in England the historic Liberal
Party was liquidated by Lloyd George. Many thought that
bourgeois Parliamentary Socialism would inherit the mantle of
Liberalism, which already before 1914 was scrapping its old
economic creed and heading for the Welfare State, deliberately
redistributive taxation, and experiments in nationalization.
This has happened—till the present—in England; but in
Europe Socialism after 1918 had to fight on two fronts, against
Communism and Fascism, and failed. Shrinking from the
Communist alternative of sudden, total and ruthless revolution, Socialism tried to preserve the existing framework while
encouraging class war and regarding capital as a static quarry,
and its record has been one of unrelieved failure and weakness.
As I recalled in Part One, already by 1929—when Hitler's
advent was still unthought of—seven European States (without
counting Russia) had adopted authoritarian régimes of varying
degrees of mildness—twenty-five years later half Europe and all
China are Communist and the Parliamentary area of Europe is
about the same in size as it was then, but much weaker.

The 1914 War broke, and the 1939 War destroyed, a
European social order which had been shaken by the French
Revolution. The old aristocracies no longer count, the
middle classes have been slowly dissolving, and power in the
democracies has been passing into the possession of new

groups. These include the upper business executive layer of the old middle class on one hand and on the other the bureaucracy and the more highly organized sections of the proletariat. It is these conflicting groups, particularly the last, which already disillusioned with Parliamentary Government and nationalized industry, are turning hopefully to " Science " and planning by economic experts as the hope for the future. A typical suggestion was recently made that the problem created by the hydrogen bomb should be submitted to the oracular ruling of a " Council of Scientists." I quote this as an extreme example of the delusion, common among the new well-meaning but half-educated public which reads the new popular press, that specialists in any field of physical science differ from ordinary mortals not only in knowledge of their special subject, but in possessing an olympian objectivity of vision in other fields.

A delusion it is. Some kinds of skill are readily transferable to other uses; thus Cornish miners were sought after in the Navy, classical scholars were described as particularly successful in the Indian Civil Service, and successful soldiers have often been equally successful in administration and business. No doubt many examples could be adduced. There does not however seem to be anything in the work of a specialist in physics or chemistry which in itself would make him better qualified than others to offer advice in political matters in their widest sense. On the contrary, the scientist (in the restricted popular sense of the word) has to overcome two handicaps. One is that the nature of his work is often far removed from ordinary affairs and contacts, requires no experience of human nature; the other is the tendency of the scientific method to over-systematization and the search for patterns everywhere. The pursuit of tidy patterns in human affairs usually ends in disaster. It partly explains why educated Germans have been so prone to fall for any form of dictatorship which has a neat theory to justify it, and why so many scientists, particularly in the U.S.A., fluttered round the Communist candle in the thirties and forties. Examples abound of the naïve innocence of specialists; one of the sponsors of Doctor Kort, in a letter to the Home Office which was published in the press, said

Doctor Kort had told him he had become mixed up with Communism in America because he believed in a National Health Service! Obviously there have been and are many men of science of mature judgement and wide knowledge outside their special subjects—but their competence in other fields is not due to their special work or helped by it. The point is that human nature with its " infinite variety " and wilfulness is only in a very limited degree suitable material for the method of pure science. Even in dealing with inorganic matter, real science is tentative and hypothetical, ready to change its judgements; but, as Bernard Rosenberg says, engineers can at least make predictions about the behaviour of steel girders without having to take into account the possibility of their falling in love with each other. Lastly, it is an important point that many scientific achievements—as in all professional success—have been due less to the method than to inspired guess work—the specialist's instinctive " hunch " or flair in his own subject.

The claims of economic experts to plan a better existence, though more relevant than those of physical scientists, must also be regarded with considerable reserve. Economists and statisticians can formulate useful general laws provided it is realized that these " laws " correspond to special periods, and are liable when the circumstances change to be scrapped with a large part of Mill and Ricardo. Similarly their statistics are useful so long as no important action is taken based on their being infallible. Professor Machlup, professor of Economy at Johns Hopkins University, has collected a striking list of unfortunate predictions during a short period, under the doubtless exaggerated title *Do Economists Know Anything?* His examples reveal, in America, remarkable conflicts of opinion on exchange rates, price controls and so on. Thus in 1933-34 Roosevelt devalued the dollar and raised the price of gold in order to raise the price of commodities and it did not rise; in 1945 price controls were abolished on the economists' assurance that prices would not rise, and they did rise. He says the United Kingdom economic plan for 1949 estimated exports for the first six months at 161 millions and the actual figure was 91; that in 1935 the American statisticians rated their imports from the United Kingdom 26·5 per cent higher than the United Kingdom authorities did; in 1945 the United States Department of Commerce raised its estimate of national income from 161 billion dollars to 182·8, by simply changing its method of estimation. I remember in the thirties André Siegfried gave a Parisian audience astonishing illustrations of the complete bewilderment of the financial authorities in October, 1929, and throughout the years of the crisis.

The conclusion is that, as Lord Keynes himself wrote, the master economist must have " a rare combination of gifts," must be mathematician, historian, statesman and philosopher, and the whole conception that the production of great industrial communities can be planned and channelled by government departments is merely one more of the attractive slogans which have obscured realities during the last forty years. The relevance of this passage is that it illustrates how people hypnotized by mass economic interests propose remedies which tend merely to intensify the disease—planning more economic restrictions instead of planning more economic freedom can only demoralize the individual still more and increase the pressure of the collective octopus. Sir Winston Churchill in February, 1948, though admittedly speaking in a Party broadcast, could not be contradicted when he spoke of 700,000 officials who, producing nothing themselves, administered 25,000 regulations never enforced before in time of peace, and of 300 officials who had the power to make new regulations apart altogether from Parliament, carrying with them the penalty of imprisonment for crimes hitherto unknown to the Law. The further implication of the passage, that the planning experts cannot be relied on to " deliver the goods " in the literal sense, is less relevant to this chapter, as the point under consideration is that the predominance of economic interests and motive in any civilization is always the forerunner of moral disequilibrium and disintegration; so that even if State planning could increase for a time the supply of commodities, it could not affect the root cause of maladjustment as seen by the modern sociologists. The experience of all past civilizations has been that material and economic decline invariably follows the loss of the higher values and the

loss of coherence and stability. A purely economic civilization, after periods of great prosperity due to increased
production and increased specialization, becomes over-compli-
cated, over-specialized, and engenders a ruthless conflict
between the mass egoism of classes and interests no longer
restrained by any other loyalties and values—with the final
issue in despair, demoralization and material collapse.

A peak period of material prosperity, such as Europe knew
in the nineteenth century, is now being enjoyed by the United
States and there is an unfortunate tendency, especially in
Continental Europe, to admire and imitate the more dangerous
rather than the best aspects of the American way of life. For
the actual prosperity of America is essentially that of the first
phase of a typical mass-civilization and is also largely due to
factors which Europe and England cannot imitate, namely, the
possession of a whole continental area full of natural resources
and without national economic barriers. On the side of the
higher values all the phenomena of European decadence are
not only fully in evidence, but in some respects further
advanced.[1] The whole attitude to life of the masses, though
genuinely sentimental and idealist, is unconsciously based on
material quantitative values. It is honestly believed that
Communism and race hatred all over the world can be
countered by money and the inspiring example of Sears-
Roebuck catalogues. The Arts and all learning outside useful

---

[1] By " decadence " I mean what some regard as " progress." The evidence
on certain aspects was summarized in *The Tablet* on January 22nd, 1955.
Approximately twenty-five per cent of American marriages end in divorce, to
which must be added a substantial number of marriages which break up
without a legal divorce. The increase of divorce is followed as always (partly
through the effect on the children) by an increase in mental illness. In 1953,
750,000 cases were treated in mental hospitals, 1,750,000 in psychiatric clinics
or private psychiatric offices, and five million others who went to hospitals for
physical ailments were found to be suffering from mental or emotional disorders. It is believed that over ten million Americans suffer from some form
of mental illness, and that in New York every tenth inhabitant will spend some
part of his life in a mental institution. New York City, which has increased its
Drug Squad from 130 to 200, started in 1952 a special hospital for young drug
addicts, of whom there are believed to be about 7,500 able to pay from six to
thirty dollars a day (say two to six guineas) for narcotics. (This attempt to
stop them developing their personalities does not seem consistent with the
ideals of progressive education!). These figures give us no grounds for
complacency, as the same tendencies are accelerating here and in Europe.

technology tend to be regarded as decorative luxuries proper to cliques and cultural oases. Already in the thirties Chicago University was offering M.A. degrees for theses on trends in hosiery advertising, styles cycles in women's underwear, or photographic studies on boiled icing, and today answers to examinations at leading Universities are recorded electrically on marked squares. The full development of the mass-civilization in Europe and England has so far been retarded by the restraining forces of tradition (of regions, classes and occupational groups) of institutions like the Public Schools and Oxford and Cambridge in England or the peasantry and the Catholic tradition in Europe. It has been impeded also by the greater slowness to act, by all the surviving restraints of an old complex civilization; by the persistence of local inherited ways of life. The partial uprooting of the dwellers in our great cities is completely achieved in the second generation of American immigrants, and the consequent psychic disintegration is correspondingly more marked. The survival —under great difficulties—of quality values in Europe and England is shown in the obstinate resistance to the spread of standardization and mass production to every field.

All this is fully appreciated by responsible thinkers in the United States, and is indeed a reason for the progress made there by students of sociology and psychology, who are in so many ways in advance of our own. Here, as throughout this chapter, I make no definite predictions; for in it I am only discussing why to so many students of social history our civilization appears to be disintegrating, or at least declining. The Sociologists find that in the past purely materialist-economic civilizations have always developed from civilizations of quality, but never developed *into* civilizations of quality; have always proceeded from integration to disintegration. I am not concerned at this stage with the further question, whether they are right in regarding this disintegration as being therefore inevitable—though it should be clear that no one who holds the traditional Christian view of man and the Universe can possibly accept the view that disintegration is inevitable. What man has done, man can undo if he knows what he wants, and wants it strongly enough.

Chapter Six

PSYCHOANALYSIS COMES OF AGE

" His mind and body kept watch in harmony together "
(St. Augustine)

It has been a national misfortune that English public opinion was—and still largely is—dominated by the pioneer system of Freud, which was introduced by enthusiastic disciples just after the First World War, when his original clinical discoveries—first published in 1894—had been made the basis of a complete superstructure of speculative theories and his leading disciples, including Adler and Jung, had already broken away from him on radically divergent lines. His philosophy was presented as making one whole with his real scientific work, and as W. H. Auden sang after Freud's death, " to us he is no more a person now but a whole climate of opinion." His system was regarded as an indivisible whole and its prestige has consequently obscured the new developments associated with Adler, Jung and the modern American and other schools of psychology.

Traditional psychology had overstressed the rôle of the conscious rational faculties, while experimental medical psychology had regarded nervous disorders as bodily diseases. Charcot and Janet in Paris—which Freud visited in 1885—by the use of hypnotism distinguished neuroses, particularly hysteria, from bodily disease, and Freud and Breuer by 1894 had founded modern psychology by concentrating on the fact that the unconscious can influence human conduct and that a neurosis can have a psychic, not a bodily, origin. (For example, they had found by hypnotism that a woman patient's inability to drink water was due to the shock of seeing a dog drink out of a cup.) Freud developed his basic theory that neuroses were due to unconscious repression of sexual impulses, and gave up hypnotism for his new technique of " free association," letting the chain of thought evoked by a leading word run freely till the original experience which had caused the symptoms came to light.

This direction of attention to the irrational sources inside the personality was a great achievement. Unfortunately Freud was a fanatical disciple of the most extreme school of nineteenth-century materialism and Darwinian biology, and his *a priori* assumptions dominate all his later work, making a useful clinical technique the starting point of a complete theoretical system of psychology and philosophy and guiding his patients' confessions to confirm his theories. In his system the personality was a bundle of separate mental states, with no continuous mental life, connected only by the impulses resulting from the original constitution of the individuals, and their past experiences. Satisfaction was the only form of pleasure, and pleasure the only aim. All desires are manifestations of the " libido," i.e., are of sexual origin, and " values " have no objective existence; they are aims which the libido makes appear valuable, i.e., disguised forms of pleasure. Deriving all the higher mental processes from biological functions, he claimed " to understand normal psychic life from the basis of *abnormal* states," and equated neurosis, perversion, dreams and every kind of culture   Accepting his Master Haeckel's long-discarded thesis[1] that the embryo recapitulates the evolution of species, he made the history of the human race parallel with that of the individual, claiming that his " Oedipus complex " is of general occurrence, which has been shown to be quite contrary to the evidence. Starting from his interpretation of dreams as " camouflaged realizations of repressed desires," he advanced to the theory that all mythology, poetry and art were similarly " substitute satisfactions for repressed desires which are alive in the soul of everyone from childhood," i.e., sub-limations of the repressed libido. (Another factor which may have influenced Freud was the strong patriarchal feeling among the Vienna Jewish community.)

[1] Professor Haeckel, long a best seller with sixpenny editions, was a classic illustration of the pseudo-scientific dogmatist. His woodcuts first published in 1868 showing that the human embryo was identical at different stages with monkeys, dogs, and even tortoises, turned out to be the same pictures with different titles and in 1891 he confessed to an " unpardonable piece of folly." Though an authority only on some branches of zoology, Haeckel disposed of the " Riddle of the Universe," indulged in wild raids into ecclesiastical history, and de-fined God as " a gaseous vertebrate." As late as 1907 I was one of his many victims.

Obviously this closed mechanical system left no room for any spiritual influences and faculties whatever, or even for the development of personality, which it arrested in the infantile stage; it never got beyond the stage of biological analysis, and found the best material for psychology in children and pathological cases. Freud found the first years of life to be the dominating influence, *not* as a result of his case-histories but because he started with a determinist philosophy and did not look for other factors. Having assumed in advance that all religion was an " obsessional neurosis," he found normal religious behaviour to be merely a deviation from the religious symptoms of the neurotics. Starting from the abnormal to explain the normal, he excluded on principle all dynamic, conscious activity and assumed that all human activity was dominated by the unconscious impersonal force of the libido working through what he called the " Id."

Though Freud occasionally disclaimed in theory that his system was completely centred on sex, it was his sex-obsession which caused the breakaway of Adler and Jung, both of whom started as biological psychoanalysts. Adler developed the school of comparative individual psychology and his influence on the trends of the later schools of psychology in America has been decisive. Adler gave psychoanalysis a fundamental change of direction by treating the human person as a total unit and as being primarily a member of society. The soul of man harbours two conflicting tendencies; one centred on himself, the other centred on society—the will is pulled both ways, and human behaviour depends on the result of this conflict. Where Freud tried to explain man's true nature in terms of the lower biological functions, and as governed by the past, Adler found man's true nature in his specific highest non-animal functions and governed by its future end. The end was more important than the cause, the future more than the past; the genius and the saint are more truly human than the imbecile and the criminal. Where Freud saw only the sex instinct, Adler saw also the will (not " impulse ") to power, and the will to live in society. Health, normality, depended on fulfilling the demands of reality (including social obligations), not on the satisfaction of impulses. From the frustration of the will to power he derived the famous inferiority complex.   The remedy lay in living in harmony with reality, with one's true nature, and treatment must therefore involve showing the patient his errors in judgement.   He stressed that a new, non-animal factor was at work in the human personality, that " values " have an objective existence; that the person can choose, and that the real conflict causing neurosis is not between impulses and environment, but is a spiritual one between man's infinite pride and his finite limitations.   The will to power (i.e., the effort at self-assertion) expresses the tendency to self-preservation, its source is the feeling of inferiority, and the problem is to enable him to assert himself within the laws of nature and society.   The abnormal pathological cases are those who, having failed to integrate themselves with their true nature and the demands of society, take refuge in unreal non-social fantasies.   When Adler left Freud in 1911, Freud was concentrating on his " Eros " instinct, the union of self-preservation and sex. When Adler developed his " will to power " as the central force, Freud adopted it as the " death-instinct," the destructive counterpart of the sex instinct but of course linked with it (through his characteristic speculation on " Narcissism "). In his tortuous mind the death-instinct became the impulse to return to the state of infantile pleasure.   The really important point however for the layman lies not in rival theories about instincts but in the fact that where Freud had used his discovery, of the active rôle of the unconscious, to reduce all the complex elements in human nature to one only of them, Adler brought out the supreme importance of the dynamic element which inspires and unifies the whole personality, its intimate relationship with other personalities, i.e., society; and the curative effectiveness of standards of value, of right and wrong.[1]

[1] A footnote must suffice for one of the most fantastic offshoots of pure materialism, the now discredited " Science " of Behaviourism.   In 1894 the Russian Pavlov published his experiments on the " conditional reflex," of which the short point was that if an animal comes to associate food with the ringing of a bell, its mouth will water at the sound of the bell alone.   The idea was taken up nearly twenty years later by a group of American psychologists,

[Continued at foot of next page

All the later developments—associated for example with Otto Rank, the Chicago school of pyschoanalysis (Alexander and French), Carl Rogers, have along varying lines developed Adler's emphasis on the social aspects of psychic life and the forces of healthy growth. Interest has tended to move away from the search for the destructive forces of repression and from combing for infantile conflicts and infantile eroticism, towards a new technique of starting with the patient's actual difficulties and trying to solve them by building new social relationships by " emotional transference " through the healer. Where Freud had insisted on pursuing his sordid inquisitions and chain-associations daily for at least two years (with obvious dangers for many self-centred neurotics), many psychoanalysts today claim results in two or three interviews, by " short therapy."

While only a minority follow Rogers' " non-directive " therapy (accepting the patient's personality as it is, in the hope that he will, in the atmosphere of sympathy, reconstruct himself), the whole tendency is to stress the factor of social and cultural relationships[1] and to take special account of the spiritual—i.e., the specifically human—aspects of personality.

Continued from previous page]

notably J. B. Watson and K. S. Lashley, who built on it the system called Behaviourism (e.g. Watson's *Psychology from the Standpoint of a Behaviourist*, 1919) which set out to explain all human conduct in terms of physiology. It was claimed that the unique human personality would eventually be explained by inference from the study of the conditional reflex hypothesis in animal life, though in the end the hypothesis was admitted to be inadequate even in regard to animals. The claim was rejected at the time by W. McDougall of Oxford, although he had himself rejected the soul as an unscientific notion and had " endowed the animal with a primitive prototype of the human mind." (Quotation from Professor O. L. Zangwill in *Psychology as the Study of Behaviour*, Cambridge, 1954.)

[1] Professor Zangwill (*op. cit.*), after pointing out that " psychology in Cambridge has moved far beyond the psychophysical tradition which gave it birth," stresses the similar work in England of Sir F. Bartlett on the influence of cultural factors on the behaviour of the individual and the extent to which conduct is determined by group membership. He wisely adds, however, that present-day social psychology is " deplorably vague," that " studies of group behaviour are still very much on trial "; and quotes approvingly W. James's reminder that in the development stage of a science " a degree of vagueness is what best consists with fertility."

It is becoming realized that mal-adaptation is often due to a loss of spiritual balance.

Meanwhile Adler's contemporary co-disciple of Freud, C. G. Jung, had created a new branch of psychology which I have always felt is more important than the healing of individual neurotics—the study of the collective unconscious. He has the great claim of having been proved right in his lifetime on a matter of universal importance when almost all his contemporaries, and longer in England than in Europe, were totally wrong. Jung's main thesis is that each individual has a personal and a collective unconscious; that mental disturbances are due not merely to infantile experiences but to primitive ancestral influences; and that the psycho-pathology of the mass is rooted in that of the individual. Impersonal collective disturbances in the unconscious are expressed as motifs, which he called " archetypes," in dreams and fairy tales or legends. Forces from the unconscious can compensate for deficiencies in the conscious if they can be integrated by the forces of order (measure and proportion), but if they flood into consciousness breaking the moral controls, they create collective neurosis and finally collective psychosis, just as in the individual. When the conscious state of a people is alienated from the natural laws of life by their being uprooted and herded in masses, the individual becomes unstable and suggestible, and the unconscious " compensates " by an upheaval of mass instincts. Before going further into Jung's system, consider some of the predictions he made on the strength of it. In 1918 he found his German patients had non-personal collective disturbances and that the " archetypes " expressed primitiveness, violence, and cruelty. He concluded that the 1914 War had been released by the accumulated pressure of the unconscious uprooted masses with their blind desires, and that the War in its course had released the hidden power of evil which remained active after the end of the War, and indeed became accentuated because the feeling of helplessness was " compensated " by the surging-up of the desire for power, and its counterpart the longing for order and discipline in the obvious easy form of dictatorship. So he wrote in 1918 that " as the unconditional authority of the Christian-World attitude loses more and more ground, we shall become increasingly aware of the blond beast stirring in its subterranean prison and threatening us with an outbreak that will have devastating consequences." In 1919 he told the British Society for Psychical Research that a breakdown of conscious hope would animate the collective unconscious and the latter would replace conscious reality. In 1927 he said the old religions lived on in their primitive forms and might at any time break out with destructive force through mass-suggestion; " our frightful gods have only changed their names—they rhyme now with -ism." In 1932 he told the Viennese that " the gigantic catastrophes that threaten us are not of a physical or biological kind, but psychic events. We are threatened in a fearful way by wars and revolutions that are nothing else than psychic epidemics. Man is exposed today to the elemental forces of his own Psyche." That was the year before Hitler's complete authority; in 1933 he said " only he can hope to withstand the overwhelming force (of the mass) who is rooted in the inner as well as in the outer world." In 1937 he said in a lecture at Yale that mass destruction of dissenters belonged " quite particularly to the future," that when people crowd together the dynamics of the collective man are set free, " beasts or demons who lie dormant in every person till he is part of a mob."

Of course this had been said before—I have quoted some instances in earlier chapters—but the merit of Jung was to provide an explanation based on Freud's, Adler's and his own psychology. Hysteria, which he defined as the disassociation or separation of the opposites (the extreme case being the split personality) in the psyche, could result, in the collective as in the individual soul, from the feeling of inferiority, and the desire to escape from it by self-admiration, lies and persecution-mania turning into the desire to persecute others. Hitler united them all, a reflected image of Germany's invasion by the subconscious. Jung held that there was a general invasion by the subconscious in Europe, but that it had occurred first in Germany because the primitive archetypes were particularly strong there. Nietzsche and Wagner had long before the First World War brought the old Teutonic myth " surging up from a remote past "; in 1936 Jung had described Wotan, the God of Storm, passion, wandering, " magical wishes," and the " possessor " of men, as a fundamental psychic factor, an archetype, and identified it with the youth movements and mass hiking, the cult of race and soil.   People explained Hitler by economic and political factors, but " Wotan explains more."   Referring to the belief current in Germany in 1936 that Hitler dabbled in black magic, Jung thought " the evil spirit had taken possession of him long before," but while seeing reflected in him the hysterical German yearning for a sombre daemonic hero, Jung also thought that many supported him from a genuine desire for order, not realizing that he personified the very weaknesses they feared—a " psychic scarecrow " and an " irresponsible ranting psychopath cursed with the keen intuition of a rat or a guttersnipe."   (An examiner might set this for discussion along with Mr. Trevor Roper's verdict that Hitler triumphs by the power of his mind—a systematic thinker . . . the most philosophic conqueror the world has ever known.)   There is truth in both views.

If the Western nations had not been obsessed by Freud, Jung's warnings might have shaken the widespread, most misleading, delusion that Nazism was a right-wing, Conservative movement genuinely opposed to Bolshevism, and not rather a more popular and also more nihilistic German version of Bolshevism.   I had a photograph once of Hitler, Goebbels, Goering and Himmler in civil clothes before their rise to power, and they had the same seedy, common, frustrated appearance as the dirty little morons in Tussaud's Chamber of Horrors.

Jung held that the European idea had been a patriarchal order which had protected the soul against the most serious psychic danger, loss of its roots in custom and tradition.   The uprooted individual, losing his instinct of self-preservation and personal responsibility, turns for direction to the State which is only an agglomeration of the non-entities of which it is composed, and " far lower than most of them as it represents mass psychology raised to the highest power."   The declared aim of psychotherapy was education of the people towards independence and moral freedom, but " at present the only attempted solution is the total incorporation of the individual into the State," on which " the parental images are projected as universal provider and authority. The spiritual order of direction which bridges the centuries and keeps cultural values alive is replaced by a political directing order which serves the power-aims of particular groups." Jung distinguished between " Society " as a condition (not the object) of human existence; the " State " as a group of individuals; and the individual, who is " the only carrier of life."

There is much more in Jung's system, but his views on the collective unconscious deserve special attention because they enabled him to see what few others did, and to foretell the greatest events of his time on the basis of his belief that " all human control comes to an end when the individual is caught in a mass movement and the archetypes begin to function."

I began this chapter by expressing regret that the prestige of the narrow nineteenth-century philosophy, which Freud had erected on top of his (and Breuer's) one original positive achievement, should have so much obscured the work of his disciples, work which is tending towards a more balanced and comprehensive view of man than had existed for several centuries. This feeling is greatly strengthened by study of the details of Freud's work, which I have had no space to quote. The underlying tone of Freudian work is mean, obsessed, often disgusting; its whole purpose is the destruction of all moral and spiritual values.[1]   It is lamentable to think that in recent years one of the most responsible organs of opinion in England, while fully admitting that the Freudian *method* in psychiatry was out of date, should say with approval that his *theories* were becoming more and more prevalent in education and social anthropology, and should speak reverently of his effect on " the mental attitude of a whole generation of progressive men and women." The effect was certainly great, and the more so as the majority

[1] Mr. C. Dawson, in the preface to his *Spirit of the Oxford Movement*, refers to the fantastic theories of one author about the personal relationships of the ascetic and religion-dominated leaders of the Oxford Movement, including Cardinal Newman and J. H. Froude!

of the progressive men and women probably knew Freud mainly through the medium of popular summaries and were primarily attracted—as Freud must often have chuckled to reflect—by the all-pervading atmosphere of sex.

I suggest that it follows from this brief sketch of psychology as a developing study which has far outgrown the pioneer Freudian stage but is still divided into various schools, that it is far from having become an agreed positive science. I mean a science of such a kind that anyone who has studied it can assume the right of pontifical judgement in particular cases as is being attributed to it by laymen.[1] An unfortunate belief has become officially accepted that any professional psychiatrist can by scientific method pronounce, with the shortest acquaintance, on a young man's vocation, his qualities of leadership and so on. This is a rare intuitive gift which has been the distinguishing mark of great headmasters and great civil or business administrators, but cannot be acquired from any existing text-books or from clinical practice with abnormal cases; and the authority given of late years to professional psychiatrists in the selection of candidates in the Fighting Services and the Foreign Service has no real warrant from practical experience or psychology itself, which must in the long run be based on common sense.

[1] There seem to be many psychological societies, some with correspondence courses and diplomas, in the English-speaking world. Professor Valentine, from whom I have already quoted, has told us of one psychological society, of which he attended a meeting by mistake, which has grafted psychology on to the tradition of evangelical revivalism. It has a rousing hymn (to the tune of " John Brown's Body ") which begins: " Practical psychology will suit your every need."

The Johannesburg Zoo, reversing the Behaviourist idea, has (according to Mr. Douglas Woodruff) engaged a psychiatrist to supervise an elephant who had tried to keep fit by sprinting with a passenger-load of children.

Chapter Seven

THE LIBEL ON THE CAVEMAN

A CARDINAL object of this survey is to suggest along various converging lines that all the new sciences dealing with man were started sixty to eighty years ago by research workers who almost all were total believers in a special philosophic theory and selected and arranged the facts to fit into it. As in Freud's case, so the other new " ologies " were developed from presuppositions held as artĭcles of faith; the reverse of the proper scientific method of looking at the facts first. Our beliefs about prehistoric man and about the historic religions (historic because we have documentary evidence) have a very important bearing on our own beliefs; the two subjects are closely inter-connected, and in regard to both, the distortion and scrambling of the evidence was specially marked because the presuppositions had a strong emotional religiously anti-religious bias.

The main presuppositions were that the whole life of man (not merely his purely physical organic make-up) has been governed by mechanical forces of natural selection working by very slow but regular progression; that the law of beneficial upward progress is universal; that therefore in the story of beliefs, conduct, and institutions, the higher form must be assumed as inevitably coming later than the lower. Though this dogma was based on the biological theory of organic evolution through natural selection, its unquestioning application to man as a spiritual rational being was, it must be repeated, unconsciously prompted by the unique conditions of security and comfort enjoyed by the European middle classes between eighty and forty years ago—I remember vividly the assumption still prevalent forty years ago, though a little disturbed by German expansion and the " Yellow Peril "—that fundamentally the course for civilization as we knew it was set fair and that no real retrogression was possible. No one would have admitted as possible the horrors of Belsen or Auschwitz with its four million murders, nor the Katyn massacre of four thousand Polish officers, nor the mass deportations of whole nations. Applied to the study of mankind, the dogma involved the presupposition that monotheism must be the latest form of religion; that primitive man had no religion and advanced through spirit-worship or ghost-worship, through magic and fetichism, to polytheism and finally monotheism; that slavery, human sacrifice, cannibalism, sexual promiscuity must be characteristic of the early stages of evolution. It meant equally that all the arts must have evolved by slow stages from zero through the lower to the higher forms. The stages of material culture were identified with stages of spiritual growth. Thus as late as 1927, when Sir A. Keith told the British Association that " man's brain has been evolved from that of an anthropoid ape and in the process . . . no new or strange faculty interpolated," Bishop Barnes preaching in Westminster Abbey said, " Darwin's triumph had destroyed the whole theological scheme, since man is merely an animal who is slowly growing in spiritual understanding." (Incidentally Sir A. Keith had also said we may confidently presume " that this individual was representative of the people who inhabited England at this remote date "—the " individual " was poor " Piltdown man " whose modern cranium and modern monkey jaw had been brought there by the practical joker who invented him!) The press announced that Bishop Barnes " had declared himself on the side of the scientists," just as his obituary referred to his " progressive opinions on original sin." The words used illustrate the emotional bias against the Christian Doctrine of the Fall and Redemption, and the ignorant muddling of material phenomena with the moral and spiritual order with which the Christian Doctrine is primarily concerned. The concept of original sin belongs to the supernatural order: it is either true or false, for all time, and words like " progressive " have no meaning in regard to belief or disbelief in it.

The closed dogmatic mental attitude of the older anthro-

pologists was strikingly illustrated by the unscientific reaction
to the series of discoveries of Palaeolithic cave art beginning
with the discovery of Altamira in 1875, and which can now
be studied in photographs in Abbé Breuil's *Four Hundred
Centuries of Cave Art*. For many years most of the pseudo-
scientists simply refused even to look at the originals of these,
in their own *genre*, superb naturalistic drawings, in Lascaux,
Altamira, La Mouthe, Les Eyzies, Font de Gaume, Les Com-
barelles, Niaux, Pech-Mirle; for they not only revealed a high
artistic achievement over 20,000 years old; they showed also
that it had *degenerated* into scribbles without form and finally
disappeared leaving no tradition. It was not until 1902 that
the members of a hostile congress of savants at Montauban
were induced to visit Les Eyzies because it was near, and the
recantation began. Even before the discoveries of the cave
art, it had been found that Neanderthal man had buried his
dead with engraved tools and weapons and magical arrange-
ments of bison's horns and rhinoceros' teeth; but the dogma
said that " Palaeolithic man had no religion," so of course the
object must have been to get rid of the deceased's belongings!
Now look at some of H. G. Wells' comments in the nineteen-
twenties, which millions of readers swallowed as the last word
in science. Basing himself on Gabriel de Morillet, a great
authority in the 1880's, Wells stated that Palaeolithic man had
no religion (the ornaments and food were put in the tombs
because " they doubted they were dead "); that the cave
drawings were drawn with increasing skill as the centuries
passed, that there was scarcely anything religious or mystical
in them, and it was " doubtful if they knew of the bow." In
fact, the cave art appeared in sudden maturity; one of the
most famous pictures is the bison transfixed with arrows;
and not only is the whole art obviously magico-religious, but
it seems clear that these often nearly inaccessible caves were
not dwellings but temples. But perhaps Wells' greatest
museum piece was that Neanderthal man had " nothing we
should call language " but " probably " made imitative
sounds! He illustrated his work with horrid pictures of the
ape-man who made the cave-drawings. Poor Neanderthal
man certainly was rather unattractive by our standards, with

beetling brows, but the size of his brain was often above some modern averages. Incidentally, the earliest Neanderthal crania are not those showing the most resemblance to the few very first men of whose supposed skulls fragments have been found in China and Java; these traits are more marked in the last Neanderthal men when their race was becoming extinct— again suggesting degeneracy. We still have no real knowledge of the ancestors of modern man. One of Wells' nineteenth-century masters was Sir J. G. Frazer, whose work, representing his whole epoch, is still being quoted and abridged. In 20,000 pages Frazer, who admitted cheerfully that he had never once met a black man, gathered together an incredible array of facts with superficial resemblances selected to prove at all costs that everything to do with primitive man was, as Professor Eliade says in his treatise on the history of religions, a monstrous mass of beastliness, cruelty, and superstition, happily abolished by scientific progress. The whole spirit governing Frazer's 20,000 pages was summed up in one perfect sentence of his: " Such tales of Virgin mothers are relics of the age of childish ignorance when men had not yet recognized the intercourse of the sexes as the true cause of offspring "! How can several generations have failed to see the comic side of this pompous idiocy ? Only because of the totally unfounded assumption that real men and women before they lived in cities could talk, make fires, and draw pictures, and yet not possess any rational faculties. The statement cannot stand a moment's critical consideration, but this humourless obser-vation expressed the underlying spirit of the whole school. But Frazer was only one of a chorus; Spencer, Tylor, Hartland, Letourneau, Reinach, Levy-Bruhl, Durkheim, and many more one could quote, all had the same un-objective approach, insisted that " higher " and " lower " equate with " later " and " older," and completely ruled out degeneration by insisting that all aberrations must be primitive.

This whole school was already out of date when Wells published his " Outline " and Bishop Barnes " declared for the scientists." The modern *cultural* history method was already in being, with the collaboration of at least

twenty-seven authorities in many countries,[1] though notably in
Germany and Austria.   The formula of the modern school is
to trace cultural elements to their meeting in new cultural
systems, creating culture-circles which expand and modify,
or are modified by, other culture-circles.   The three main
types are primitive and primary cultures, and their mixture
in secondary and tertiary cultures.

The primitive culture, still represented by degenerate
survivors in Australia, the Arctic, and places in Asia, Africa
and South America, was based on hunting and wild produce.
The primary culture appeared simultaneously in three culture
circles each of which was based on active production, whether
by more skilled hunting (combined with the totem and magical
practices), or by nomadic cattle-raising, or by horticulture.
When they begin to mix, the secondary and tertiary cultures
appear.   Each of these culture circles corresponds to a prehistoric stage in the geological record, and each developed its
own form of religion.   An outstanding conclusion of this
modern anthropology is that monotheism is the essential
feature of primitive culture.   Some primitives have only one
God, the others have one Supreme Being who has created any
lesser spirits.   The Supreme Creator is regarded as eternal,
omniscient, good, shining like light.   It is a social religion,
with liturgical prayers, ceremonies, festivals, youth initiations;
sacrifice of first fruits is universal, but no human sacrifice and
no offerings to the dead; morality is organically related to the
religion, and it includes strict monogamy, and support of
the old and sick.   Land is held by family-units, the father
of the family is the public authority.   Wars of conquest are
unknown, as are torture and cannibalism.   In short, though
their life was simple, the assumption of their moral and
spiritual inferiority is as contrary to the evidence as it is to say
that a millionaire is necessarily more moral and spiritual than
an agricultural labourer in a poor country.   This does not
mean that " when wild in woods the noble savage ran,"

[1] Quatrefages, Andrew Lang, Ratzel, Frobenius, Graebner, Ankermann,
Foy, Schmidt, Koppers, Krickleberg, Vatter, Boas, Dixon, Kroeber, Swanton,
McLeod, Rivers, Hocart, Codrington, de la Boullaye, Metraux, Nordenskiold,
Birket-Smith, Rassmussen, Krohn, Breuil, Menghim.

" everything was lovely in the garden." Technologically
primitive man was far removed from the later city-dweller
but not so far as he was from all other living creatures by his
use of fire and bone and horn implements and the faculty of
speech.[1] His chief material advantage was having plenty of
room in a period of natural abundance. What it does mean
is that he not only had the same spiritual and rational
capacities but was a higher type morally and spiritually than
many of his successors, and that to assume he was brutish and
nasty because his technical equipment was rudimentary is the
same as assuming that a man with two cars is a higher moral
type than a man with one car, and that a man with no car
is more inclined to polytheism and human sacrifice than a
man with one car. Technology and the soul are entirely
separate matters.

On the contrary, it is found in early cultures that as the
economic conditions improve, the anti-religious forces of greed
and egoism, " keeping up with the Jones'es," begin to disturb
the social equilibrium, and when the horticultural-agrarian
circle becomes established in the river valleys, the first big
move is made towards debased forms of religion. This culture
becomes matriarchal—it centres on the woman, Mother Earth,
the Earth Goddess, soon identified with the (female) moon.
Blood sacrifices, and soon sacrifices of heads and hearts, are
needed to awake fertility; disembodied souls and other spirits
take charge of the plants, must be propitiated by sacrifices.
Animism, which Tylor thought was the origin of religion,
appears first in this matriarchal primary culture. Belief arises
in a dark underworld, ruled by the Earth Mother or Dark
Moon; as rewards and penalties become dependent on ritual
human sacrifice, cannibalism, and magical incantations,
religion is divorced from morality. Meanwhile, in the
patriarchal totem culture of the higher hunters, the clan-
totem develops animal-worship, while magical rites to increase
the animals' fertility, and to secure their capture, develop

---

[1] It was, I think, G. K. Chesterton who said the point was not how the
faculty of drawing had evolved from the blue-faced baboon through the caveman to Michelangelo, but that the caveman and Michelangelo both knew how
to draw, and the baboon did not!

worship of the Sun, source of all power. Here again, the will to power, through magical acts, diminishes respect for the Supreme Being and increases the separation of religion from morality. Finally the cattle-raising culture, starting with breeding of reindeer and horses, then camels, fosters the large patriarchal family and the succession of the elder son; while the vulnerability of the herds to drought and pestilence maintains the sense of dependency on the Supreme Being. Hence the pastoral cultures tended to preserve the essentials of monotheism, and when the three culture-circles began to mix, the pastoralists sometimes degenerated, sometimes held their own. From the amalgamation arose the first city and village-states, often ruled by a governing-class of pastoral conquerors. In most cases the sun and moon mythologies were both adopted, and the magical practices of all three cultures fused into a vast and intricate system.

This fusion was the basis of nearly all the historic religions. Here we enter the domain of written records; yet once more, scientific fact-finding was obstructed by generations of theory-ridden scholars. Preoccupation with the slow upward evolution of man's spiritual and rational faculties came up against the unique religious originality of the Jewish nation, which therefore had to be denied along with the antiquity of their Scriptures. It came up against the supernatural claims of Christianity, so the Church had to be shown up as an omnium-gatherum of borrowings from all cults however dissimilar from it in their actual results, and as having rapidly developed into "magical superstitions and thinly veiled polytheism." So Professor Harnack referred to the seventh-century Church, forgetting that Suetonius and cultured pagans generally had seen the earlier Church also precisely as a "magical super-stition." For a still earlier generation of higher critics the Synoptic Gospels had to be later than the fall of Jerusalem *because* they had prophesied it.

If the "higher" critics had approached Jewish history with no fixed ideas and had dispassionately studied their records, they would have found a small people who for nearly 2,000 years—including the conquest of both its kingdoms by Assyria in 721 B.C. and Babylon in 586 respectively—with

polytheists of their own Semitic race all round them, clung,
despite frequent popular lapses, to their primitive belief in
one God who was not only the God of Israel but superior to
those of their great neighbours. Their oldest documents treat
Jahveh as the creator of the world. Their books imply that
monotheism had in the third millennium extended from Lydia
in the West through Assyria to Babylonia and Elam, but
eventually was confined to Israel and finally to its minute
southern kingdom. They not only guarded their monotheism
but also their unique Messianic belief in a New Covenant
which would be shared by the rest of the world. Their writers
constantly used figurative language, and personified peoples
and events, but never invented divine heroes who had taught
the arts and become the subject of grotesque legends, such as
are found in most religions. Their attribution of the origins
of agriculture and pastoralism, architecture, music and metal-
working, to Cain, Abel, Tubal and Tubal Cain clearly implies
a knowledge of a period previous to them, and of a progress
from stone to bronze and iron. In ascribing the institution
of polygamy to Lamech, they correctly associated monogamy
with an earlier, economically poorer age. Their special
institution was the long line of prophets; men and women of
all classes, recognized as having special illuminations from
God through dreams and visions which they did not always
understand themselves. One thing they did understand, their
mission was to denounce all other gods but Yahveh, all
idolatry, all human sacrifice; that Yahveh was a personal,
righteous, paternal god who worked according to a settled
plan. While all other nations looked back to a golden age,
the Hebrew prophets definitely looked forward to a Redeemer
who would found a Universal Kingdom—Renan's impressionist dogma that the Semites were monotheist by character
(" the religion of the desert ") was entirely false; the nearest
neighbours, the Canaanites, were deep in polytheism, child
sacrifices, sorcery, ritual prostitution. " Moloch horrid king
besmeared with blood " was propitiated by burning children
throughout the Semitic world, in Arabia, Canaan, Tyre and
Carthage; " Astarte Queen of Heaven with crescent horns "
was worshipped from Babylon and Moab to the Mediterranean

shores as goddess of sex, maternity and war, with her court of consecrated temple prostitutes, male and female. Solomon's foreign wives lured him into polytheism, Jezebel nearly replaced Jahveh by Baal. *Prima facie*, Israelite monotheism stands out as a unique fact in the World's history, not only as monotheism but in its insistence on interior purity. The " higher " critics would not have it; the history of the patriarchs *must* have been written a thousand years later, Abraham was a lunar hero, and so on.

The unique character of the Israelites' stand against polytheism, idolatry and human sacrifice, can only be appreciated against the background of almost all the other historic religions, of which space only allows a few illustrations. The great twin civilization of Babylonia and Assyria which flourished on the Tigris-Euphrates plain for three thousand years was an amalgam of small city-states inhabited by people who shared a common ancestry with Israel. Each city-state had its local god, all forming a hierarchy, with, at the top, the Sky-god and his colleagues, all of whom had goddess-wives; and Ishtar, goddess of war and fertility (Astarte of the Canaanites) and Tammuz, later the Greek Adonis, the spring god who died annually and was rescued by Ishtar. In Assyria, which borrowed her religion from Babylon, the head god was Asshur, his wife Ninlil corresponded to Ishtar. One series of incantations calls on 150 gods. Counter-witchcraft by incantation was a central feature in religious observance; for sickness and disaster were inflicted by evil spirits as punishments for offences against some god, so to get forgiveness and cure (the two were identical) you recited all the likely faults, and called on all the gods most likely to be concerned. Divination, a special personal gift among the Jews, was in Babylon and Assyria the trade of a vast hereditary profession, interpreting the stars, entrails of sacrifices, dreams (" if a ewe gives birth to a lion with a pig's eye, the princess will die! ") and many other magical techniques. There is, to their credit, no proof of human sacrifice. The whole theology is full of grotesque stories of drunken or cowardly gods (" like dogs with drooping ears "), of Tiomat who gives birth to dragons, and is shot by her husband Marduk, who uses half her body to hold up the upper waters. Yet generations of " critics," with the Hebrew books under their eyes, seriously maintained that the Jews got their religion from Babylon.

The Jewish wanderings took them to Egypt—what did they find there? Egyptian religion, which lasted nearly four thousand years, was a composite system of local cults (Heliopolis, Memphis, Thebes, the principal). Herodotus' description of them as " the most religious of men " is confirmed by the fact that all their surviving monuments are concerned with religion. Over the local gods and goddesses were the Supreme Sun-god, Osiris (the Nile), Set (the enemy desert-god), Isis and so on, but in the thousands of years no systematic doctrine with fixed principles and logical conclusions ever developed. Theology was a fantastic mythology, and the real religion was centred on the Book of the Dead, one of the world's oldest texts, which prescribed the technique for the soul's entry to Amenti, the Kingdom of the Dead, including elaborate " cramming " for the oral examination of Osiris and his forty-two assessors. (One of the stock tips was to announce " I know all your names! ") From early times many of the Egyptian gods had animal heads—rams', hawks', jackals', bulls'. This was probably a relic of totemism, but when the decadence set in from the seventh century, B.C., the system became an animal cult. Serpents, fishes, crocodiles, birds, cats, originally symbols, were mummified and buried with divine honours—cats in particular were buried with more ceremony than their owners' own parents. By the time of the Ptolemies it was thought safer to let a snake kill you than to hurt it; a Roman was lynched for killing a cat by accident, local wars were occasioned when rival towns killed each other's sacred animals.

The classic illustration of how far human aberration can go and of how easily increasing technology can accompany increasing beastliness, is the religion of the Mexican Aztecs. The federation of Tenochtitlan (Mexico City), Tlacopan, and Tetzcoco had conquered the culturally higher Toltecs. There were four chief gods, nine underworlds and thirteen heavens. Four previous worlds having perished through the sky falling down, etcetera, one, among the big four, Quetzalcoatl, created mankind by kneading old bones with blood from his own and his brothers' generative organs. Which heaven or underworld the soul went to depended on the place and manner of death. Women who died in childbirth became eventually evil night-ghosts especially haunting cross-roads. Quetzalcoatl, who had taught the techniques of living, wearing while on earth a green featherdress and snake mask, had become the god of sea and sky, but the Aztecs' chief god was Uitzilopochtli, sun and war god. Before he took precedence over Quetzalcoatl, the sacrifices had been of birds, butterflies, snakes, plants; by the end of the peak period of Mexican High Culture (eighth to fifteenth centuries, A.D.) human sacrifice had become the central feature of the system. It included the drowning of small children, but the routine was for specially dressed victims to climb to the top of a pyramid, where the priest tore out the living heart and offered it to the sun, while the corpse rolled down the steps, to be eventually ritually eaten. The priests of both sexes were celibates and had long seminary training; they were painted black, their unkempt hair stiff with blood: sometimes dressed in the skins of flayed human victims! There were 25 pyramids in Mexico City alone, the chief one with a courtyard holding 8,600 people. The theory was that the sun was nourished by human hearts, which were therefore in special demand at eclipses and high festivals; so tribal war was a constant instrument of policy, to secure prisoners for sacrifice. The latter often felt honoured, for they became divine themselves and the deity entered the person who ate them. The Spaniards, who built a cathedral on the site of the chief pyramid, have been often reproached for their destruction of this interesting culture.

Space does not allow even a cursory consideration of the 5,000 years' story of religion in China, or of Brahminism and Buddhism, and the higher, official creeds of those systems fall properly within a later chapter. It must suffice to say that the primitive Chinese who came from Western Asia about 3,000 B.C. are agreed by all commentators to have been strict monotheists, with a general cult of the souls of the dead, that they sacrificed oxen, and only learned fetichism and magic later from the aboriginal tribes. Of the early Indians, before

the growth of orthodox Brahminism, it can only be said here
that though polytheists, they knew nothing of the later caste
system, suicide of widows, the pessimistic doctrine of reincarnation with its discouraging effects on social reformers, and the
universal popular phallic worship and cult of fantastic diabolical
idols; all of which became, outside the upper circle of Brahmin
and Buddhist initiates, the real religion of the mass of the people.

The point of this canter through a number of the great
religions has been to bring out the fundamental differences
between their character and the spirit animating the Jewish
religion, and secondly to illustrate how ritual murder, ritual
cannibalism, ritual prostitution, polytheism and the cult of
evil forces, have constantly appeared in expanding, materially
progressing societies; and though cannibalism is found in some
savage tribes, there is a presumption of its being either a
survival from a higher culture or a mark of degeneracy.

Now the first point is even more clear from an objective
comparison of the Christian Church with the surviving Asiatic
cults with which it has so often been compared.   Leaving the
ludicrous comparisons between the Christian tradition of Our
Lady and the obscene cults of Astarte, Isis and so on and their
crude mythologies, we find equally radical differences with the
Gnostic and Manichaean heresies or the soldiers' cult of
Mithras.   The fanciful doctrines of the many sects of Gnostics
and Manichaeans originated in the fusing of local religions
after Alexander's conquests.   They were marked by a division
between the elect initiates and the mass of worshippers; by a
central idea (borrowed from Persia) that matter was essentially
evil and eternally opposed to spirit which it tended to overcome; that the material world was governed by groups of
Eons or Archontes or Demiurges always tending to be regarded
as demons, and with a fantastic mythology in which the
Supreme Creator, being spiritual, played only a remote
part.   The essential feature of regarding all matter as evil in
itself, reappeared in the mediaeval Albigensian heresy and has
always lurked in the background of puritanical heresies.

I included slavery among the institutions which accompany
a materially rising standard of culture.   Of all the people
who have lived, a majority have been slaves or without full

legal freedom. Where there has been equality among citizens
in high cultures, it has been a dead level equality before the
State, as when the later Roman Empire extended the use of
torture from slaves to all citizens, including senators; in all high
cultures, that is to say, before the Christian European.
Further, the growth of slavery was actually a leading factor in
the progress of the high cultures, typically in the Greek city-
states, where the whole fabric of democracy and the artistic
life was built on it. Professor Gomme estimates there were in
431 B.C., at the peak of Greek civilization, 115,000 slaves in the
small city of Athens, of whom 65,000 were in domestic service,
50,000 in industry (10,000 in the mines). Thanks to them the
free citizens, who regarded slavery as marking the gulf between
themselves and the " Barbarian " world outside Greece, were
able to spend much of their time in the theatre, the baths or
stadium, or endlessly arguing about politics or philosophy.
Aristotle, who said that some men were by nature slaves, said
also that " menial and mechanical occupations unfit a man for
citizenship." It was the same in Rome, where four centuries
later the great expansion of the Empire flooded Italy with
slaves, incidentally squeezing out the free farmers who had
made Rome and creating in Rome itself a huge cosmopolitan
proletariat. We know that slaves often did retail trade,
could own property and even other slaves; that freed men
could rise to the highest official posts, and that household
slaves were on a different footing to slaves in the mines. But
we know also that the owners legally had literally absolute
authority; that if the satirists may have exaggerated (like
Bernard Shaw on the treatment of children in England) St.
John Chrysostom preached about jealous wives insisting on the
flogging of female slaves; and that the unlimited powers of
masters and mistresses were accepted as natural by the most
urbane and highly cultivated figures in history—Cicero, Virgil,
Horace, Tacitus, by the Stoic philosophers and leaders famous
for their clemency and generosity (by Roman standards) like
Julius Caesar. It is relevant, too, to note that the barbaric
public games and the mass slaughter of the arena were directly
associated with the growth of imperial luxury and the need to
gratify the new urban proletariat.

It frequently happens that when one has made some study of
the most recent evidence on a subject, one encounters the
conclusion in some casual remarks written many years ago by
G. K. Chesterton against the whole spirit of his age.   Thus,
writing in 1908 in a review owned by my stepfather, he said he
suspected that human sacrifice was much more a decadent or
diabolist innovation than an old and simple custom, and that
cannibalism, though sometimes done by starving savages as by
starving Europeans, was rather an overcivilized product than a
simple one.   " There is much more kinship between cannibalism and the art of Aubrey Beardsley than between
cannibalism and the art that scratched the reindeer on the
rock . . . I use my own common sense, for I am talking of
my own family." Progressives, he said, regard the past not
only as hostile but as inhuman, and talk about brotherhood in
the future; there have been " high places of horror, cruelties
incredible and indecencies . . . but while the modern pedant
looks at those heathen heights from a greater height of super-
ciliousness, as things he has passed for ever . . . we can only
cry that we know not the depth of our own darkness, and pray
that we be not led into temptation but find deliverance from
evil." In less than thirty years after G. K. C. wrote those
words, slavery, torture and mass murder had been revived by
Nazis and Communists on a scale unknown in all pagan
antiquity, and we ourselves were soon to accept the total
destruction of all enemy cities as a routine technique in
warfare.

Chapter Eight

WHAT ARE THE *WESTERN* STANDARDS OF VALUE?

WHEN a number of authorities contribute a " symposium " to the B.B.C. on a set subject some of them may think it unfair to be judged some years later by their necessarily compressed remarks in such circumstances. Nevertheless such a series can have lasting value and significance as illustrating the various types of thought fashionable at a given period, and their general trend is of more than ephemeral interest. Some six years ago the *Listener* published a series of broadcasts of this kind on the Western political tradition.[1]

The significant feature in the series was that none of the contributors, except Mr. Christopher Dawson and Canon Demant, even attempted to offer a coherent analysis and defence of the traditional Western culture, beyond a general

---

[1] Sir Ernest Barker restated the formerly orthodox view, at least of all classical scholars, that there was a tradition three thousand years old, built on the Hebrew Prophets and the Gospels, the Greco-Roman heritage, St. Augustine, St. Thomas Aquinas, Locke and Jefferson. It was not one of " Democracy " in either of its modern forms; its essence was the Rule of Law instead of caprice; " a life of expectability." Professor Toynbee said there was no Western tradition; a Western tradition was still in the making. Professor Barraclough said the idea of the triple heritage—Greece, Rome, Christianity— was " a reflection of the liberal ideology . . . a plush and mahogany relic of the rather resplendent prosperity of the late nineteenth century." Professor Barraclough seemed, however, a little shaky on Europe, as he also said— notwithstanding the examples of Belgium, half Holland, and half Germany— that " where Catholicism is politically ascendant the living conditions of the people are intolerably low and its standards of education lower still." The one point of agreement of all the contributors was that they personally valued their own freedom above all else. For Professor G. D. H. Cole " the living tradition of our Western civilization sets the final value on the individual sentient human being; Hegel's idea of the State was mystical nonsense; the great faith of our Western civilization is that men and women matter . . . in the last resort nothing else matters." Mr. A. J. P. Taylor, on the other hand, while he also " cared for liberty above all other political causes," thought it " a strange delusion that the rise of Christianity did anything to improve the position of the individual . . . the only constant thing in European history is that the individual, the ordinary man, has been always pushed around, always exploited." Bertrand Russell's values were intelligence, kindliness and self-respect, but he admitted that science cannot prove that these things are good; still he can believe in ultimate values without giving a reason, " since the matter is not one for rational argument."

opinion that freedom was a good thing. I have italicized the word " Western " values precisely because it has become the fashion in some intellectual circles to refer to them as a meaningless formula (using sometimes the pejorative abbreviation of " W. V's "!). Canon Demant, after referring to the Roman idea of a universal law for all men, and to the Greeks having taught men to get outside the stream of Nature and grasp reality by thought, said that Christianity by insisting on man's special position as a creature made in God's image, had made these two facts a working habit of mind. By giving things a meaning outside society and the State, it gave the human person a significance unknown outside Europe. The overall existence of the Church, something exterior to tribe and class and state, was the root of the European belief in freedom. Man, seeing himself as part of a " cosmic spiritual drama," and feeling his power to make history, developed an historical and scientific habit of mind; and the fact of a common culture without political or economic uniformity, produced the unique diversity in unity which has been Europe. The trend now is to political and economic uniformity without cultural and spiritual unity. Mr. Dawson, summarizing the views he has since brilliantly expanded in his *Understanding Europe*, said the Western tradition is the tradition of Christian peoples, and had represented a new way of life and an abrupt break with the past. The differences between Christians and Pagans or Moslems had not been one of race or language, but a gulf between two spiritual worlds. The transition had been a change not only of religious beliefs but of laws, customs, art, even a new script. For one thousand years citizenship in Western society had been primarily membership of the Church, not the State (which scarcely existed in the modern or Roman Empire sense). The secularist tendency of the last three centuries had detached some Christian principles from their context—the rights of man, liberty, equality (before God), social justice; when the lack of an independent basis for these ideas was realized, men turned to nationalism, class, or race, starting a new world of exclusive antagonistic ideologies which undermine the very existence of Western civilization. For Europe has never been a natural unity, and no political or economic ideology can do what Christianity did. Everything therefore depends on whether our culture and our religion can be reintegrated.

Neither Mr. Dawson nor Canon Demant had space to treat of the Greek and Roman contribution, which in fact fitted into the tradition with remarkable appropriateness; although that heritage has often been described, it is becoming obvious that many intelligent people are unfamiliar with its fundamental importance to us. The unique and novel qualities of the Greek mind were their instinct for relating concrete things to general principles, for seeing things as wholes, their longing for balance, form, symmetry, and their habit of associating moral, aesthetic, and intellectual values. They used the same word for " beautiful " and " honourable," the same word for " base " and " ugly," for " word " and " reason," for " wisdom " and " self-control." Their deep sense of the essential dignity of man and of his weakness before the inexorable ordered pattern of the universe produced Greek tragedy; they founded (as the very names remind us) Drama, Epic Poetry, Mathematics, Philosophy and History. Their idea of the city-state was a small " cosmos " based on the rule of Law, which even " tyrants " had to respect. The rule of Law meant security of personal rights, and this was their primary distinction between Greeks and " barbarians "; Greeks were free men, Barbarians were slaves by nature. Their second distinction was the contrast between their sense of form and balance, of orderly cosmos, and the " chaos " of Asia. They were well aware of the luxury and high culture of the Persian and other oriental monarchies; by " barbarians " they meant, not savages, but people who were both servile and unable to see things whole, in the round. Though they tended to rely too much on pure reason at the expense of fact-finding, they did by its means arrive at the essential grammar (again a Greek word) of philosophy and the sciences. Throughout their greatest period their professed ideals were quality before quantity, honour and all-round competence before wealth, and the amateur instead of the professional in the Army, Law and Politics.[1] The decay of the city-state—before,

---

[1] Plato's Guardian—the professional ruler-philosopher—reflects the decadence of the classic city-state.

and leading to, the Macedonian conquest—was due to the growth of specialization, the breakdown of the traditional morals, and the Athenian attempt at Naval Imperialism instigated by a fusion of commercial and demagogic interests.

Though all this has been said many times, the series in the *Listener* and much other evidence show that it needs re-saying; an outstanding feature of our present crisis is precisely the wide rejection of the Greek insistence on form, balance and general principles. The legacy of Rome is equally discounted. The Roman was, and at heart long remained, a farmer-soldier with a deep sense of devotion to duty and personal responsibility, expressed in the untranslatable words *gravitas* and *pietas*. Though later writers insisted that religion had been the foundation of Roman power, the Roman did not try to impose his ideas, but instead had a genius for making conquered peoples agitate for Roman citizenship. Of his Empire at its peak, Mr. Asquith wrote that " in the one thousand years which followed the birth of Christ, there was no era in which the external conditions of life were so favourable to the happiness of mankind as the reign of the Emperor Hadrian "; and Gibbon thought the period in the history of the world in which the human race was most happy and prosperous was " without hesitation " that from the death of Domitian to the accession of Commodus. This Empire, with its ten-thousand mile frontier, was protected—not held down—by a long-service professional Army of Roman legionaries and local auxiliaries, the two together amounting to well under half a million, and the legionaries were not merely soldiers, but engineers, surveyors, farmers. There were no tariffs between the forty-three provinces, there was no colour-bar or race discrimination; many of the most important later authors were Spaniards or Africans. The Roman roads need no recalling, but the genius for townplanning is obscured by the extent of destruction. The Palatine (hence our word " palace ") was 490 feet long, 160 feet high, 390 feet wide, the Circus Maximus held several hundred thousand people, and not a fragment of either remains; but in solitary places, provincial towns have been excavated, with their rectangular streets, special quarters,

baths, theatres, libraries.[1] When one has had the good
fortune to visit several dozen Roman and Greco-Roman
cities, the cumulative effect (even if the literature had perished)
is an impression of the strength and grandeur of that civilization
which becomes one of those axiomatic certainties so difficult
to communicate to the many who have lost the tradition of it.
Today nearly nine hundred millions live under Roman law
—Turkey, latest recruit, has taken hers from Switzerland; its
basic principle of fixed legal rights for each individual was in
as complete contrast to the arbitrary corrupt practices endemic
in the East as it was to the collective guilt of the German clans
and tribes. The Roman Empire never " fell," in the sense
of any sudden military catastrophe or complete invasion.
There was a long period of decay while the smaller landowners (as usual, the larger ones adapted themselves better),
strangled by overtaxation and an immense parasitical civil
service, abandoned their land to the State, which " froze "
labourers and tenants in their jobs and by degrees applied
the same control of labour to industry; and there was a similar
gradual spasmodic infiltration of barbarians, whose ideal was
to imitate, not destroy, and who adopted the religion of their
new subjects and fused with them. Professor Toynbee, in
speaking of the imposition by the barbarians of their religion
on the Roman Empire is no doubt thinking of Asia Minor.
With the real barbarian invaders it was the other way round.
Few historic myths have more seriously misled opinion than
this of the wholesale invasion, conquest and clean sweep of
the Roman Europe by hostile Germanic tribes; it has masked
the central point that the Empire was gradually transformed,
pari passu with a slow decay of its material wealth (which had
begun long before), into the feudal Christian Europe of the
Dark, and later the Middle, Ages. The Church and the new
barbarian aristocracies tried consciously to salve what they
could, and did in fact preserve the basic elements, above all
the Latin language, so suited by its clear, logical epigrammatic

---

[1] A classic example is Timgad, which I briefly described in a former book;
because I stressed it was now in a " desert," a reviewer explained with heavy
sarcasm that it was not in the Sahara—as though all deserts must be on the
sea level!

character to become the language of all the educated in a common international culture (as it was till recent times) and the perfect vehicle for the new synthetic Christian philosophy built on the Greek Aristotle and the Roman Saint Augustine. Only those who had to translate English into Latin and Greek at school can fully appreciate how difficult it is to be woolly and ambiguous in either language.

In an earlier chapter I referred to some of the darker sides to the Roman character—the absolute legal subjection of the slaves, the monstrous cruelty of the public games. One must also notice the underlying theme of sadness and pessimism which pervades the thousand years of Greek literature, the seven centuries of Roman literature, and the often exquisite funeral monuments. The cultivated Greek and Roman was at heart melancholy, with a pessimistic view of the universe. As regards their own world, the most progressive and energetic people in history (before modern Europe) were always looking back to a primitive Golden Age. This fact emphasizes the curious character of the famous prophecy in Virgil's Fourth Eclogue, which led to his being adopted by mediaeval Christendom as a sort of honorary Christian; " Behold the last age of the Cumaean prediction has come . . . behold the Virgin returns, the reign of Saturn begins again, a new progeny is sent down from heaven," and so on. Though no one can be sure how far Virgil was really prophesying in the line of the Hebrew prophets, only the usual prejudice and lack of critical intuition could have led nineteenth-century scholars to believe that by the " Virgin's son who would inaugurate a new era " a man like Virgil could really mean the son of the Consul G. Asirius Pollio, because he had dedicated the Eclogue to him, and young Pollio said it meant himself!

I have dwelt on the Greeks' concentration on form, balance, symmetry, on their instinctive urge to link fragments into intelligible wholes—qualities which the Romans adopted and passed on to the Romanized barbarians—because they are deeply relevant to the theme of my previous chapter, and to the underlying motive of the Second Part of this book. I am convinced that the dividing line between " Western " civilization and Asia, Africa, and pre-Columbus America was for well over two thousand years the Western search for form, balance, wholeness, and on the other hand the constant tendency to fragmentation, deformity, disunion elsewhere; and secondly that one of the deepest currents under our present crisis has been the slow invasion of the Western mind by these disruptive, dissolving tendencies. In my seventh chapter I stressed the constant growth in the historic religions (Judaism and Greece and Rome excepted[1]) of a preponderant interest in the propitiation, leading to worship, of evil powers, a growth associated with ritual cruelty and bestiality on the grand scale. This cult of evil is associated with a second characteristic, that it generates an artistic expression which revels in the ugly and the heterogeneous, the very spirit of chaos and contradiction. If Greek art is the most free of all arts from diabolism because of its ideal of harmony, reason, and beauty of form, the best example of the other extreme is that of the Aztecs, Mayas and Toltecs in America. The representations of their hideous gods, with which I became familiar during two years in Mexico, produce in a sensitive European a feeling of nausea. Unity of line hardly exists, distortion, abnormality and sheer ugly wickedness are the rule, and the nearest approach to rhythm is a sort of hysterical "jitter-bugging." A similar—though less frightening—riot of the grotesque and unnatural sprawls all over countless temples and shrines in India, mingled with the ubiquitous phallic emblem. The cosmic dancer Siva, father of Ganesa, lord of mischievous monkeys, is both creator god and destroying demon, uniting, Freud would say, the Eros and the death instincts. In his temples the holy o holies is the Linga-shrine, his followers carry the symbolic phallic stone about with them. The temples of the rival popular cult of Vishnu and his " avatars," Radha and Krishna, are equally decorated with phallic pictures and symbols. Siva has his still worse consort, the magical bloodthirsty Kali; small wonder that Ruskin found cruelty a predominant streak in Hindu art. The same association of artistic deformity with the cult of evil is found in the decadent periods of China's long

[1] Of course I only bracket the three under this special heading. The Judaic religion differed radically in its Messianic tradition and in its persistent rejection in principle of polytheism and idolatry.

history, as during the Chou Dynasty (twelfth to sixth centuries B.C.) when the growth of sorcery, polytheism, and slaying of servants to follow their masters (or even to give them the latest news), astrology, and mass executions (Professor Grousset says 400,000 in one year) was accompanied by an art of bits and pieces joined in meaningless patterns.

Now it is a curious fact that the long decline in the West of the inherited standards of value—including, as we have seen, the very processes of thought—is now associated not only with the cult of size and speed and change as substitutes for quality or truth, but also with an increasing prominence in art of an element alien to all Western tradition but characteristic of pessimism and the cult of evil in all times and places. Indeed this element is, amid the many variations of contemporary art— variations typical of a civilization without a common culture and spiritual basis—the specifically " modern " and " advanced " form of art. My comments are based on the principle that purely aesthetic standards are not enough: the artist cannot claim immunity from ethical, philosophic, spiritual judgements.

I am not thinking of the comic excesses of the obviously lunatic fringe which made so much noise (literally in their famous concerts) especially just before and after the 1914 War—Futurism, Dadaism, Expressionism, and so on. I mean the central, typically modern theory of abstract geometrical art combined with, and inspired by, the supposed primitive art of Africa. For practical purposes the movement dates from George Braque's exhibition in 1908 of " Cubist " pictures based on the suggestion—made long before by Cézanne though not practised by him—of the representation of nature in terms of cones, cylinders and spheres. In the previous year Picasso emerging from his " blue period " had painted his " Demoiselles d'Avignon,"[1] with the now familiar

---

[1] Called by M. Raynal " one of the great landmarks in the advance to modern art . . . the work without which Cubism could never have come into existence . . . Picasso concentrated on breaking up the subject piecemeal, then turning and analysing its basic elements as he reorganized them along the lines he fancied . . . reintegrated into a fresh and startling edifice." Quite; but what motive or view of life prompted his fancy to rebuild the elements of the Demoiselles into these grotesque creatures wearing gas-masks ? Nature, M. Raynal explains, had to be made over, as it were, for creative ends—but what are the final creative ends of this art ?

characteristics of dehumanized bodies in dissolution. The background to modern " abstract " art is of deep significance. The broad theoretical object was to interpret abstract ideas independently of accidental detail, using geometrical forms and arranging them in accordance with the dictates of the artist's unconscious. More important, however, in the present connection than the theory itself was the background fact that it was frankly based on admiration for the mask of the African medicine-man and the Ju-Ju idol with its wooden cylinder body and cylinder arms and legs.

I called this the " supposed " primitive art of Africa, for the fetish art which delighted " Les Fauves " fifty years ago was not a genuinely primitive art but the art of degenerate tribes enslaved by witchcraft and diabolism. If the artist claims the right to represent what is in his mind by geometrical forms, the question arises as to what is in his mind—and the outstanding feature is that what they have in their minds is what was also in the mind of the old Oriental, American, and the modern African, devil-worshippers. The interest is not in composition but in decomposition. It is a very disquieting novelty in the Western World to find a real artist like Picasso dedicating himself to the piecing together of nightmare enigmas with no rational principle except unnatural incongruity and disharmony. It is the equivalent of deliberate dissonance, " scientific atonality," and general cacophony in music. Of course the juxtaposing of incongruities (Judge in wig slips on an orangepeel) is a characteristic form of humour, just as a paradoxical Oscar Wildeism is a form of wit; but the spirit of this kind of art is not witty or humorous. A special feature of it is the gloomy malignant relish found in disintegrating and distorting the human face and body, in deliberate contemptuous caricature of the Western tradition of the human personality. Surrealism is closely akin, indeed the word was coined by Apollinaire, the first propagandist of Cubism. It meant originally the discovery of relations between incongruities and became the expression of dreams, phantasies, the unconscious. Sometimes there are significant reminders of the witches' sabbaths of Hieronymus Bosch, whose work was specially   recommended   to   Madame   Cerruti,   Italian

Ambassadress in Berlin, by Himmler the supreme artist in sadism of the Nazi hierarchy. These sinister evocations of the spirit of chaos and disunion have not yet become "popular" in the West but they have long ago gained the first stage by becoming fashionable; large prices are paid, and still-secretly-shocked Philistines mechanically repeat catchwords about "significant form," though the significance of these monstrous patterns is precisely their hatred of "form."

In saying that sometimes there are significant reminders of Hieronymus Bosch I mean no more than that; for in the whole history of Western art over several thousand years there is I believe no analogy at all to Cubism in its various forms. The Beast of the Apocalypse with his seven heads and ten horns, leopard's body and bear's feet, is certainly a queer beast, but definitely a beast. Placed side by side with a fashionable "nude" with two eyes on one side, ears between the nose and the mouth, and propellers or guitars screwed on to represent legs and arms, the Beast would look in comparison like a regimental mascot, or might be preparing to take human children for a ride in the Zoo. Western art has only very occasionally been interested in diabolism—this is one of its distinguishing characters—but when it has in the past taken interest, the evil spirits have been represented either as comic characters with pitchforks or as pigs, goats, monkeys, flying creatures, or horrid little men. The adoption on principle of the real diabolist tradition—the chaotic, the incongruous, the breaking of line and of continuity—is a new phenomenon in Western art.

At first sight it might seem curious that the great revolutionary anti-Western system—the Soviet Empire—should have totally suppressed the whole "left-wing" movement in Western art since the Impressionists. It was, however, logical. For the ruling group, the stability of the new régime and the rapid build-up of industry and war-potential were priorities. The one thing they most wanted to check was any new subversive tendency; they must suppress all novelty not only as potentially dangerous to a totalitarian system but also as likely to distract the citizen from singleminded devotion to four- or five-year plans. The decision was purely one of expediency and policy.

In literature one interesting form of a somewhat analogous tendency is obsession with the subject of evil. Mr. Alan Pryce-Jones, an acute modern critic, has analysed this in a broadcast on " The Cult of Evil." " One of the things about modern literature," he said, " which would most astonish our forebears is the special importance attached by writers to the fact of evil and the peculiar consolations drawn by many of them from that fact . . . a twist shared by writers as various as Mauriac, Graham Greene, Koestler." He refers to Sartre's *Saint Genet Comédien et Martyr*, a preface of 600 pages to works which would be sold by booksellers as *curiosa* to amateurs of the erotic. " Sade has now become an important thinker, a subject for grave biographical studies." Mr. Pryce-Jones says that this new writing starts from either of two premises. One is that categories of good and bad are eliminated straightway, and " in a world where everything is absurd . . . the real Saints are those who accept and exploit their loneliness and sickness . . . the thief, the pervert, the murderer, as soon as they become aware of their exceptional advantages in Society, are already well on the way to Sainthood." The other premise is the theme of reconciling the old theology with extreme naturalist realism, with an implication that only the saints have freewill. This Mr. Pryce-Jones sees as the approach of Graham Greene and Julian Green—and he says that Aldous Huxley, George Orwell, Angus Wilson, Marcel Jouhandeau and the serious American novelists almost to a man agree " that in a life where all is uncertain, one governing factor at least can be relied on; the supreme importance of evil." He shrewdly suggests that this insistence on evil is a consequence of a reluctance to admit the reality of sin, which presupposes an absolute, a perfection to fall from, " whereas evil needs no absolute." After getting so much help from Mr. Pryce-Jones, I am reluctant to disagree with his conclusion. When, however, having advised young writers (very properly) to get back to Scott and Fielding and regain a standard (which their characters could then violate), he says this would at once eliminate the artificial cult of evil, I fear he is under-estimating the gravity of the situation. I fear this attraction to evil is more than a passing literary fashion; it seems another symptom of a general movement, or rather lapse, away from all the canons of art, morals, and reasoning which survived for three centuries the break-up of the spiritual unity of the West, a unity which in its day had inherited them from the classical world and improved them. It had improved them by integrating all that was best in the Greek and Roman cultures with the spiritual world of Christianity and the vitality of the former Northern barbarians; and the growing rejection, and worse, the forgetting, of all this is at the heart of our crisis.

This means that our crisis, on the reality of which all the sociologists cited in Chapter Four agree, is essentially a spiritual crisis, only secondarily a political or economic one. It is not primarily biological. Although the characteristic symptom of denatality,[1] a characteristic symptom of all materialist societies, has had obvious effects on the French national character it is itself only a symptom; and if it were merely a matter of national senility, one should not find it in the United States, where in fact all the signs are rather strongly in evidence. To say that Europe never was a political or economic, but a spiritual, unit, does *not* mean that the Western tradition is identical with Europe—far from it.   Man is everywhere essentially the same; no people is sealed hermetically to the universal appeal of charity and reason, and every people which has really accepted Christianity, and with it the Greek and Roman mental discipline, is a member of the Western tradition.   The tragedy is that the great impact of the West

---

[1] Though sterility is of course sometimes due to biological causes, it is much more often deliberate, i.e. the result of ideas—of a change in standards of value. Mr. Colin Clark, Director of the Institute for Research in Agricultural Economics at Oxford, has recorded that at the World Population Conference of 1954 the exponents of the Anglo-American propaganda for restriction of populations found themselves very much in the minority and that this outlook is earning us a great deal of dislike in Asia and Africa.   The Communists are now telling Asians and Africans that the Anglo-American Imperialists are spreading contraceptive propaganda among them to weaken their military strength.   So far as agricultural resources are concerned, Professor Dudley Stamp showed that the world was at present cultivating only about one-third of the available cultivable land; and the economists representing many African, Asian and Latin-American countries, so far from anticipating a world crisis due to shortage of food and raw materials, complained that they saw no real prospect of their countries earning a satisfactory livelihood by selling such commodities. (*Sunday Times*, March 6th, 1955.)

on Asia, and later on Africa, set in at the very moment when the West was already rejecting its own standards and denying the sources of its own vitality, losing its balance and making material progress its only value. (I have so often heard American friends say that Communism and Xenophobia would end if only every Russian and every Asiatic could see a Sears-Roebuck catalogue!) Thus far I am with Professor Toynbee. I differ profoundly with him when he identifies this cult, and sole export, of technology with the historic Western tradition; and with Bertrand Russell when he identifies the Western tradition with power politics and economic exploitation. I differ because these self-criticisms seem to me contrary to the facts. They ignore the astounding mass-successes of a handful of missionaries in India and Japan (mainly frustrated by the Dutch Calvinistic traders). They ignore the lively interest of Chinese and Indian Emperors in the society and knowledge of the Jesuit missionaries; the Great Mogul rejoiced in public debates between them and the Indian theologians. In recent times, there have been many evidences, especially in China and in Japan, that there is no inherent bar in the Far East to Christianity when presented as a living Faith—not as mainly a purveyor of material benefits in the Baptist-Y.M.C.A. tradition—that only breeds Sun Yat Sen and Chiang Kai-shek and his followers. (Legendre in his *Civilisation Chinoise Moderne* quoted Bertrand Russell as writing in the 1920's that " the young reformers of China were about to set up a human society and a culture infinitely better than the worn-out organism called European civilization." Alas! these young reformers can now only make their new society in Formosa!) The failure to convert Asia has been due to the growing contrast between the missionaries' creed and the increasingly materialist European culture of the last centuries, exemplified in the frankly commercial Empire of the early Dutch and British traders.

These sweeping charges against the Western tradition, of power politics and the sole export of technology, break down under the detailed examination which modern historians have brought to bear. Thus, recent North American scholarship has destroyed a false legend about the Spanish conquest of America

which has had far too long a run. The long conflict between
England and Spain and the fundamental differences in character and temperament between the two peoples have resulted
in an unusual amount of mutual misunderstanding, and there
are few historical subjects on which English opinion has been
so one-sided as that of the Spanish Colonial Empire. This is
highly relevant to the question of the alleged identification of
the West with the exploitation of other peoples. In later
mediaeval Spain, earlier a nursery of Parliamentary Government and Federalism, society was regarded as a cultural
apostolate based on the extension of Spanish authority, not on
the basis of imperialism, sovereignty, and the modern State.
The Law of the Visigoths, the " Fuero Real " and " Seven
Partidas " of Castile, the " Usatges " of Barcelona, the Customs
of Tortosa, were all derived, not from Roman Imperial Law
but from the Visigothic customs and the doctrine of St.
Augustine and Aristotle, finally interpreted by a long line of
Spanish jurists and philosophers from de Vittoria to Suarez.
The Dominican de Vittoria was the true father of International
Law from whom Grotius derived his main system. They
insisted that the norm of government must be justice; government should be a directing agency acting always in obedience
to God in charity and justice. The ideal was the " social
pact," defined as a union of hearts, will and concord. The
Spanish Crown and the jurists set themselves to impose these
concepts on their tough conquistadores in Spanish America;
their inevitable partial failure was the material for the very
partial polemics of Las Casas, also a Dominican, who was the
source of much of the prejudice against Spanish colonialism.
The Spaniards argued among themselves as to the validity of
their title, but in general they accepted the Bull of Alexander VI
as a just title. In practice they insisted that the Indians,
though a part of Spanish society, had separate interests and
must therefore have separate institutions, which were not to be
identical with the Spanish. The Indies were incorporated
(1519) into the Crown of Castile, implying juridical equality
of Castile and the Indies, equal rights for individuals, and
separate institutions. Resisting the temptation to set up an
imperial hierarchy, a Federal system was developed. Economic

development, far from being left to the natural greed of
individual colonists, was the subject of scientific policy with
surveys and census—the *Ordenanzas de poblaciones* of 1573 was
at once a legal code and a whole philosophy of colonization.
There is no equivalent to the efforts of the Spanish Crown to
protect and develop the Indians in the colonization of North
America.   The result can be seen in the survival and
actual predominance of the Indians in all the Republics where
they were already settled at the conquest;   in the general
survival throughout Latin America of a solid social framework
based on the family, which has counteracted the political
instability resulting from mixed populations and local climatic
factors.   Finally, it is usually forgotten that the moral and
intellectual condition of the Latin American Indian and
Mestizo must be compared not with any European nation but
with that of their own ancestors before the Spanish conquest—
and with the fate of the North American Indians, who have
now dwindled to a negligible fraction of the population.   Far
from giving the least credit to the Spaniards for their crusading
spirit and unique achievement, our sympathy was secured for
the buccaneers, whom Andrew Lang accurately described as
" the most hideously ruthless miscreants that ever disgraced
the earth and the sea," with illustrations of " their almost
incredible wickedness."

" Thence we sailed against the Spaniard with his hoards of
plate and gold which he wrung with cruel tortures from Indian
folk of old," sang Kingsley;   but when L'Olonnois was taken
in Nicaragua by the poor Indians they, " being entirely on the
Spanish side, tore him to pieces and burnt him."   It was
L'Olonnois who would " tear out a Spaniard's heart and gnaw
it with his teeth like a ravenous wolf," and Braziliano, who
according to Esquemeling was " beloved and respected by
all," shared Morgan's habit of roasting Spaniards alive on
wooden spits;   Morgan's more appalling cruelties were " not
fit to be told."   One of the poor Indians' favourite devices was
feathering prisoners with thorns wrapped in oily cotton and
set on fire.

This glance at Spanish colonial policy is directly relevant to
the argument that the West has always stood for naked

exploitation and technology; and it has needed dispropor-
tionate space, because the myth of the ill-treatment of the poor
Indians by the " devil-dogs of Spain " is so deep-rooted that a
general statement would be dismissed offhand.[1] But the
fallacy about European exploitation is not merely a misrepresentation of the true Western tradition; it depends on a
still greater misrepresentation of Asiatic history, which needs a
chapter to itself.

[1] If space allowed, it would be easy to show that the case is stronger still in
regard to the Portuguese colonial empire, which, though it made Portugal for a
time one of the richest countries in Europe, was from the beginning *primarily*
a missionary empire. Among the great viceroys in India, João de Castro returned penniless and Constantine of Braganza destroyed a tooth of the Buddha
for which the King of Pegu offered a sum which would have paid off the public
debt of India. The welfare of the natives in Africa, India and Brazil was a constant element in Portuguese policy, and the effect has survived in the obstinate
refusal of the Goanese to unite with the new India. The discoveries of the
great African explorers in the nineteenth century, unknown to them or the geo-
graphers, had been marked on old Portuguese maps by early Portuguese
missionaries centuries before.

Chapter Nine

THE WESTERN HERITAGE: THE ATTACK
FROM WITHOUT

" Thou hast set up altars of confusion " (Jeremias xi.13)

H UMPTY-DUMPTY, a pioneer in mass-suggestion, said that
" if I say a thing three times, it *is* so." Constant
repetition has created the widespread acceptance of a
picture of the world in which the spiritual East, pacific and
tolerant, stands in noble contrast throughout history to the
greedy, materialist, machine-minded, intolerant West. Daniel
Halévy described a typical lecture by Rabindranath Tagore in
Paris when he contrasted " the East which is all spirit " and
" the West which is all machine "; his lecture was followed by
a long murmur of submissive admiration and approval and in
general conversation afterwards Tagore, who had constantly
referred to " love " in his lecture, " hardly concealed from us
his hatred and eager expectation of the catastrophe of Europe."
It was also Tagore who predicted that India would be asked to
" bring her vessel of holy water to sweeten and purify the
human race." Okakura wrote that " Asia is nothing if not
spiritual " (the prisoners-of-war in his compatriots' camps and
jungle roads did not share his opinion). The doctrine offered
by the leading Indian propagandists and their Western
fellow-travellers is a kind of modernized Hindu–Buddhism in a
Western form. Gandhi talked of Ruskin and offered a
" purified religion " including the Bible and the Koran and all
the prophets of the world, just as Coomaraswamy talked of
Blake and Walt Whitman, but to his own people Gandhi
preached acceptance of their own tradition received from
Brahma, including the caste system, idolatry, the Sacred Cow,
and that " the only effort needed is to drive out Western
civilization "; while Coomaraswamy quoted with approval a
Japanese prediction that equality in peace could only be built
on the ruins of the annihilated Western States amid the ashes
of the vanished European peoples. Their gospel of universal

tolerance and a universal amalgamated religion was essentially dishonest, as their propaganda could only have, and was meant to have, a dissolving influence on the utterly incompatible Christian system, while anything they themselves borrowed (it was precious little) is lost in the dreamy bottomless chaos of Indian speculation, itself the prerogative of the high-caste theologians. It is quite impossible to summarize the religion of the Indians as you can the doctrines of Christianity. The popular religion of the mass of Hindus, yes; but over and above it is the fluid stream of subtlety spun on subtlety by the hereditary exclusive Brahmins and their offshoot, Buddhism, a stream of dissolving pictures with no firm basis in reason or revelation. Buddhism ignores Brahmă (the neutral spirit which is the source of Brahmā) and the Vedic ritual and offerings and is concerned only with the *élite* brotherhood seeking Nirvana, but it is based on the essential Brahminical doctrine of the cycle of rebirths which can only be broken by the renunciation of all desire, the rejection of life, and so absorption into the original impersonal All-God.

The high Indian religion, whether Brahmin or Buddhist, is therefore the most pessimistic which has ever occurred to the human imagination. Its whole point is to eliminate the personality, which on the contrary is the mainspring of Christianity and the source of all its activity. Western man has wished to exist, to control nature, to develop his personality in harmony with nature; he has gloried in precise thought and action based on it. For the Brahmins and Buddhists, existence and personality are evil, the world of appearance is unreal, an illusion, and irreformable. All orientalists agree that the Western system of logic is unknown to them, and that the terms used in Sanskrit and European philosophical writings have no reciprocal equivalents. The Western idea of Law does not exist, any more than the idea of the free person and the corresponding ideas of a common good, of the permanent power of renewal and recovery.

The practical consequences of this profound Oriental pessimism and depersonalization have been immense, and I believe they account (apart from climatic factors, also important) for the passivity, stagnation and squalor—a squalor inconceivable to those who have not travelled East—now being presented as spiritual pacifism. First, if life is radically bad and the one goal is escape from personality, there can be no point in seeking justice and social reform. Secondly, the doctrine of Karma—reincarnation—explicitly means that your lot in life, your place in the community, is the penalty or reward for your actions in a previous existence. Caste is therefore the working of inexorable law, and the new Indian democracy still has, in practice and whatever the laws may say, even her sixty million "untouchables." Thirdly, it has always happened—not only in India—that overstressing of the spiritual, subjective side and over-denunciation of the material, lead through the loss of balance between matter and spirit to disorder, followed by passive—or grateful—acceptance of lawless arbitrary authority; and ambitious practical people exploit the situation. They exploit it without any restraint, for the religious guides, having given up matter and everyday life as hopeless, can give no lead in practical matters. This is one reason why arbitrary despotism has been endemic all over Asia, from China to Russia.

The way had been prepared for the appeal of the Gandhis and Tagores by the similarity of Indian thought to some deep tendencies in the divided mentality of Germany. Schopenhauer had predicted that Indian wisdom would flow over Europe and transform our science and our thought from top to bottom, and Fichte had said it was the mission of Germany to link up with Asia. There was a close affinity, a likeness of mental climate, with German philosophy in general, and after the shock of the First World War the German Intelligentsia turned vociferously eastwards, led by Curtius, Keyserling, Scheler, and others, while Romain Rolland led a fifth column in France itself. In England the most important effect has been, characteristically, a sporting feeling—with a streak of unconscious patronage—that we have been taking an unfair advantage over those clever, pacific people; for the higher flights of Brahmin and Buddhist fancy, even in the diluted form of Theosophy, are quite unintelligible to the normal Englishman. The more he understood them, the less he would like them—but usually and wisely he does not try to understand them. The extreme form of the *Mea Culpa* tendency is that popularized by Bertrand Russell. He argues that people who talk about Western values are grossly underestimating the rôle of power politics and exaggerating that of belief and opinion; that power politics have been the mark of the West, and that toleration and love of freedom have been much more practised in the East than in the West, where they were not thought of till the rise of science in the seventeenth century. This is going a lot further even than Professor Toynbee, and both as regards East and West it seems totally unhistorical. The conception of personal freedom within the Law—as expressed for example in the American Declaration and Constitution—is a heritage of the European Middle Ages, derived from St. Augustine and ultimately Athens and Jerusalem, which held its own during the seventeenth century against the Divine Right of Kings and the revival of the Roman Imperial Law, with no help at all from the scientists; but it has never existed in Asia except during our brief period in India. Throughout Asiatic history the one thing that stares you in the face is that the passive resignation of the masses has had its inevitable counterpart in the unlimited tyranny and corruption of their masters, from the kings and emperors down to the lowest official. Until the partial disintegration of Europe threw up Hitler, the West had known no equivalent of the Tartar Khans; but the human-skin lampshades of Belsen or Buchenwald were quite in keeping with Oriental history. Today India and Pakistan are ruled by English-trained idealists of unimpeachable democratic orthodoxy; they were unable to prevent popular massacres—according to their mutual recriminations, on a vast scale—leading to the flight of millions from their respective territories. I quoted earlier the figure of 400,000 executions in one year under the Chou dynasty in China; who knows what the figure of " liquidations " has been under Mao-Tse-Tung?

The element of truth in the theory that Asia has been the home of toleration lies in the character of most of the Oriental religions; the fluid, fanciful speculations of the *élites* and the innumerable polytheist fancies of the masses have turned China and India into a vast exhibition or patchwork of cults.

In China, Buddhism, Confucianism (really an ethical system held by the governing class of the educated), Taoism (also a religion without God), Shinto, have all existed side by side mainly because the governing classes, whether they followed Confucius or Chu Hsi, having no theological dogmas and being only interested in social stability, patronized all the popular cults and the innumerable, often very beautiful, popular festivals, as a matter of expediency. Though the official religion was for seven centuries completely materialist, the young emperor Henry P'u-i performed the sacrifice to heaven for the last time in 1934. Taoism—the 2,400-year-old system of Lao-Tzu—after masses of theory about Yu and Wu (Being and not-Being), Yin and Yang (darkness and light and a good many other things) and K'i (breath), concluded that activity was useless and that the duty of sovereigns is to abstain from activity, and leave the natural course of events alone, except by making sure that their subjects have empty brains and full stomachs. Buddhism, we have seen, is interested only in the Buddhist brotherhood seeking extinction. In short, Chinese religious toleration was based on indifference— provided there was no disturbance to authority and custom—a rather big proviso, as missionaries have frequently found.

In India, the peaceful co-existence of the innumerable sects has been the natural result of the incoherent fluid nature of the religion itself, with no official centre of authority, an enormous mass of sacred books written during several thousand years of which the authentic parts have never been distinguished from the unorthodox, and above all, lacking in precision and logic, form and unity. If your only firm ideal is a general desire to lose yourself in Brahmă, you can well be indifferent to variations in popular religion.

In any case the advocates of this theory of Eastern tolerance apparently overlook Islam, which dominates half Asia and would not be grateful for the intended compliment. None of the great religions keeps such a tenacious hold on the masses as Islam, and though it gets into increasing difficulties whenever a Moslem Government adopts Western institutions and technology, it is actually expanding in Africa and parts of Asia. Has it a message for us? Mahomet started under Jewish and

Christian influences, and though he frankly changed his views on many subjects, and became definitely anti-Christian during his second, or Medina, period, there are curious resemblances. Thus the duty of almsgiving is called " purification," linking it with atonement for sin; the six great previous prophets (out of a hundred) are Adam, Noah, Abraham, Moses, David, Jesus, perhaps seven with Elias; Jesus was the son of a virgin mother,[1] " every human being at birth is touched by Satan except Mary and her son " (though original sin is unknown to the Koran). Ramadan is the Moslem Lent. Before the end of the world an Anti-Christ will march on Jerusalem and Jesus will descend and kill him. Devotion to the saints is officially forbidden, but anyone who has lived in Moslem countries knows that it is extensively practised; the tomb or relics of a holy man convey all the virtues comprised in the untranslatable Arab word *baraka*. These borrowings, however, are only incidentals. The essentials are, first, belief in God, the angels, the holy books, the prophets, the resurrection and judgement, predestination, the prayers five times daily; and secondly, the doctrine of the Holy War. This is not an accidental development mixed up with politics or popular pressure as so much Christian persecution has been, but an integral part of the Islamic Constitution. Mahomet laid down that the faithful " must slay the unbelievers wherever they found them," that fighting for Allah was the most meritorious of all actions. Mahomet said he would have no monks; " Holy War is the monasticism of Islam." The practice of Islam has been that once conquest is achieved, the unbelievers are an inferior subject minority, not privileged to fight but made the main source of revenue. This incidentally made a great economic appeal to its converts in Asia Minor, by relieving them from Byzantine taxes and debts and making them one with the

---

[1] The officially secular Turkish Government have recently built a motoring road to the traditional mountain-top home of Mary and St. John the Divine, near Ephesus, and though this is of course meant for Christian pilgrims, the shrine is visited by Moslems who light candles and buy medals. There is also an interesting Moslem cult of the Carmelite Saints. The wife of a high Turkish official told me she wore a medal of St. Thérèse of Lisieux, and Sidky Pasha, an Egyptian Prime Minister, made a large donation in the Saint's honour to a Carmelite church.

conquerors. But conquest whenever possible is a duty. Hell is the irrevocable penalty of all unbelievers, while Moslem sinners after a temporary period in Gehenna reach heaven and are served by eternal youths with a wine which gives the elect no headaches (" nor shall their wits be dimmed ") and by gazelle-eyed maids " with modest glances and swelling breasts " who would remain miraculously virgins. Wine, games of chance, the representation of living creatures, are forbidden (the Wahabis added music, dancing and all games); polygamy up to four wives, and unlimited slave concubines, are allowed.

The greatest Moslem philosopher, Averroes, who tried to reconcile Islam with Plato and Aristotle, agreed that the Divine Law revealed by Allah (the Shari'a) should be the complete foundation of the ideal Moslem State, and distinguished between the intellectual *élite* with an intelligent faith, and the masses who must have uncritical faith in the external literal sense of the beliefs; otherwise confusion and even schism would arise. Averroes however also boldly said that the inferior position of women was one of the reasons for poverty, as it made them a burden on the men.

I think the conclusion is that the strength of Islam lies in its simplicity, its easy attitude to sex for men, and in its essential fanaticism which creates a real feeling of brotherhood among the elect. Its weaknesses lie in the lack of a rational foundation, in the incompatibility between its practices and the balanced use of all our faculties; both weaknesses result in an inherent conservatism which makes adaptation to more complex forms of society impossible. Islam is a great fighting faith which up to a point improves its pagan converts, and its members were just defeated in time at Poitiers, Lepanto, and again in 1683; but it has no spiritual or intellectual message for the West. I, too, have " heard the East a'calling," and feel profoundly its fascination; but here I have to concentrate on the relevant point that the whole thesis of the spiritual and ethical superiority of the " East," over the Western tradition (until its recent weakening), breaks down wherever we disregard general statements and get down to the concrete facts.

Chapter Ten

THE WESTERN HERITAGE: THE ATTACK
FROM WITHIN

I HAVE left to the last the problem of the attack from within, because I think it is the real core of the whole subject. The society of Christian peoples inhabiting the Eurasian peninsula have always had in their midst a factor of division and disorder; I mean the still unfinished conflict which divides the soul of one of Europe's most vital and energetic peoples, the Germans. It is nothing less than a struggle between the Christian order and the old Germanic mythology for the soul of a people.

Germany has never had a "geographical personality." Open on both east and west, with no natural frontiers, no natural centre or capital, her nationality depended on race and language. The struggle between foreign influences and self-preservation, the mutual hatred of the German tribes, could only be controlled by authority, ideas, and will-power. The greatest disaster in European history was the loss of Varus' three legions in the Teutoberg Forest in A.D. 9 which resulted in only Western Germany being incorporated in the Roman Empire. This was not in the least inevitable. The German invaders of Gaul had been defeated by the Romans at Orange and Aix-en-Provence, and later by Caesar; Germanicus, after Varus' defeat, reconquered the land up to the Elbe, and the eventual Germanic infiltration of the declining Empire did not take place for several centuries. In a criticism of Professor Toynbee's emphasis on spiritual values, Bertrand Russell wrote that " What really happened was that the barbarians beat the Romans in battle." I think it would be more accurate to say that until the moral breakdown of Roman society the Romans were not only capable of beating the Germans, but would have imposed their civilization for good, as in Gaul, the Rhineland and Austria, if the emperors, haunted by the memory of the lost legions, had not voluntarily withdrawn to the Rhine, so that only the Rhineland and Austria were integrated into the European tradition. Owing to this fateful decision Christianity never thoroughly got hold of the German soul, and the resultant schizophrenia, the inner contradiction of " the two Germanies," intensified by the rise of the non-German Baltic Prussians, has been a major cause of Europe's decline.

The primitive German soul has been profoundly analysed by modern French historians, and with especial penetration by the Swiss historical philosopher Count Gonzague de Reynold, and I make no claim to originality in this summary. The spirit of the Nordic (i.e., Germanic and Scandinavian) paganism remained very much alive in the emotional sub-conscious of the German people, was deliberately fostered as a protest against foreign, chiefly Latin, influences, and in the last two centuries reappeared as the real inspiration of the German philosophy which has so deeply influenced the West. From the sixteenth century onwards the old pagan spirit rose nearer and nearer the surface, and boiled up as Nazism after the crash of 1918. The original mythology which expressed this soul before any foreign influences came was heroic, pessimistic and dynamic, an outlook dominated by catastrophe, predestination, and perpetual movement. Valhalla must be stormed by the elect few, whose only moral virtues should be force and fidelity to leader and group. The mental climate was pantheist, full of intangible shadows, with no interest in stability or finality; the exact contrary of the Greek paganism with its clear-cut statues and innate longing for order and definiteness. The fundamental feeling was for action for the sake of action, for perpetual " becoming " (rather than for " being," which implies ideals of balance, measure, and stability). It was the ideal religion of the born revolutionary, wanderer, and pessimist. The ancient hatred of limitation by definite forms was manifest in the panic fears of " encircle-ment " before the 1914 War; a kind of claustrophobia. This religion of action for its own sake, of pantheism (i.e., no personal God outside man and nature), of fatalism and pessimism, was kept alive by the Nibelungen, and blossomed out in German philosophy from Kant and Hegel to Nietzsche, in the Romantic movement in literature, and reached full recognition in Wagner and the " Aryan " race-worship. The keynotes of German philosophy are avoidance of pure reasoning, and concern with the " Eternal Becoming." The World is Will; in the Beginning, as Goethe said in *Faust*, was Action. Tending always to make nature itself divine, it slipped naturally into Fichte's making a god of German nationalism, and Hegel's making a god of the Prussian State. The ultimate " Thing in itself " being unknowable, German philosophy lapses easily into pure materialism and instinct, whether the economic materialism of Marx, Nietzsche's will to power and superman, Schopenhauer's total pessimism, or the Nazi deification of soil and blood. The close relationship to the Hindu and Buddhist world-view is obvious, and both Indians and Germans have fully recognized this. It led inevitably to the gospel of the mission of the German race to regenerate the decadent Western world, which was the motive of Wagner's vast drama, wherein music, poetry and thought combined to exalt the restlessness and heroic pessimism of ancient Germany. It issued in Pan-Germanism, anti-Semitism, and finally Nazism. Wagner was an admirer of the Aryan-Race philosopher Conte de Gobineau, and it was no mere coincidence that his daughter married Houston Stewart Chamberlain, the spiritual father of Hitler and Goebbels.

After the voluntary withdrawal of the Roman Empire to the Rhine, a series of efforts were made to unify Germany on a Christian-European basis. It was attempted by Charlemagne, whose Frankish Empire disintegrated under his grandsons; by the Saxon Holy Roman Emperors, whose efforts failed through their quarrels with the Papacy; and finally by the Austrian Habsburgs. The Habsburgs represented the " other Germany " and the unity of Central Europe against Pan-Germanism and the " Balkanization of Europe " by the Slavs. In the sixteenth century the Emperor Charles V failed, having to deal on two fronts with the German Lutheran princes and the invading Turks. In the seventeenth century the Thirty Years' War ended in a draw, after reducing Germany to ruin and semi-barbarism for well over 100 years, because Richelieu, thinking exclusively in terms of French national advantage, threw the weight of France behind Gustavus Adolphus and the German Protestant princes. Had the latter been winning, he would presumably have backed Austria in order to prolong the war and keep Germany divided. The failure of the Habsburgs left the field clear for the Prussian State and Army to unify Germany as a militant anti-European empire. Prussia, originally a Slav tribe, was for centuries a State with an army but without a nation, a political idea incarnated in the Hohenzollern dynasty.[1] Their dominions were scattered—Prussia, Brandenburg, Pomerania, Cleves and others—and their assets were discipline and the will to succeed. What they accomplished, the Germans themselves had failed to do because they could never decide between the rival attractions of racial mysticism and Western Christianity.

The real turning point was in the consequences of the German Reformation and its French offshoot, Calvinism, which in turn produced the French civil wars of religion, Dutch Calvinism, Scots Presbyterianism, and the English Puritan sects. Of course the German Reformers at first professed to be entirely concerned with theology, so much so that at first the outbreak was thought to be a monkish dispute between two schools of Augustinians; the immediate, and still more the later, consequences are a classic example of the way revolutionary movements and ideas take charge of events and sweep on by their own momentum. For (excluding for the moment all but historical considerations) the German reform led to the complete despotism of the princes, with the clergy as their servants; to the division of Germany into two hostile camps, excluding Austria from Germany but admitting Swedish and French intervention; to an appalling fall in the

[1] A striking feature of the rise of Prussia was the gradual ascendancy obtained in the German Universities—beginning naturally with Berlin—by the schools of philosophers and historians who made a cult of the Prussian State and the Hohenzollern Dynasty. This bias of the historians is too well-known to need amplifying, but a curious illustration is given by the Conte de Chambrun from the domain of theology. Professor Harnack, best-known in England of all the German theologians and " Higher Critics," referred during the bicentenary celebration of the Berlin Academy to Kaiser Wilhelm as " an Instrument of Heaven," and a " Minister of God," and expressed his gratitude to his " Sublime Protector King and Master."

general social level. Outside Germany, the French religious
wars favoured the over-centralization of the monarchy, the
long quarrel with Austria, the French Revolution, the division
of nineteenth-century France into two hostile camps, and with
that, the dechristianizing of French State Education, and
ultimately the paralysis of will and government in modern
France.

As with all revolutions, we have to distinguish between
Luther's actual beliefs; the practical driving-force which led
to success when so many forerunners had failed; the actual,
mostly unforeseen results; and in his case, his personality has
to be noticed as well. In the form of his beliefs Luther had
first and last a purely theological and scriptural outlook in
the most narrow and literal sense (" a reactionary heresy with
its eyes fixed on the past "), and was fiercely opposed to
rational argument. " Logic is nowhere necessary in theology
because Christ does not need human inventions "; in spiritual
affairs " Reason is the devil's greatest whore . . . a whore
eaten by scab and leprosy who ought to be trodden under
foot and destroyed . . . banished to the filthiest place in
the house, the closets." Aristotle was " the Godless bulwark
of the Papists . . . an urchin who must be put in the
pigsty." He is largely responsible for the widespread fallacy
that Faith and Reason are opposed to each other. He broke
with Zwingli (" the incarnation of lying, deceit and
hypocrisy ") originally because Zwingli had said Socrates
might be saved, whereas Luther said the Gospel was useless
if its benefits covered heathens. As Professor Pollard wrote
in the *Cambridge Modern History*, " Tolerance was not in his
nature and concession in Church or State was evidence of
indifference or weakness." Luther's hatred of reason was a
necessary part of his doctrine. His teaching was based on the
principle that the human will is impotent and that God is
directly responsible for the evil in the world. Man being
radically vicious owing to original sin, could gain nothing
(except in the world) by actions and works; salvation depended
exclusively on baptism, faith and the grace of God. The new
Protestant doctrine of faith without works, when established
and spread from Geneva by Calvin, in his special form of

predestined election, had far-reaching social effects. It reversed the mediaeval teaching which had regarded avarice as far worse than improvidence or idleness, and had made charity a prime duty. As Sir G. N. Clark says, " types of character or conduct were now admired and imitated which had not previously been held up to admiration "; the proverb " as cold as charity " would have been unintelligible in the Middle Ages. The now familiar discovery by Max Weber, Troelsch, Werner Sombart, Mumford, and R. H. Tawney of the organic link between Calvinism and modern capitalism must not obscure the fact that capitalism in itself was already in existence; the point is that capitalism and eventually the Industrial Revolution would have developed in a different form and spirit, more slowly and equitably. Mediaeval businessmen like mediaeval kings, were expected to be " under God and the Law," and this was not a pious expression but a real pressing climate of public opinion. Bishop Pecock had thought it necessary to insist that " the rich *as such*, are not hateful to God." This is less a matter of laws and institutions —though these were completely changed—than of spirit—the difference between Dick Whittington feasting among his retainers and the Victorian businessman in his six-storey house with the servants hidden, when not on duty, in the basement and attics; between the spirit of the mediaeval guild and that of the prison-workhouse and the " grim satanic mills." The abstraction of money was substituted for the ideal of welfare.

If Luther would have been furious to hear that he would one day be widely hailed as a champion of rational free enquiry, he would have been hardly less angry at being regarded as a pioneer of democracy. To quote again Professor Pollard in the *Cambridge Modern History*, " Luther in fact saved the Reformation by cutting it adrift from the failing cause of the peasants and tying it to the chariot wheels of the triumphant princes." Professor Pollard says the peasants' demands were " purely agrarian and extremely reasonable," that it was the lords who were the revolutionists and the peasants the reactionaries; and that there is no reason to suppose they would have used force if they had not been opposed by force.

What was Luther's reaction? In his tract of May 1525 he urged the princes to kill the peasants " like mad dogs," and (in Mahomedan fashion) he promised heaven to those who fell in the holy work. In fact at least 100,000 peasants were killed; in Kitzingen 59 townsfolk were blinded by Margrave Casimir of Brandenburg. Quite apart from the peasants' revolt, Luther said that all servants should be treated like " other cattle," and Melanchthon said serfdom was too mild for the Germans and that the masters' rights of punishment must be unlimited. The princes' wishes came to be regarded as divine, and in the famous case of the Landgrave Philip of Hesse's bigamy, Luther and Melanchthon advised him that it was legitimate but must be kept secret. " The secret yes must for the sake of Christ's Church remain a public no."

Contrary to general belief, Luther did not himself assert the infallibility of the Bible, but only of the parts with which he agreed, and this brings us to the effect of his own personality which accounted for his tremendous impression on the German soul. He said he did not admit that his doctrine could be judged by anyone, " even by the angels," and that " he who does not receive my doctrine cannot be saved." Carlyle called Luther " a Christian Odin, a right Thor," and he did in fact personify the primeval German soul. He personified it in his love of music (shown in his greatest achievements, his hymns and his German Bible), his hatred of logic and reasoning, his imagination, his restless overflowing exuberant energy, and above all in his stark egoism. For Luther was a pure Romantic, governed by his will and his feelings; he did not think-out a system and then revolt; the revolt came first, and it was against his monkish vow of celibacy. There has been almost a conspiracy to ignore all the sensuous side of Luther's character, but he did not try to hide it himself. It was not only that he said " What is needed to live in continence is not in me," and " it does not lie in my power to live without a wife." He also said that " Nothing can cure lust, not even marriage," and that " the work and word of God tell us clearly that women must be used for marriage or prostitution . . . let them die so long as they bear children, they are made for that." As Denifle says, some of his writings are of a type rarely found even in the most depraved authors, and one of his observations, which I learned over 40 years ago, was so obscene that I have never felt able to repeat it even orally. He wrote to Catherine Bora boasting that he gorged like a Czech and soaked like a German, and he habitually and conscientiously mixed up his evangelical teaching with frantic abuse, obscenities, and defence of lying in a good cause. Duke George of Saxony called him the coolest liar he had ever known, and he said himself in connection with Philip of Hesse's bigamy, what harm would there be in telling a good big lie for the sake of the Christian Church?

Though his doctrine was of universal application, based on original sin and predestination, Luther tried to set up a German popular National Church; instead he left the Church as a department of State. He left also an intensified serfdom, and a state of Anarchy which only ended when the Thirty Years' War had destroyed half the population of Germany. But he also left a revival of the old German spirit, a profound reaction against the Western culture represented by the Austrian, still nominally Holy Roman, Empire; and fatally encouraged the primeval German instincts to pessimism and the will to power. (Incidentally, his last sermon four days before his death was a furious invective against the Jews, demanding their expulsion from Eisleben.) Professor Pollard concluded that " the Reformation began with ideas and ended in Force," but this was true in a deeper sense than the merely political fact of the Peace of Augsburg (which laid down that the religion of each state must be that of the prince). The bearing of all this on the Western heritage cannot be better stated than in the words of the late Dean Inge, writing in the *Church of England Newspaper* on August 4th, 1944: " If we wish to find a scapegoat on whose shoulders we may lay the miseries which Germany has brought upon the World . . . I am more and more convinced that the worst evil genius of that country is not Hitler or Bismarck or Frederick the Great, but Martin Luther. . . . There is very little to be said for this coarse and foul-mouthed leader of a revolution. It is a real misfortune for humanity that he appeared just at the crisis in the Christian World. Even our own burly

Defender of the Faith was not a worse man, and did far less mischief."

The Reverend A. M. Fairbairn, Principal of Mansfield College, writing on Calvin in the *Cambridge Modern History*, said that Luther being entirely German had no sense of intellectual consistency, and that " the personal cause which most of all contributed to the creation of the reformed Church as history knows it, was John Calvin." For Calvin, a Northern Frenchman, was a fine scholar, a born administrator, and an only too clear thinker. By a set of curious historical circumstances, he was able to establish a political and missionary headquarters at Geneva, which he made into a model totalitarian theocracy. The party which accomplished the revolution in Geneva were called the Confederates or " Eygenots," and Calvin's French missionary pastors—at least 161 were sent out between 1555 and 1566—spread the " Huguenot " fifth column all over France, then converted Holland and Scotland. Geneva was organized on the basis of his theology. Man being born in sin, and his nature corrupt, so were all his actions. He could do nothing for his own salvation. God did it all (if He wished), therefore the State must be a pure theocracy, and its civil law a branch of moral theology. The ministers were to be under the State in purely civil matters, the magistrates under the Church in all Church matters. A synod meeting every three months, and a consistory which met every Thursday, were charged to have their eyes on everyone, with the right of entry and investigation and no appeal. The offences included obstinate refusal to communicate and absence from church, " dressing a bride too gaily "; card players were put in the pillory, and a woman was flogged through the streets for singing a secular song to a psalm tune.

A volume could be written filled with illustrations of the moral and social effects of these appalling doctrines and the wars and persecutions which filled the century after Luther and Calvin. I have alluded to the economic effects. Sir John Adamson, Professor of Education at London University, wrote in 1920 that " the immediate consequence of the Reformation was not favourable to public education:

Universities and schools suffered a declension which persisted
for more than a generation . . . the most successful schools
of the period following the beginning of the Reformation were
the Jesuit Colleges." Professor E. O. James, Professor of
Religious History and Philosophy in London University, says
in his *Marriage and Society* that the return by Luther and Calvin
to the Jewish Scriptures revived the patriarchal conception of
the family " under the despotic rule of the male progenitor
with a corresponding disparagement of women as the inferior
sex." Luther denied the sacramental character of marriage,
" and condoned polygamy in theory," as did Milton and others.
The Calvinistic interpretation of the Fall, continues Professor
James, implied the complete subjection of the wife, and
therefore as civil marriage took shape, legislation limited the
right to own property to the husband. " In short," he
concludes, " the Protestant bid for freedom was essentially a
masculine conception of the rights of man in which women
shared not as independent personalities but as the adjuncts
of the all-powerful male." An interesting study might be made
of some curious analogies between Islam and the early Puritans.

A remarkable product of the German and Geneva
Reformation was the veritable obsession with demonology and
witchcraft, and the wave of persecution which had no analogy
in the previous ages. In Scotland, for instance, the first Act
of Parliament imposing the death penalty for witches, in 1563,
was expressly instigated by John Knox, and Melvill tells of
one wretched woman who before being burned had to endure
one of Knox's sermons: " the Quhilk Mr. Knox—that maist
notable servant of God—dealt from the pulpit, she being set
up at a pillar before him." The storm which prevented Ann
of Denmark arriving for her marriage with James VI (First
of England) was revenged by a holocaust of witches. Some
estimate that there were during the period fifty thousand
executions in Germany, Belgium, and France. The difference
from the mediaeval period was first the vastly increased scale
and secondly that it was due to official religious guidance
rather than to popular initiative. Further, though witch mania
infected all Europe, it was particularly associated with the
followers of Luther and Calvin; in Denmark and Transylvania

witch-burning only started after the Reformation, and Lecky in his History of England said that " more persons have perished on that ground in a single year in England and Scotland than in the whole recorded history of Ireland."

My object in bringing out these facts has been to underline that the Lutheran movement in the form it took and in the intention, was in no sense a movement for freedom of enquiry and discussion, the scientific spirit, political democracy, or social reform.   Puritanism was a violent setback to all these; its ideal was an aristocracy of the born saints, living under despotic princes in Germany, or a theocracy in Geneva. " Nor do I name of men the common rout, but such as thou hast solemnly elected," sang Milton; as G. K. Chesterton said, Milton was so successful with the character of Satan because he was rather like Satan himself.   Above all, the whole movement was inspired by what the historic Western Christendom had considered the one supreme sin—spiritual pride.   " Our soldiers had the sins of men, wine and wenching," said the cavalier to the Roundhead, " yours had the sins of devils, spiritual pride and rebellion."   The whole outbreak was a stab in the back to the Western tradition, and its after-effects are still expanding.

Chapter Eleven

SO WHAT?

THE underlying theme of this book is that the crisis of our civilization is primarily a spiritual crisis and that our political and economic difficulties are its surface manifestations. Failure to realize this is natural if the crisis is itself ultimately due to false ideas about the nature of man and society. Modern psychiatry is tending to act on a basis which is consistent with the central Christian tradition; the tradition that man is a composite creature of body and soul or, in modern terms, of body and psyche. In his biological functions man belongs to the animal world, but at some unknown date a biped physically resembling man acquired a human personality and became thereby a unique creature different in kind to all other living things, a personality or body-spirit so varied and paradoxical that his reactions cannot be measured or predicted on any mechanical scientific basis. He is capable of the most opposite extremes. On one hand of unlimited self-sacrifice for spiritual motives, of analysing his own mental processes and the Laws of the universe; of attaining to a balanced harmonious integration of his whole person and of expressing it in creative work marked by form, balance and harmony. Capable on the other hand of unlimited cruelty, selfishness and materialism, of conflict and divisions inside his personality expressed in creative work which is formless, disconnected, incongruous; capable—and this has been the normal state of the majority—of living in ignorance and making no mental effort beyond the minimum required by his daily work. The contradiction between his unlimited aspirations and his finite limitations is an unending source of internal conflict, mal-adjustment, discontent and perversity. The way to self-control and integration is through humility and self-denial; the negation of this is spiritual pride and revolt, ultimate source of wrong thinking and wrong action.

2. This spiritual personality has not essentially varied since

it first appeared. In his various civilizations man has acquired (and often lost) a great knowledge of nature and made great technological achievements, but there is no evidence that his mental *capacity* and moral *nature* have undergone any evolutionary modification. Christian heresies which insisted that his moral nature was totally corrupt and depraved, " humanists " who believed in his infinite perfectibility by his own sole efforts, were both wrong, but the former had the more factual justification. The outstanding fact in man's moral history is his constant tendency to lapse into moral degeneracy culminating in a conscious cult of evil; this is not a primitive trait but apt rather to coincide with an improvement in material technique.

3. This conception was totally rejected in the later nineteenth century by a new philosophy which in practice superseded the older rationalisms. It applied to mankind the dogma of evolution through natural selection, asserting as a scientifically established fact that man in all his aspects had evolved by a purely mechanical process from an animal condition. It assumed a natural transition from organic to mental life and a gradual broadly continuous moral progress and growth in creative capacity. This was a speculative theory suggested by the analogy of the physical sciences, but it was accepted as a proved scientific law and became the basic axiom of all the new or re-created sciences dealing with man.

4. The five main human sciences—psychology, anthropology, the comparative history of religions, history, and sociology—were all given their modern form by men who accepted these philosophic assumptions as proved facts. One of my main objects has been to suggest that these branches of study were initially falsified by the fixed idea that the facts must be forced to conform to the *a priori* theory; that later workers in each department have been building a different picture, and that in each case the resulting tendency is leading back, often unintentionally, to the central Christian tradition of man's nature and destiny.

5. Modern psychology undoubtedly dates from Freud's emphasis on the unconscious, on the influence of the irrational sources on conduct and ideas. Unfortunately all his work

was based on the presupposition that the forces moving human nature were exclusively biological and that all mental phenomena were derived from impulses. His system contained a substratum of selected manipulated mostly abnormal facts, a string of scientific hypotheses, and a whole elaborate philosophy of life based or rather superimposed upon them. His system assumed that satisfaction was the only form of pleasure; it left no room for a continuous mental life, no room for the ego or soul, no room for freedom or free will. He derived the whole structure of the personality from his one constructive force, the "libido." I have tried to indicate the successive stages of the development of modern psychology; Adler's work on the social factors (the will to community against the will to power); Jung's work on the collective unconscious and in developing the psychotherapist's true aim of educating the individual to moral freedom and independence; finally the tendency of the later American and other schools to act on a constructive theory of the personality as a coherent whole, at once physical, social and spiritual, with a dynamic purposeful unity which is the source of all behaviour and the whole psychic life.

6. In anthropology and the overlapping study of comparative religions, the early history of culture and religion was turned upside down to suit the presuppositions. Obvious facts like palaeolithic art or the beliefs of existing primitive peoples were ignored or given absurd explanations—as that primitive men did not know about sex and did not know when people were dead. The theory implied that the life of primitive man was, as Hobbes said, "nasty, brutish and short," without morals, religion or art; that later he gradually "evolved" through superstition and magic to polytheism and then monotheism, from scratching doodles to the art of Phidias and Rembrandt, from imitative sounds to Cicero and Demosthenes, from communal promiscuousness to monogamous marriage, and so on. If one thing is superior to another, it must for that very reason have come later. Sometimes, owing to the absence of written records, the early anthropologists had more excuse than the scholars who—again from *a priori* assumptions—distorted and discredited the unique documentary records of the most

important of all religious histories, that of the Jewish nation and early Christianity. Their tendentious pseudo-criticism which they called " Higher Criticism " had a specially undermining effect among the Christian clergy,[1] inspiring a revival of ancient heresies incompatible with Christian ideology, under the attractive but unwarranted label of " Modernism." The general trend of the evidence indicates that magic and polytheism, and all the derivative ritual of human sacrifice, phallic worship, sorcery and general diabolism, are comparatively late lapses from primitive monotheism; that they are apt to be associated with material progress; and that this is equally true of polygamy and slavery. This is not to say that they invariably coincide with material improvement; but that there is no equation between material and moral improvement. Neither is there any support in fact or logic for the particularly silly theory of a gradual progressive development by minute stages of the power of artistic creation.

7. History proper—the study of man based on his documentary records—has not escaped the befogging influence of the myth of inevitable progress. Historians have tended first to justify success as both inevitable and right, secondly to attribute it to the action of the ideas which it finally comes to represent, thirdly to justify its further effects because they are its effects and therefore also right and inevitable. In discussing the old perspectives in history I cited the French Revolution as a classical case of a false historical legend. Misrepresentation of that great upheaval has clouded the judgement of succeeding generations on their own current affairs. Because the French Revolution was judged to be both inevitable and the result of conscious volition, and therefore right, its disastrous consequences have been condoned, including the economic wastefulness of conscription with its logical conclusion in " total " war; the implacable unreasoning hysteria of modern nationalism (Europe's boomerang gift to Asia); the dogma that you and I have absolutely no rights whatever which a majority vote cannot lawfully take away

---

[1] " Modernism " is now so " dated " that it is hard to believe that as late as 1925 Dr. Jacks could write in the *Hibbert Journal* that the *future of Christianity* depended on the result of a controversy between Loisy and Harnack!

from us. It is regarded as axiomatic that it was at least an immense benefit to France; yet France, once the greatest nation and the cultural model for Europe, now has half the population of Germany (which was unified and nationalized by the French Revolution), and has been torn for nearly two centuries by a corrosive " cold " civil war; has enjoyed 13 Constitutions since 1789, had 93 Governments during the 65 years of the Third Republic, and 16 Governments in the last seven years, and, out of these seven years, six months altogether during which there was no Government at all. Depopulation, political instability, religious war, class-war, and German supremacy, have been among the direct fruits for France of the Revolution; these are indisputable facts, but the official textbooks of the French Republic and English and American Liberalism have consistently disregarded them.

8. Ideas play so great a part in affairs that the analysis of their subtle far-reaching effects should be the historian's most important duty; but too often their action has been over-simplified, exaggerated or minimized. An aspect of their influence which is frequently ignored is the effect of subversive criticism, not in spreading a definite new belief, but in creating a climate of doubt and bewilderment and thereby under-mining the self-confidence of the active minorities who influence the course of affairs. I have cited as illustrations the spirit created in the eighteenth century by the French Intellectuals— hardly any of whom anticipated or desired the Revolution —and the effect on ourselves in this century of H. G. Wells and Bernard Shaw and, one might add, of Sigmund Freud after they had lost hope. Shaw had incomparably more wit and mental fertility than Wells, but Wells with his second-hand and second-rate ideas exerted equal or greater influence through his great power as an imaginative novelist; and he never wrote a better novel than his *Outline of History*, which carried into millions of English homes a colourful rehash of the Rationalist Press Association's outfit of thirty years earlier. The active executive politically conscious minority became unable to see where they are going or to be sure of what they want; they cease to give an intelligent lead, and instead look themselves for a lead from mass " public opinion." Nineteenth-

century Liberalism had given the active minority (apart from those who had the moral courage to oppose it) a clear fighting creed of which the backbone was the passion for personal liberty. Unfortunately it adopted as well the principles of equality and unlimited majority rule, which when fully developed in association with a completely materialist standard of values seldom " coexist peacefully " with personal freedom. In Europe it also took over from the French Revolution, as a main tenet, a fanatical secularism, and worked for the exclusion from all influence of its opponents, though not often so indiscreetly as in the " Affaire des Fiches."[1] It used all the resources of the State, especially through education, to undermine belief in the unique value and dignity of each human soul, although in the last resort this belief is the only rational justification of personal freedom. Liberalism was a useful corrective but a bad master; it could not control the forces it had released and it perished in the shock of the First World War, leaving the way clear for its opposites—Nazism, Fascism, and Communism.

9. My chief motive in Part One of this book was not so much to advance particular opinions as to illustrate the woolliness and confusion of twentieth-century opinion attributable to the general breakdown of standards of judgement and the undue influence of uninformed mass opinion. I cited the confusion between diplomacy and foreign policy, muddled thinking about the relations of armed strength and foreign policy, and the historically unprecedented degree in which from 1918 onwards shams and catchwords uncritically reiterated were substituted for reality in international affairs. There has never been an age in which the fable of the emperor and his clothes was so applicable. In the case of England I

---

[1] In 1905 it was revealed in France that some of the most promising Army officers, including the future generals Foch and de Castelnau, were systematically spied on and denied promotion if they attended religious services. The President of the Council of the Grand Orient, Lafferre, boasted that " cette surveillance traditionelle de ceux qui ont la charge de gérer les intérets de l'état a toujours été une des obligations et des préoccupations de la franc-maçonnerie," which had " le droit de controler et le gouvernement et les fonctonnaires et les députés et les senateurs." The President of its Assembly, Augagneur, said at the same time that " La Maçonnerie a un rôle supérieur à tous les partis politiques."

contrasted the irresponsible treatment of the colonial peoples
with the sane and progressive policies of smaller nations
applying the Roman imperial tradition. The modern English
attitude to their colonial responsibilities is an example not
only of confused thought and unrealism, but of a curious
mingling of lack of self-confidence with an arrogant over-
confidence in the virtue of British Parliamentary institutions.

10. A valuable corrective to orthodox history and all social
sciences affected by the Progress myth has been supplied by
the modern sociologists. No one of the various cycle theories
agrees in its classifications with the others and is factually
adequate in itself; or indeed can be, for all such theories are
inherently pessimistic and exclude both chance and free will.
They have however established an important body of significant
facts, analogies and rhythmic patterns, and though no two
systems or classifications coincide, the points on which they
do agree carry great weight for that reason. Points on which
they all agree are first that the long line of past civilizations
have passed through certain broadly similar stages and have
each in turn perished by a process of disintegration of which
the causes and symptoms have had a marked similarity, and
secondly that the symptoms associated with disintegration in
former civilizations are all notably present in our *Western*
civilization—which in fact they unanimously agree is in its
last stage.

11. I have italicized the word *Western*, as its precise meaning
is a cardinal point in my argument. By the Western tradition
I mean a particular set of values which happen to have found
their chief home in Europe, but which are not confined to
Europe. It was the values which made Europe, not the other
way round. They are independent of race, climate, geography,
and their assimilation by any people anywhere has a transforming effect just as their renunciation must in the long run
effect a transformation in the contrary sense. Either way it
is a moral and spiritual revolution; for they represent values,
not a technology, although the people who had adopted them
are in fact responsible for a great part of mankind's technical
achievement. The true Western tradition is an integrated
whole; its chief components have been the Greek sense of

form, balance, harmony, the Greek search for quality and distinction, all transmitted through their art and literature to Rome; the Roman sense of law and order and the ideal, common to both, of the free complete man (though they denied it in the case of slaves and barbarians); and thirdly, the Christian concept of the unique human person, free to live in harmony with his supernatural destiny, though tending always to lapse into spiritual revolt and variations on all the deadly sins. These three main sources were integrated into one great central tradition during the Middle Ages, much stimulated by the infusion of the new blood of the tough adventurous Northern Barbarians.

12. During the centuries when Europe was a community of peoples united by a common belief in this tradition, these peoples were emerging from six centuries of barbarism which followed the disintegration of the Roman Empire; technical resources and technical knowledge were only beginning to be rebuilt. Their material conditions which were a legacy from the past, have obscured the gigantic possibilities and actual advances which were diverted into other channels by two quite different, but constantly confused, revolutions; namely the catastrophe of the religious wars, and the conquest of the European mind by a mental atmosphere in which man became the centre of the universe, technical achievement became the supreme good, and unlimited confidence was placed in human reason. The growth of this attitude was of course stimulated by reaction to the devastation of the religious wars. The real meaning of the two revolutions is only in our time becoming apparent, because the moral framework of the old unity was—illogically—partly maintained, and indeed some of the chief values, such as the rule of law, personal freedom, spiritual equality, though torn from their context, were even exalted and pursued with greater fervour. The world became full of isolated Christian principles running wild. Even the façade of European unity was maintained until the French Revolution, by the international use of Latin and French, by the international " Front " of the governing classes and the scholars, above all by the maintenance in all Western countries till recent times of most of the traditional

Christian morality with its insistence on the supreme importance of the family as the essential pillar of society. The chief exception had been the radical change in the attitude to wealth and industry, which, largely as a result of Luther's insistence on justification by faith alone without " works," became divorced from morals and charity, and became in themselves the test of respectability and virtue. Anatole France's secretary relates how the satirist found in an old book the words " the Widow C. was wealthy and respectable." He rewrote it in a story of his own as " The Widow C. was wealthy and therefore respectable "! In that one word " therefore " he summed up the change in values inherited from the sixteenth century.

13. It was not realized that outside Western Christendom the vast majority of mankind did not accept the moral values which the men who were gradually discarding the ideological basis of those values, imagined would nevertheless be permanent and self-evident. Outside the Western tradition the tendency has been to regard man as the hopeless victim of an irredeemedly evil and hostile universe; a profound pessimism expressed in the Hindu Karma, the Buddhist ideal of self-annihilation, Moslem fatalism, the Slav obsession with evil, the Teutonic cult of action and destruction, the magic of the ancient West Asian civilizations, the Egyptian obsession with death, or the hardly-veiled devil-worship of the Aztecs or Phoenicians. All these pessimistic systems tend logically to the rejection of the personal dignity and freedom of choice of the individual, the passive acceptance of tyranny and capricious authority, the propitiation of evil spirits and deities associated with sex and fertility. It seems to be a law that an exaggerated emphasis on the spiritual and subjective, and corresponding depreciation of the body and the world of Nature, lead in practice, through pessimism, to their opposite reaction in the acceptance of evil. The rule of law—what Sir E. Barker calls the reign of " expectability "—cannot exist, the family loses its strength, dignity, and stability, in a world of slavery, polygamy, child marriages, the omnipotence of corrupt and capricious authorities, and the general prevalence of squalor and undernourishment among the masses.

14. The gradual realization that Christian moral ideas had no real authority without their theological basis took shape in the two most influential nineteenth-century philosophies— Utilitarianism—the " greatest happiness " principle which became the unavowed creed of the triumphant bourgeoisie— and Marxism, which frankly made economic determinism the basis of everything but combined its dreary philosophy with an irrational Messianic gospel of an earthly paradise to be won by class warfare, and has become after half a century the only live and aggressive survivor of all the modern philosophies. One of the great paradoxes of our time is that a doctrine based solely on materialism has been, through the peculiar genius of Karl Marx, coupled with a messianic irrational promise, and inspires its devotees with a fervent religious emotion quite inconsistent with the doctrine itself. The breakdown of traditional moral values accelerated by the disillusionment caused by the Great Wars—in fact the final revolt against the surviving Christian ideals—at last has had its counterpart in the revolt against rationalism itself. Every possible intellectual " ism " had been worked out and gone out of fashion; it remained only for the Pragmatists, Logico-Positivists, Phenomenologists, and Existentialists to deny at least by implication the validity of reason itself, to reject the possibility of any absolute standard of truth and value; the reasoning conscience has followed the moral conscience into the abyss.

15. Great historical events, themselves both causes and symptoms, have contributed to the break-up. Luther's purely theological revolt, locally successful through his alliance with the German princes and made permanent by the organizing genius of Calvin, undermined the mystical dogma of " charity " by his exaltation of faith against works, and was ultimately responsible for the form taken by the Industrial Revolution; because the latter took shape from an already existing background of ruthless competition and the concentration of wealth and investment-capital in a few hands. Because the Industrial Revolution came *after* the partial breakdown of the Western system, the great advances in technology— admirable in themselves—created an inhuman social structure

and like Frankenstein's proverbial monster have escaped from
human control, culminating in the supreme example of the
nuclear bombs.   They have been allowed to create conditions
which man cannot control, and to which he has failed to
adapt himself.   In another direction, the religious wars turned
the scale inside Germany in the endless conflict between the
European idea—then represented by Austria and its allies,
now by the Party of Dr. Adenauer—and the old Teutonic
mysticism of race and conquest, and decisively favoured the
rise of the military Baltic State of Prussia as the eventual
creator of German unity.   The French Revolution completed
the influence of Luther by the levelling of the German States,
by provoking the German reaction towards romanticism, by
the impulse it gave everywhere to the new religion of
nationalism.   For a time the new German Empire, the old
Austro-Hungarian, Russian and Ottoman Empires, thanks
partly to an efficient diplomatic technique, maintained an
uneasy equilibrium and stability over Central and Eastern
Europe; their collapse in 1918 finished the main work of
the French Revolution and set the stage for the Soviet Empire,
Nazism and the Second Great War.   All these things are
facts; to state them is not to disparage the great technological
advance of the last two centuries, nor does it imply advocacy
of a spurious neo-mediaevalism, nor of Gothic post offices.
The point is that the evolution of the Western world during
the last four centuries has been bedevilled and deviated by the
gradual abandonment by Western man of the values which as
a whole had created him, and that the ultimate consequences
have been accelerated by the Wars of Religion in the sixteenth
and seventeenth centuries and the revival of German paganism,
radically different though these were from the general intellectual revolt.

16. Whatever may be thought of this thesis—and many
presumably will disagree—as to how our present condition has
come about, it is difficult for thinking people to have very
different opinions about the nature of our condition or to deny
the plausibility of the sociologists' pessimism.   It is obvious
that we have entered a phase of mass civilization in which
standards of mass, quantity, speed, and mediocrity have

become the accepted standards of value. While our Western countries are committed to unheard-of expenditure on education, the educational machines are set for mediocrity and to act as a brake on quality or distinction. It is not the ideal of the " educational ladder " which is at fault, but the content of the education itself. Its character grows ever more technical, and those who try to pursue humanist studies find themselves, at the universities, equally in an atmosphere of narrow specialism. The idea of a " liberal " education is dying out, and with it the old intellectual fraternity between the educated people of the different Western peoples; the last link in their spiritual unity is being broken. Artistic creation— the visible or audible manifestation of every great civilization —is becoming either a stylized repetition of old models or a gradual reversion to the formless, disconnected, disharmonious art of the great pessimistic cultures. The urbanized masses, uprooted and cut loose from their own social traditions and ancestral memories, get no guidance; though their common-sense may reject the gospel of Marx, they can make no alternative faith out of academic subtleties or the false pseudo-sciences of fifty years ago which are still being hashed up and which have become the mental background of millions who have never read the original authors and have not heard of their successors. For Europe the Christian tradition has become associated in the mind of the largely dechristianized masses with the bourgeois " camp," although in fact the long campaign against Christianity has been directed from within that camp. It has also been narrowed by an over-literal verbalistic and unhistorical treatment of the Bible which ignored the figurative language of Eastern writers and inter-preted it without reference to the whole body of Christian tradition to which the books belonged, and many of the clergy and their followers, demoralized by the flood of pseudo-scientific propaganda, have exactly reversed Luther's principle of faith instead of works and have abandoned religious faith in favour of ethical works.

17. In the modern urbanized mass, uprooted and without any positive guidance, the subconscious non-rational instincts of the herd—Jung's " archetypes "—must inevitably come to

H.S.—P*

the top. In the individual the loosening of the opposites—
the disassociation of the conscious elements in the personality—
leads to hysteria and if unchecked, through neurosis to insanity.
In a collective group, when the controls internal and external
are weakened, the same process is at work. In the gradual
weakening of all forces of resistance—school and university,
the family, the local groups, the leadership of the educated,
the press, above all, of the Churches—one institution alone
grows stronger and claims more and more insistently the
heritage of all the rest—the State. Its claims are becoming
unlimited and its self-deification, which is already a fact in
the whole Communist orbit, is beginning in the Western
countries. In many respects its power is already unlimited,
and while all criticism of the old values is both permitted and
fashionable, criticism of the State and its actions is becoming
dangerous and is well on the way to being made illegal—as it
already has become in time of war.

18. The sociologists seem to be justified in thinking that
nothing short of a moral and spiritual revolution can now
arrest the flood tide of materialism, loss of critical standards,
and the final omnipotence of a parasitic bureaucracy enthroned
over a dying civilization—unless a short cut is taken by mutual
mass-destruction. That is however the central issue—the
sociologists have formulated a universal law of the cyclical
rise and fall of civilizations and do not believe that the chain
of historical cause and effect can be broken by moral and
spiritual revolutions. For they believe that the values men
hold are themselves the manifestation of the particular phase
or life-period on which a civilization has entered; that the
return of a society to the outlook of an earlier period is no
more possible than for an old man to recover his youth, or an
old woman to have a child. This analogy with the life of an
organism—and it is implicit in the theories even of those
sociologists who condemn it in Spengler—can only be really
refuted by those who hold the old Western and Christian
concept of man as a unique personality with the gift of free
will. It is this which has accounted for the extraordinary
exuberance and energy of Western man, his incessant creative
activity and changes of mind while the great civilizations of

Asia remained stagnant and conservative until they were overthrown by the merest handful of Western men and then galvanized into new activity and taught to revolt by the ideas imposed by their new conquerors—ideas which no other conquerors had ever dreamed of instilling into the conquered.

19. Western men—the first in history who have attached serious value to time—can "set the clock back" if they wish —what they have made by false ideas, they can unmake if they will return to the right ones. Our "Western" civilization is tending to disintegrate through the gradual rejection of the spiritual values on which it was built—the values represented by the fusion of the best elements in Greek form and Roman character with the central Tradition of historic Christianity; and the disintegration can only be arrested by our conscious re-acceptance of those values. At first sight the prospects of such a return do not look bright, for the opposing forces seem to be accelerating and consolidating; but as their real nature becomes more evident, the realization is bringing into existence a reaction by active intelligent minorities which hardly existed a century ago. When the great sultan in Chesterton's epic was awaiting the approach of Don John of Austria before Lepanto, he warned his staff of the great issues at stake:

> It is he who says not Kismet, it is he who knows not Fate;
> It is Richard, it is Raymond, it is Godfrey in the gate!

No one can assume the mantle of Peter the Hermit or St. Bernard, but we have something to learn from the spirit of the men whose great castles dotting the Near East still witness to the driving force of a living idea. There is still—far more indeed than there was a generation ago—a great fund of good will, an anxious feeling that we are on the wrong road. My own contribution to an answer is very small, for I have had to choose between a book which would put off the general reader by its length, and a book which is too short to contain more than a fraction of the evidence and illustration needed to defend myself against hostile specialists. (" He doesn't seem to have heard of so and so! ") I accept the risks— including that of falling between two stools and pleasing no one—in the hope that some others may pursue the lines of enquiry I have suggested and may know better how to present the same conclusions.   People want guidance and are deprived of it by " the treason of the clerks," the orthodox academic intellectuals who can pick holes, analyse, quote each other, snigger at the now unorthodox traditional values, but too often are happy in a purely negative rôle and boast that they can give no coherent inspiring message.   Though Milton meant the words in a very different sense to mine, they are not inappropriate today:

> The hungry sheep look up, and are not fed,
> But swoln with wind, and the rank mist they draw,
> Rot inwardly, and foul contagion spread.

BIBLIOGRAPHY

Author's Note

As this book is based on many years' reading, I have had to restrict the list of authorities to those specially relevant and of which I had kept notes. The assembling of the list has suffered from two handicaps. In making notes I often omitted the date of publication and sometimes the title of the book or article, and whether it was a translation or the original. Secondly, I lost over two thousand volumes by fire during the Second World War. The consequent difficulty of identifying the editions I had used has been increased by the fact that many of my sources had been in European or American reviews and books not published in England, and also that books sometimes bear no date. Though I succeeded in most cases in identifying the editions used and their publishers, I was advised that uniformity is expected, and have therefore omitted the names of London publishers.

Limits of space exclude references to two categories: that of very well-known recent works, such as Sir Winston Churchill's on the Two World Wars, Chester Wilmot's *Struggle for Europe*, and leading text-books; and that of sources in the *Dictionary of National Biography, Notes and Queries, Révue des deux Mondes, The Tablet, New Statesman, Economist*, and many works of biography and history to which I am in debt. I have cited critical commentaries rather than the works criticized, when the latter are obvious and well known. The names of some publications have been omitted although I had studied them with care, because I wished to avoid even the appearance of recommending works, however significant, which I consider false, misleading, and sometimes dishonest.

RUSSIA—TSARIST AND SOVIET

The Dynamics of Soviet Society. Rostow, 1953.
" Some factors in the Development of Russia." R. M. Fleming in *Studies in Regional Consciousness and Environment*, 1930.
L'Empire des Tsars et les Russes. Leroy Beaulieu, 1899.
L'Ame Russe. T. Legras. Flammarion, 1934.
Histoire de la littérature Russe. Hofmann, 1934.
La Russie en 1839. Marquis de Custine.
" Voyageurs étrangers en Russie du Xme au XXme Siècle." *La Table ronde*, 1947.
Russia—a History. S. Harcave, 1953. Lippincott.
Lettres de France et d'Italie. Herzen.
Dostoievsky. N. Berdyaev, 1936.
Journal d'un Ecrivain. Dostoievsky. Fr. tr., 1927.
Letters from the Underworld. Dostoievsky. Eng. tr., 1913.

The Possessed. Dostoievsky. Eng. tr., 1914.
Speech at Unveiling of Monument to Pushkin. Dostoievsky.
The Brothers Karamazov. Dostoievsky.
Travels in Russia, 1839. Tschaadaev. Fr. tr., 1862; Eng. tr., in U.S.A.
" Centenaire de Tolstoy." A. Hardy. *Rev. Cat.,* Brussels, 1928.
" L'erreur de Tolstoy." P. Bourget.
" Simplicity & Tolstoy." G. K. Chesterton.
" Tolstoi." H. Bugija in *Blackfriars.*
La Russie et les Russes. Tourgeniev, 1847.
" Ame Slave ame russe." A. Chedel in *Synthèses,* 1950.
La Tsarine Elisabeth Petrovna. M. Paléologue, 1939.
Karl Marx. Isaiah Berlin. Oxford, 1949.
Theory and Practice of Marxism. R. N. Carew Hunt, 1950.
Marxism Past and Present. R. N. Carew Hunt, 1954.
La Revolution russe. Kerensky, 1928.
The Russian Revolution. N. Berdyaev, 1931.
The Prophet armed: Trotsky, 1879-1921. Isaac Deutscher. Oxford, 1954.
Problems of Leninism. J. Stalin.
Betrayal of an Ideal. G. A. Tokaev, 1954.
Soviet Imperialism. G. A. Tokaev, 1954.
The Peoples of the Soviet Far East. W. Kolarz, 1954.
The New Soviet Empire. D. T. Dallin, 1952.
Soviet Policy in the Far East. Max Beloff. Oxford, 1953.
Stalin's Heirs. Gordon Young, 1953.
Oil in the Soviet Union. Hassmann, 1953.

DIPLOMACY AND POLICY

Diplomacy. Sir H. Nicholson, 1939.
L'Esprit de la Diplomatie. Ch. de Chambrun, 1944.
L'Ecole des Ambassadeurs. J. Jusserand, 1934.
Diplomacy and Peace. R. B. Mowat, 1935.
Diplomatic History, 1713–1933. Sir C. Petrie, 1946.
Enfances diplomatiques. Cte V. d'Ormesson, 1946.
La Diplomatie francaise d'Henri IV à Vergennes. P. Rain. Plon, 1945.
Talleyrand. Louis Madelin. Flammarion, 1944.
Le Diplomate. Jules Canbon. Hachette, 1926.
Histoire de la Diplomatie. Potemkine and others (Soviet book).
Cambridge History of Foreign Policy: 1783–1919.
English Saga 1840–1940. A. Bryant, 1942.
Le Siècle de Louis XV. P. Gaxotte, 1933.
Frédéric II. P. Gaxotte, 1938.
Crimean War & Diplomacy. Henderson, 1947.
A Balanced Economy. L. S. Amery, 1954.
Democratic Ideals and Reality. Sir H. J. Mackinder, 1919.
The Private Papers of Douglas Haig. 1952.
" Dr. Melchior." Lord Keynes in *Two Memoirs,* 1949.
Conflicts. L. B. Namier, 1942.
R.A.F. 1934–45. Vol. I, 1954.
Je les ai bien connus. E. Cerruti, 1954.
The Generals and the Germany Monarchy. E. Eyck. Roy. Hist. Society, 1951.
La troisiéme République. J. Bainville. Paris, 1935.
Histoire de deux Peuples. J. Bainville. Paris, 1933.

EUROPEAN EXPANSION

" Students from the Colonies." *P.E.P.,* 1954.
World Health Organization Report on Africa, 1953.

" Lessons of the Congo." *The Times*, July, 1954.
" Le Nigérie inaugure Sa troisième Constitution." Andre Blanchet, *Libre Belgique*, December, 1954.
Short History of Nigeria, and *How Nigeria is governed*. C. R. Niven. 1952 Editions.
" Portuguese Africa." H. D. Livermore (in *Portugal & Brazil*, Oxford, 1953).
" Goa ": in *British Surveys*, 1955.
South Africa under King Sebastian and the Cardinal. S. R. Welch. Cape Town, 1949.
Twentieth Century Empire. H. V. Hodson, 1948.
" Background of Macaulay's Minute." E. H Cutts, *American Hist. Rev.*, 1953.
Spanish Colonial Literature. B. Moses; Hispanic Society of America. New York, 1922.
Spain. Sir C. Petrie, 1934.
Latin America in World Politics. Prof. Rippy, 1928.
The Spanish Plan of Civilization. Marie Madden, 1930.
Political Theory and Law in Mediaeval Spain. Marie Madden, 1930.
Adventurers of the Buccaneers. Andrew Lang, 1926.
De Soto and the Conquistadors. T. Maynard, 1928.
" Spanish American Empire " in *History*, 1952.
" The Mau-Mau Rituals." *Manchester Guardian*, May, 1954.

THE LEGACY OF GREECE AND ROME

The Legacy of the Ancient World. W. G. de Burgh, 1947.
The Root of Europe. Various authors, 1952.
The Legacy of Rome. Various authors. Oxford, 1928.
The Romans. R. H. Barrow, 1953.
Slavery in the Roman Empire. R. H. Barrow, 1928.
Invasion of Europe by the Barbarians. J. B. Bury, 1929.
Roman Society from Nero to Marcus Aurelius. S. Dill, 1904.
The Legacy of Greece. Various authors. Oxford, 1942.
Companion to Greek Studies. Cambridge, 1905.
Ancient Greece. H. D. F. Kitto, 1951.
Grammar of Greek Art. P. Gardner, 1905.
Le Monde grec et Sa Pensée. G. de Reynold, 1944.
" Le Miracle grec." H. Berr in *En Marge de l'Hist. Universelle*." Paris, 1934.

EUROPE AND THE ENEMIES FROM WITHIN

Making of Europe. C. Dawson, 1932.
Understanding Europe. C. Dawson, 1952.
" Education and the Study of Christian Culture." C. Dawson, in *Studies*, 1953.
Mediaeval Religion. C. Dawson, 1934.
La Grande Clarté du Moyen age. G. Cohen, 1943.
The Thirteenth Greatest of Centuries. J. J. Walsh. New York, 1913.
Le Colline inspirée. M. Barrès.
L'Inquisition médiévale. J. Guiraud. Eng. trans., 1929.
L'Inquisition. E. Vacandard, 1913.
Formation territoriale des Etats de l'Europe Centrale. Himly, 1894.
L'Ame Allemande. L. Reynaud. Paris, Flammarion, 1933.
D'où vient l'allemagne? G. de Reynold. Plon, 1939.
" Luther " in *Trois Réformateurs*. J. Maritain. Eng. trans., 1928.
Luther. H. Grisar. Eng. tr., 1930.
Luther et le Lutheranisme. H. Denifle. French tr., 1916.
Un destin: Martin Luther. L. Febvre, 1928.
L'Allemagne et la Réforme. Janssen. Paris, Plon.

" National opposition to Rome in Germany." A. F. Pollard in *Cambridge Modern History*, Vol. II, Ch. 5.

" Social Revolution and Catholic Reaction in Germany." A. F. Pollard in *Cambridge Modern History*, Vol. II, Ch. 6.

" Conflict of Creed and Parties in Germany." Idem , Ch. 7.

" Calvin and the Reformed Church." Rev. A. M. Fairbairn in *Cambridge Modern History*, Vol. II, Ch. 11.

The Wealth of England, 1496-1760. Sir G. N. Clark.

The State of the Poor. Sir M. Eden, 1797.

Marriage and Society. E. O. James. London University, 1952.

" Milton and his Age." G. K. Chesterton in *Oxford and Cambridge Rev.*, 1909.

Religion and the Rise of Capitalism. R. H. Tawney, 1926.

Origines de la Réforme en France. Imbart de la Tour, 1904.

Wycliffe and the Beginnings of English Nonconformity. K. B. McFarlane, 1953.

" Loss of Confidence." A. W. Krutsch in *American Scholar*, 1953.

The French Revolution. G. P. Gooch, 1920.

Causes of the French Revolution. A. Cobban, 1946 Historical Association.

" The Anti-Revolutionary Rousseau." G. H. McNeill in *American Historical Rev.*, 1953.

La Révolution francaise. Madeline, 1911.

L'Ancien régime et la Révolution. A. de Tocqueville, 1856.

Les Origines de la France Contemporaine. H. Taine.

L'Ancien Régime. Funck Brentano, 1926.

La France et le monde 1715-1789. Préclin et Tapié, 1952.

La Révolution francaise. P. Gaxotte. Fayard, 1928.

L'Avénement de Bonaparte. Vandal.

L'Europe et la Révolution francaise. A. Sorel.

Lectures on the French Revolution. Lord Acton.

Robespierre on the French Revolution. J. M. Thompson, 1952.

" Centenaire de H. Taine." G. de Reynold. *Rev. Cat.*, Brussels, 1928.

Souvenirs sur Taine. P. Bourget.

In *Le Correspondant* 1904-1906 :—
  " Catholicisme et Romantisme." E. Faguet.
  " Du Romantisme à l'anarchie." F. Pascal.
  " Eugène Sue." F. Pascal.
  " Georges Sand." H. Bordeaux.

Friedrich Nietzsche.—*See* " Psychology and Philosophy " section.

Essays on Contemporary Events. C. G. Jung (*see* " Sociology ").

Essai sur l'inégalité des races humaines. Gobineau. 1854: 1933.

Vie et Prophéties du Conte de Gobineau. R. Dreyfus, 1929.

The Roots of National Socialism. R. d'O. Butler, 1941.

Défense de l'occident. H. Massis, 1926.

Histoire de deux Peuples. J. Bainville, 1933.

Germany's Revolution of Destruction. H. Rauschning, 1938.

An introduction to American Politics. D. W. Brogan, 1954.

The Two Nations. Christopher Hollis, 1937.

PSYCHOLOGY AND PHILOSOPHY

" Freud: 1856-1939." *Times Literary Supplement*, Sept., 1953.

Psycho-Analysis, Behaviourism and the Gestalt. R. H. Furbey (U.S.A.).

La Methode psychanalytique et la Doctrine freudienne. R. Dalbiez. Paris, 1936.

The New Psychologies. R. Allers, 1932.

Psychology of Character. R. Allers, 1931.

Réflexions sur la Pathologie du Conflit. R. Allers, 1938.

New Ways in Psycho-Analysis. K. Horney. New York, 1939.

Essays on Contemporary Events. C. G. Jung, 1941–6.
Psycho-Analysis and Personality. J. Nuttin, Louvain, 1950; Eng. tr., 1954.
St. Augustine's City of God. J. Rickaby, 1925.
" Death Instinct and Western Man." F. C. Palmer. *Hibbert Journal*, 1953.
God and the Unconscious. V. White, 1952.
Factors in the stages of Moral Development. C. Baudoin, 1953.
Prolegomena to Ethics. Green, 1887.
Ethical Studies, Essays 3 and 7. Bradley, 1876.
Jeremy Bentham. C. K. Ogden, 1932.
The English Utilitarians. Stephen, 1900.
Varieties of Religious Experience. W. James, 1902.
A Pluralistic Universe. W. James, 1909.
Studies in Humanism. F. S. Schiller, 1907.
Les Pages Immortelles: Selections from Nietzsche. H. Mann. Paris, 1939.
Friedrich Nietzsche. F. Copleston, 1942.
Philosophy of Nietzsche. Modern Library, New York, 1905.
Pensée allemande de Luther à Nietzsche. J. E. Spenlé. Paris, 1934.
Pensée philosophique Allemande depuis Nietzsche. B. Groethuysen. Paris, 1926.
Nietzsche ou le déclin de l'esprit. G. Thibon. Paris, 1948.
Principia Ethica. G. E. Moore, 1903.
Language, Truth and Logic. A. J. Ayer, 1936, 1953.
Critique of Logical Positivism. Joad, 1950.
Two Memoirs (Second). Lord Keynes, 1949.
Place of reason in Ethics. S. Toulmin, 1950.
Existentialism and Modern Man. F. C. Copleston, 1948.
Metamorphose de la littérature de Proust à Sartre. Boisdeffre. Paris, 1952.
Monument to St. Augustine. Various authors. 1930.
St. Augustine's City of God. J. Rickaby, 1925.
An Augustine Synthesis, 1936.
La Philosophie au Moyen age. E. Gilson. 2nd Edition, 1944.
Mediaeval Philosophy. F. C. Copleston, 1952.
Scholasticism old and new. M. de Wulf. Eng. tr., 1907.
St. Thomas Aquinas. G. K. Chesterton, 1933.
Primauté du Spirituel. J. Maritain. Plon, 1927.
" St. Thomas et l'Unité de la Culture Chrétienne." Address by J. Maritain
    in Germany, 1928.
" Political Philosophy of Edmund Burke." J. A. McGann in *Thought*, 1929.
Science and the Modern World. A. N. Whitehead, 1926.
Essays in Science and Philosophy. A. N. Whitehead. New York, 1947.
" The Authority of the Expert." M. C. D'Arcy in *Thought*, 1927.
" Social Science and the Humanists." B. Rosenberg in *American Scholar*, 1953.
Orthodoxy sees it through. Various authors, 1934.
" Do Economists Know Anything ? " Prof. Machlup in *American Scholar*, 1953.
Science and Religion. C. A. Coulson. Cambridge, 1955.
Psychology as the Study of Behaviour. O. L. Zangwill. Cambridge, 1955.

SOCIOLOGY—MASS PSYCHOLOGY

History of the Philosophy of History. Prof. Flint, 1893.
" Historicism," etc. Karl Mannheim in *Essays on the Sociology of Knowledge*,
    1952.
Human Nature in Politics. Graham Wallas, 1909.
" Human Nature and the Historians." G. K. Chesterton in *Oxford & Cam-
    bridge Rev.*, 1908.
Psychologie des Foules. G. Lebon, 9th Edition, 1905.
L'Evolution Actuelle du Monde. G. Lebon. Flammarion, 1927.
Effects of Tropical Light. Pearson (U.S.A.).
L'Homme et le Climat. A. Misserand. Plon, 1937.

Decline of the West. O. Spengler. English Edition, 1934.
The Hour of Decision. O. Spengler. English Edition, 1934.
End of Our Time. N. Berdyaev, 1933.
Nouveau Moyen Age. N. Berdyaev, 1927.
History of Civilization & Culture. F. R. Cowell, 1952.
Social Philosophies of an Age of Crisis. P. A. Sorokin, 1952.
Théories Sociologiques Contemporaires. P. A. Sorokin. Paris, Payot, 1938.
The World and the West; A Study of History, &c. A. Toynbee.
Bilan de l'Histoire. R. Grousset. Plon, 1946.
Suicide E. Durkheim. Eng. Edn., 1952.
Man the Unknown. A. Carrel, 1935.
" Western Political Tradition." Symposium in *Listener*, 1948.
Time and Western Man. Wyndham Lewis, 1928.
" Estrangement of Western Man." B. Russell in *Sunday Times*.
" Why Fanaticism brings defeat." B. Russell in *Listener*, 1948.
G. B. S. By various authors. 1946.
Some Errors of H. G. Wells. Downey, 1920–1929.
Companion to Wells' Outline of History. H. Belloc, 1926.
Mr. Belloc Objects. H. G. Wells, 1926.
Mr. Belloc still objects. H. Belloc, 1926.
Four Hundred Centuries of Cave Art. Abbe Breuil, 1952.
Social Evolution. Benjamin Kidd, 1895.
Essays on Contemporary Events: C. G. Jung:—containing

    " Psychotherapy Today," 1941.
    " Psychotherapy and a Philosophy of Life," 1943.
    " After the Catastrophe," 1945.
    " Individual and Mass Psychology," 1946.
    " Epilogue," 1946.

Picasso: by Maurice Raynal. Skira Art Books, 1953.
Le Mythe du Moderne. C. Baudoin, 1950.
March of the Moderns. W. Gaunt, 1949.
" Loss of Confidence." A. W. Krutsch in *American Scholar*, 1953.
" How far is Class Warfare a Myth ? " R. H. S. Crossman. *Listener*, 1948.
Noble Castle. C. Hollis, 1941.
Christianity and Class Warfare. N. Berdyaev. Eng. trans., 1933.
" Cult of Evil." A. Pryce Jones. *Listener*, 1954.
Primauté du Spirituel. J. Maritain. Plon, 1927.
Religion and Culture. J. Maritain. English edition, 1931.
Le Crépuscule de la Civilisation. J. Maritain. Ottawa, 1941.
The Open Society and its Enemies. H. R. Popper. Vol. 2, 1952.
" The Anti-Clerical tradition in France." Articles in *Le Correspondant*, 1906–1912.
" Mon temps." G. Hanotaux in *Revue des deux Mondes*, 1936.
Understanding Europe. C. Dawson, 1952.
" Education and the Study of Christian Culture." C. Dawson in *Studies*, 1953.
Universities, American, English and German. Dr. Flexner, 1930.
Progressive Education in U.S.A. Colliers. May, 1954.
" Weaknesses of Scientific Education." R. Birley at British Association, 1953.
Some Economic Consequences of the Great War. A. L. Bowley, 1930.
The Road to Serfdom. F. A. Hayek. Eng. edn , 1944.
Eugenics. A. M. Carr-Saunders, 1925.
" The Aristocratic Idea." D. Woodruff. *Listener*, 1948.
Britain's Future Population. R. F. Harrod. Oxford, 1943.
Historical Inevitability. I. Berlin. Oxford, 1954.
Apologie pour l'Histoire. M. Bloch. Paris, 1952.

COMPARATIVE HISTORY OF RELIGIONS

Pre-History. F. C. Burkitt. Cambridge, 1921.

" Religion of Earliest Man." P. W. Schmidt. *Studies in Comparative Religion*, Vol. I, 1935.
" Religion of Primitive Peoples." *Idem.*
Four Hundred Centuries of Cave Art. Abbé Breuil, 1952.
Dawn of Civilization. Maspero, 1901.
Age of the Gods. C. Dawson, 1928.
Religion and the Rise of Western Culture. C. Dawson. Gifford Lectures, 1948.
Essays Ancient and Modern. T. S. Eliot, 1936.
The Bible and the Early History of Mankind. H. Johnson, 1943.
Picasso: by Maurice Raynal. Skira Art Books, 1953.
" D. H. Lawrence." Dilys Powell in *Life and Letters*, 1930.
Marriage and Society. E. O. James. London University, 1952.
March of the Moderns. W. Gaunt, 1949.
Origin and Growth of Religion. P. W. Schmidt. Eng. tr., 1930.
L'Étude comparée des Religions. Pinard de la Boullaye.
Les Races humaines. Lester & Millot. Paris, 1936.
Les Races et l'histoire. E. Pittard. Paris, 1932.
Noble Castle. C. Hollis, 1941.
" The Jews in Biblical Times." H. Frankfort in *History*, 1952.
" The Jews." T. L. McKenzie in *Catholic Commentary on the Scriptures*, 1953.
" Religion of Babylonia and Assyria." A. Condamin. *Studies in Comp. Religion*, Vol. 2, 1935.
Religion of Ancient Egypt. A. Mallon. *Ibid.*
Religion of Ancient Egypt.. C. Flinders Petrie, 1906.
Religion of Babylonia and Assyria. R. W. Rogers, 1908.
La Mesopotamie. L. Delaporte, 1923.
Etudes sur les religions Semitiques. M. T. Lagrange, 1905.
Religion of Ancient Syria. S. S. Hitchcock. *History of Religion*, Vol. I, 1910.
" Semitic Religions," " Patriarchal and Mosaic Religion," " The Hebrew Prophets." J. M. T. Barton in *Studies in Comparative Religion*, Vols. 2 & 3, 1935.
" Religions of Mexico & Peru." G. Holtker. *Studies in Comp. Religion*, Vol. 1, 1935.
" Religions of Ancient Persia." A. Carnoy. *Ibid.*, Vol. 2.
" Religions of Early Rome." C. C. Martindale. *Ibid.*
Religions of the Manichees. F. C. Burkitt. Cambridge, 1925.
Church and Gnosis. F. C. Burkitt. Cambridge, 1932.
The Legacy of Israel. Various authors. Oxford, 1948.
Early Christianity and its Rivals. S. H. Box, 1929.
Legacy of Islam. Various authors. Oxford, 1931.
The Koran. Trans. by J. M. Rodwell, 1909.
" Religion of the Koran." E. Power in *History of Religion*, Vol. 4, 1911.
" Religion of the Koran." A. Vincent, *Studies in Comp. Religion*, Vol. 5, 1935.
Religious Attitude and Life in Islam. D. B. Macdonald. Chicago, 1909.
Islam. E. Denison Ross, 1927.
Islam. H. Massé. Paris, 1930.
Influence of Islam. E. J. Bolus, 1932.
" Averroes." E. I. J. Rosenthal in *Bulletin of Oriental and African Studies.* London University, 1953.
Mediaeval Religion. C. Dawson, 1934.
" Gnosticism, Marcionism, Manicheism." J. Lebreton, 1935.
Religion of Mithra. C. C. Martindale, 1910.
The Legacy of India. Various authors. Oxford, 1938.
Philosophies Indiennes. R. Grousset. Paris, 1931.
" Hinduism." P. Johanns. *Studies in Comp. Rel.*, 1935.
Hist. de l'extreme Orient. R. Grousset. Paris, 1929.
Standard translations of Indian Sacred Books. Rhys Davids, Max Müller.
Indian Philosophers. Prof. Radhakrishnan, 1923.

Way to Nirvana. De la Vallée Poussin. Cambridge, 1917.
Nirvana, Dogme et philosophie. De la Vallée Poussin. Paris, 1930.
" Buddhism." De la Vallée Poussin. *Studies in Comp. Rel.,* Vol. 1, 1935.
" Hinduism." E. R. Hull. *Hist. Relig.,* Vol. 1, 1910.
Traité d'Histoire des Religions. Mircea Eliade. Paris, 1953.
Histoire des Croyances religeuses en Chine. L. Wieger, 1917.
" Religion of China." L. Wieger. *Hist. Relig.,* 1911.
" Brahminism," " Buddhism." C. F. Aikin in *Cath. Encyclopedia.*
" Religion of Japan." J. Mullie. *Studies in Comp. Relig.,* 1935.
Reincarnation. W. Donnelly, 1941.
Danse de Civa. Ananda Coomaraswarny, 1924.
Religions et les Philosophies dans l'Asie centrale. Gobineau, 1854 and 1933.
" Compendium of Buddhist Doctrine." Trans. W. H. D. Rouse, 1922.
Histoire de l'extreme Orient. R. Grousset. Musée Guimet.
Le réveil de l'Asie. R. Grousset, 1923.
L'Inde civilisatrice. S. Levi, 1938.
Travel Diary of a Philosopher. H. Keyserling, 1925.
Philosophie de H. Keyserling. C. Sénéchal.
Spiritualism. H. Thurston, 1935.
" Diabolism." H. Thurston in *Studies,* 1927.
" The Author of the Golden Bough." V. White. *Listener,* 1954.